T0298776

History of Insurance

Volume 5

History of Insurance

Volume 5

LIFE

Edited by
DAVID JENKINS
and TAKAU YONEYAMA

Routledge
Taylor & Francis Group

LONDON AND NEW YORK

First published 2000 by Pickering & Chatto (Publishers) Limited

Published 2016 by Routledge
2 Park Square, Milton Park, Abingdon, Oxon OX14 4RN
605 Third Avenue, New York, NY 10017

Routledge is an imprint of the Taylor & Francis Group, an informa business

Copyright © Taylor & Francis 2000

All rights reserved. No part of this book may be reprinted or reproduced or
utilised in any form or by any electronic, mechanical, or other means, now
known or hereafter invented, including photocopying and recording, or in
any information storage or retrieval system, without permission in
writing from the publishers.

Notice:
Product or corporate names may be trademarks or registered trademarks, and
are used only for identification and explanation without intent to infringe.

BRITISH LIBRARY CATALOGUING IN PUBLICATION DATA
The history of insurance
1. Insurance — Great Britain — History
2. I. Jenkins, David T. II. Yoneyama, Takau
3. 368.9'41

LIBRARY OF CONGRESS CATALOGING-IN-PUBLICATION DATA
The history of insurance / edited by David Jenkins and Takau Yoneyama.
p.cm.
Includes bibliographical references and index.
Contents: v. 1 16791816 — v. 2 17971877 — v. 3 16711762 — v.4 17741826 — v.5
18281848 — v.6 18481887 — v.7 16011910 —v.8 18101811.
ISBN 1-85196-527-0 (set)
1. Insurance — Great Britain — History — Sources. 2. Insurance companies —
Great Britain — History — Sources. I. Jenkins, David (David Trevor). II.
Yoneyama, Takau, 1953

HG8597.H574 2000
368'.00941—de21

*Typeset by Techset Ltd.,
Gateshead*

ISBN 13: 978-1-13876-089-9 (hbk) (Vol-5)

CONTENTS

Volume 5

Chadwick,
Article on the Means of Insurance

[Edwin Chadwick], *An Article on the Means of Insurance* (London: Samuel Bentley, 1828)

This discussion from the *Westminster Review* is ascribed to Edwin Chadwick. Chadwick (1800–90) was a physician and social reformer who played a leading role in social welfare reform and sanitary improvement. He was secretary of the Royal Commission on Reform of the Poor Laws (1834–46), helping to design the new organisational system for the administration of poor relief. He was a commissioner of the Board of Health (1848–54) and helped steer the Public Health Act of 1848. His *Report ... on an Enquiry into the Sanitary Condition of the Labouring Population of Great Britain* is his best known published work. His writings included discussions of interment practices, methods of representing the duration of life and the causes of mortality, and various aspects of sanitary science.

This discussion on insurance predates these other interests and publications. His views on life assurances are related to the *Report of the Select Committee on Friendly Societies* and the consequent debate. But he also uses the opportunity to discuss William Morgan's account of the Equitable Society that had just been published. Amongst Chadwick's concerns, expressed here, are those about the continued support for the Northampton Life Table which had for long formed the basis of actuarial calculations in life offices. He refers to the indifference of actuaries 'to the reception of any new facts, and the consequent incompleteness of their information for any practical purpose' and to their 'incompetency to weigh evidence, free from bias, in most cases of direct monied interest'. Chadwick also attacks the waste of public money in the Government annuity scheme, which was based on the excessive mortality calculations of the Northampton Table.

His essay on insuring against sickness, decrepitude and mortality is an early indication of his concerns for poverty and social reform, long before he became strongly involved in the reform movement.

PREFACE.

An impression of the annexed article was printed separately for private circulation soon after its publication in the year 1828. That impression has been long out of print, and the article is now reprinted in consequence of the increase of Benefit Societies and Sick Clubs, created by the operation of the Poor Law Amendment Act, having suggested to the writer the expediency of again endeavouring at this time to call attention to the general incompleteness of the tables of insurance, on the completeness of which the stability of all such provident institutions must mainly depend. The existing Government has made one important addition to the older provident institutions, by the establishment of Annuity Societies for the Labouring Classes. But much yet remains to be done for the advancement and proper security of such institutions. If the time of the writer had permitted, he would have endeavoured to show the importance of increasing the usefulness of Savings' Banks, and of giving to the labouring classes the like conveniences and securities in the application of their small amounts of savings that the larger banks afford to the wealthier classes in the management of their capital. He would also have endeavoured to trace the effects of such contributions upon wages and the investment of capital. He was, however, utterly prevented doing more than to reprint the article with some corrections, and with the addition of such notes as he could easily make. Being fully convinced that much misery will be created by the failure of institutions founded on inadequate data, he felt that he would have been a party to future suffering if he did not do as much as was in his power to obviate it by endeavouring to recall attention to the subject.

Nearly all the notes are additions to this impression.

LONDON, *September* 12, 1836.

ARTICLE
ON THE MEANS OF INSURANCE.

Art. V.—1. First Report from the Select Committee of the House of Commons on the Laws respecting Friendly Societies—July 1825.

2. Second Report on the same subject—June 1827.

3 A Treatise on Benefit or Friendly Societies, containing a statement of laws respecting these institutions; the probabilities of sickness, mortality, births, and other casualties; with practical instructions for the formation of Rates, and their general management. Read before the Mathematical Society of London. By James Mitchell, LL.D., F.S.A. E —Richardson.

4. A View of the Rise and Progress of the Equitable Society, and of the Causes which have contributed to its success. To which are added, Remarks on some of the late misrepresentations respecting the rules and practice of the Society. By W. Morgan, F.R.S., Actuary to the Equitable Society.

Among the most important duties of a government intent upon the accomplishment of what some writers have stated to be its chief end, "security for the full enjoyment of life and property," we should include the attainment of means to enable the community to provide, at the least expense, against the casualties of sickness and mortality, and to avert or dissipate those attendant evils by the apprehension of which life is embittered and impaired. Of those means the most readily attainable are, first, collections of complete information relative to the circumstances under which sickness arises, together with accurate accounts of the deaths consequent upon those circumstances; and, next, the formation of equitable tables of assurance for individual contribution, by which the evil effects of such events, when they do happen, will be mitigated, in proportion to the degree in which they are shared amongst large numbers. Accounts of this description, which perhaps at present a government alone has the power to obtain in the requisite degree of perfection, would form an invaluable acquisition to science, and would direct the public exertions in removing those circumstances which shorten life, and in promoting those under which it is found to attain its greatest and most happy duration. Our go-

vernment has hitherto paid little or no attention to this important subject, and has only concerned itself with such accounts
as means of indirect taxation.

We shall not attempt to investigate the fairness of the terms
on which the Assurance Companies deal with the public ; we
shall on this occasion concern ourselves as little as possible
about such interests.* We propose to exhibit the present state
of the information possessed relative to the casualties of sickness
and mortality, and the conduct of the government respecting the
departments of the public expenditure appropriated as means
to diminish the evil effects of those casualties.

It is perhaps requisite we should call upon our readers to bear
in mind the truisms, that the value of any table of sickness or
mortality is proportionate to the extent and accuracy of the information obtained relative to the class of persons from the
number of whose casualties it is formed ; and that the degree in
which such table is applicable to determine the number of casualties that may be expected to happen amongst another class of
persons, must depend upon the similarity of the circumstances
under which the two classes are placed.

Of the tables of mortality now in use, the oldest, and that
which is most generally adopted, is called the Northampton
table.   It was formed by Dr. Price, from bills of mortality kept

---

* *All* the provisions for insurance, whether for rich or for poor, we think,
demand the especial care of a good government.   We believe that it is only
by an enlightened and trustworthy government that the means for the purpose can be perfected.   The means of insurance by Joint Stock Companies,
though better perhaps than would have been instituted by the government
whilst the whole subject was imperfectly understood, are too frequently de-
fectively constructed, and managed with the view to narrow and immediate
advantages,—to the life interests of paid directors and secretaries, rather
than to the ultimate interests either of the shareholders or the security of
the insured.   It is to be feared that some of these offices admit indiscri-
minately bad lives upon inadequate terms ; that speculations are made on
various hidden contingencies to defeat even just claims : that the solvency of
some of the companies is not well assured ; and that, in others, the liabilities
of the actual shareholders, as well as of all those who have ever been shareholders, are greater than they are ever made acquainted with.   A large proportion of the Joint Stock Companies founded for the purpose of insurance
have from time to time failed.   It is to be feared that some of the existing
companies are fraught with the elements of eventual ruin and extensive
misery to families.   We speak advisedly when we state that there are good
grounds for a searching government investigation into the constitution and
management of this class of institutions.

in the parish of All Saints, Northampton, during the years
1735 to 1780. This parish contained little more than half the
number of inhabitants of Northampton. A table formed upon
the casualties happening to such a proportion might have been
applicable to determine the chances of mortality in that town,
provided that the parish of All Saints was not inhabited exclusively or disproportionately by rich or by poor; and provided
also that the population was stationary during the period included in the returns, which there is evidence to prove was not
the case. But a table formed on so narrow a basis as that afforded by half the population of a small town is obviously inapplicable to determine (of itself) the chances of mortality amongst
the general population of the kingdom. This, however, is the
table adopted by most of the Assurance Offices, as the one on
which they depend in the insurance of lives of the middle or
wealthier classes.

The next table, or set of tables, called the Swedish, was constructed in a very satisfactory manner upon returns carefully
collected in the years 1755 to 1776, from the whole population
of Sweden and Finland. These tables have been corrected by
others, deduced with equal care from other returns, officially
compiled during the years from 1775 to 1795, and from 1801
to 1805. These tables may be trusted, as accurately exhibiting
the chances of mortality amongst the whole population of the
two countries, but not the relative chances amongst the different
classes of that population. But the climate and soil of those
countries, the alternations of good and bad crops, the severe
and rapid changes of the seasons, and the other circumstances
influencing health and longevity under which the Swedes were
placed, differed so greatly from the circumstances of this country, as to render this set of tables, if unaided by other evidence,
insufficient for the determination of the average mortality amongst
our population.

The third table, or rather set of tables, is that formed in
France by Monsieur de Parcieux; of which set, one table was
calculated from the mortality found to prevail (mostly during the
years from 1689 to 1696) amongst the nominees of the French
Tontine; four were formed from the registers of deaths among
the monks of four monastic orders in Paris; and the sixth table,

which was the first ever calculated separately to show the duration
of female life, was formed from the registered deaths of the nuns
in Paris.   Each of these tables was deduced from the casualties
happening amongst classes of select lives, differently circumstanced from the general population of France, and therefore
bad, as data, for shewing the probable mortality amongst that
population, and still worse for the purpose of estimating mortality amongst the population of this country, which probably
differs in its circumstances more widely from the monks and
nuns of the old French regime, than did the general population
of that country at that period.

The next, called the Carlisle table, was formed from the results of observations made during the years from 1779 to 1787,
upon a population of eight thousand persons in the town of
Carlisle.   The facts were carefully collected by Dr. Heysham,
and the calculations founded upon them accurately conducted
by Mr. Milne.   A basis of observations upon eight thousand
persons is evidently too small to form tables applicable to the
whole kingdom ; and the period of nine years, during which
the observations were made, as it might have been attended by
a greater degree of good or bad health than usual, was far too
short to form a correct average, even with regard to that town.

These were the tables in most general use before the appointment of a Committee of the House of Commons in 1825, to
inquire into the general management of Benefit Societies.   The
chief presumption (and in the absence of other evidence it must
be admitted as a strong one) in favour of these tables, as representing the average mortality amongst the population of this
country, was the degree in which they corresponded with each
other, though formed independently.   The Northampton table
is the one adopted by the greater number of the Assurance
Offices for the purpose of assuring to persons the payment of
certain sums of money on the deaths of other persons.   This
was the table strongly recommended to the Committee as the
best adapted to shew the average mortality among the whole
population ; and as peculiarly applicable to govern the assurances against risks among the labouring classes, by whom chiefly
the Benefit Societies are formed,—it being on the safe side ;
that is, not representing the duration of life too favourably, so
as to call for premiums too low to cover the risks incurred—too

low to ensure the stability and prosperity of the establishments. The witnesses in favour of this table were the practical men, extensively conversant with the business of assuring against such contingencies. They urged that Dr. Price had corrected this table by information which he had collected of the casualties in other towns, and that its general applicability was confirmed by subsequent experience.

Opposed to these witnesses were several others equally eminent, who not questioning the correct formation of the Northampton table, or its applicability to display the probable length of life at the time when it was made, contended that the duration of life had since increased, and was now far greater than the Northampton table represented.

The theory which the latter class of witnesses maintained of the increased duration of human life has for several years past gained ground; and it appears to us that strong *primá facie* evidence may be adduced in its favour, independently of any proof derived from population returns or mortuary registers.

Dr. Price laid down the position, that mortality invariably follows the rate of sickness; or, in other words, that mortality is always proportionate to the causes of mortality. Persons of age and observation bear testimony, that a great improvement has taken place in the general mode of living among the people of this country even within the last twenty years. The higher classes are acknowledged to be much more temperate—less addicted to those gross sensual excesses which characterise a people who, in the earlier stages of civilization, are not aware of the pleasures to be derived from useful pursuits, and who have few intellectual amusements as a resource against ennui, " the disease of unfurnished minds." The vice of hard drinking is no longer fashionable; and he who should now seek distinction as a six, or even as a four bottle man, would be classed with those persons of humble station and more limited means, who are occasionally celebrated in the newspapers by the announcement of such exploits as eating a whole leg of mutton, and a proportionate quantity of candles by way of dessert. The physical condition of the aristocracy has been greatly improved; partly, doubtless, by their better habits, and partly by their plebeian alliances, and obedience to the general law of nature which is found effectual for the improvement of the lower animals. The

satire of Swift is only applicable to by-gone times. A lord, if
an Hidalgo of the " true-blue Castilian blood," is no longer
known by his spindle shanks, as in the days of Fielding, and
the younger of the aristocracy are in general taller and better
made than their parents.

The habits of the labouring classes have (as was stated in
evidence before the Committees of the House of Commons
which sat in the years 1816 and 1817, to inquire into the police
of the metropolis) undergone considerable improvement within
the same period. It must be admitted that the reduced circumstances of some classes of workmen militate against this position ;
but there are very few of them who have not been sustained, and
even advanced in condition, by a better application even of diminished means. They have gained somewhat in knowledge, in habits
of various and more temperate enjoyment, and have in the same
proportion been recovered from that tyrannical control of single
appetites and passions, from that propensity to seize with avidity
and to use without restraint the means of immediate gratification,
which distinguishes all ignorant people of whatever rank.   The
sailor when he returns from a voyage, the ill-educated heir to
an estate when he becomes of age, and the workman who by
three days' labour obtains enough to maintain him in idleness and
dissipation during the remainder of the week, are influenced by
very much the same class of motives.   The most decisive and
gratifying proof of the improvement taking place in the habits
of the labouring classes, is the increase of Benefit Societies and
other institutions directed to the same end, which before the
middle of the last century were scarcely known.   It appears
from returns made to Parliament, and cited in the Report before
us, that so early as 1802 there were no fewer than nine thousand
six hundred and seventy-two Friendly Societies, and that in
1815 the members of these institutions in England alone were
enumerated at nine hundred and twenty-five thousand four
hundred and twenty-nine.   In Scotland the numbers in proportion to the population were still more considerable ; and in both
countries they have subsequently much increased.   We may
add also, that during the last year (1827,) the deposits in the
Savings Banks amounted to upwards of sixteen millions of money.
Of this sum a large proportion, though not probably so large as
is generally supposed, consists of deposits from mechanics and

other labouring men. The prosperity of these institutions is gratifying, as affording evidence that large classes of the labouring community possess surplus means beyond what are requisite to procure them the necessaries of life ;—it is cheering, as indicating the growth of improved habits of foresight and self-restraint, which must exercise an important moral influence over all their actions and relations in society.*

Considerable improvements have taken place in the domestic habits of artisans : they are less filthy and irregular, their houses are better constructed, they have acquired some notion that fresh air is conducive to health, and the streets where they reside are less filthy and pestilential than formerly. When to this enumeration of the causes of diminution in the amount of mortality are added the extensive reductions which must be occasioned by vaccination, less injurious nursing in infancy, and improved medical treatment, enough of classes of particular facts have been indicated to sustain the general conclusion, that were we to admit that the condition of several classes may have been deteriorated, the sum of improvement in the entire community will be found to preponderate considerably.

The opinion, that the value of life had improved, was, until the last year or two, treated as a " mere theory;" by which term of derision was meant an hypothesis or doubtful speculation, and the supporters of it were of course viewed as men whose opinions might be listened to, but ought not to be carried

---

* A philosophical writer characterizes the great progress of these institutions as " one of the most striking manifestations of virtue that ever was made by any people." He observes, that " For persons merged in poverty, and totally deprived of education, as the English population heretofore have so generally been, it is not easy or common to have much of foresight, or much of that self-command which is necessary to draw upon the gratifications of the present for those of a distant day. When a people thus situated have a provision made for them, to which they can, with certainty, have recourse, as often as they themselves are deprived of the means of earning their own subsistence ; and yet, notwithstanding this security, choose to form themselves almost universally into Benefit Societies, in order that, by taking something from the means of their present scanty enjoyments, they may in sickness, disablement, and old age, be saved from the necessity of having recourse to public charity, and may continue to live to the end of their days upon the fruit of their own labour, no burthen on the public, or dependant upon its bounty ; they exibit a combination of qualities, the existence of which could hardly be credited if it were not seen ; above all, in a country in which the higher ranks too often display an eager desire to benefit themselves at the public expense."—*Sup. Ency. Brit.*, Art. *Benefit, Societies*, p. 263.

into practice.   A minority of witnesses, who, as actuaries, prac-
tically conversant with the tables of mortality, came under the
denomination of " practical men," being of opinion that there
was no foundation for the theory, their evidence held the Com-
mitte *in dubio* during the first year of its sitting.   Before we
give any specimens of the opinions received from these witnesses,
and treated as evidence by the Committee, we shall offer a few
general observations on the value of the opinions of average
" practical men," on all questions of change or improvement.

The common reliance on the testimony of this class of witnesses is founded upon an assumption, that those who have been
long engaged in a particular pursuit must necessarily have obtained, or at least are most likely to possess, the whole of the
existing knowledge relative to that pursuit, and must, therefore,
be the most competent to form a correct estimate of it, in all its
bearings.   This assumption of completeness of information, as
predicated of the whole class of practical men, is untenable.   By
nothing are they so much distinguished, as by their indifference
to the progress and result of any investigations which may be
carried on relative to that pursuit, and to the utility of any new
facts that may be elicited with respect to it.   Thus the chief practical man examined as a witness before the Committee was asked,

' Do you know of any actual observation or collection of facts
subsequent to the final adoption of the Northampton tables by Dr.
Price, whereby those tables have been confirmed?—To which he
answered, " I know of none since the year 1791, that was the
time in which he died.   He proved the tables made at Holy Cross,
and at Chester, and at Warrington, and compared them with those
of Breslaw.   Chester is the best town for making observations,
for it is a town where the inhabitants, at the time Dr. Price formed
his tables, neither decreased nor increased much.'

He was then examined in the following manner :—

' Are you acquainted with the table published by Mr. Francis
Baily, shewing the number of persons living at the several ages
according to the observations at London, Stockholm, Chester, and
other places?—No; I know nothing of the table.'

' Are you acquainted with a table published by Corbaux of the
same nature?—I never heard of him : there was a Swedish table
published by Mr. Baily, but that, I " believe," is nearly the same
with that given by Dr. Price for males and females.'

Ask, in like manner, the practical agriculturist, the practical
merchant, or the practical tradesman, about any book relating

to his avocation, which furnishes new facts, or presents the old facts in better method and order for practical purposes, and you will find him equally ignorant and careless on the subject. It is obvious that the practical man whom we have just cited had made up his bundle of opinions in 1791, and did not care to open it for the purpose of substituting in the place of those which were old and rotten, others that were new and sound. Since the Northampton table worked well for him, produced to himself a good salary, and to the parties for whom he acted a good bonus, what motive had he to investigate? What mattered it, whether or not the circumstances of society had been altered and the duration of life extended since 1791? Thus it will be found, in the great majority of cases, that, the routine of practical men being given, you have the whole of their information relative to their avocations. To their indifference to the reception of any new facts, and the consequent incompleteness of their information for any practical purpose, may be added their incompetency to weigh evidence, free from the bias, in most cases of direct monied interest; and in nearly all cases, of the interest arising from the loss of reputation which would be incurred by acknowledging that others were in possession of superior information, or were capable of making a better application than themselves of the information already possessed: while all experience proves that even the interest occasioned by the disinclination to change old habits is of itself sufficient to counteract a considerable monied interest, when that interest is not immediate and obvious to the senses. " The great bulk of mankind," observes Paley, " act more from habit than reflection;" and most especially must this be the case during the prevalence of systems of education which perform by the memory alone, all which the memory alone can be made to perform,—which teach everything by rote, nothing by reference to first principles. Under the evil influence of the habit of parroting, which is acquired under a common education, almost every person is taught his avocation according to fixed rules, and is made to believe that the existing practice, whatever it be, is the best possible. Before he has time to form an opinion for himself, the associations and belief chosen for him by others become so strongly impressed on his mind by habit, as in a great measure to destroy his power of forming, or even of en-

tertaining, any new combinations on the subject. Hence, perhaps, it is, that the most important improvements in the arts
and sciences have been made, not by the " regularly-educated
practical men," but by persons trained up to other pursuits.
The greatest improvements in agriculture have been made by
persons bred up in cities. The best laws are made by persons
who are not practical lawyers. The same causes will, perhaps,
account for the circumstance so frequently observed, that whenever a man of superior mind arises, the last thing benefited by
the exercise of his powers of invention will be the pursuit to
which he was " regularly educated." As an instance of the
operation of the causes to which we have alluded so often, incapacitating men of extensive practice, and even of something
more than mere routine, from forming a conception of any
change or improvement, we may mention the recent case of
Sir James Scarlett. It may be recollected, that a short time
ago, a complaint was made in Parliament that the fees extorted
from prisoners at the sessions were so considerable, that the
court and jury, from motives of compassion, conspired to convict a poor man in order that he might be fined a shilling and
be discharged from further payments. Sir James Scarlett hereupon rose : he candidly admitted and lamented the existence of the evil, but declared (and we fully believe in the
sincerity of the declaration) that he could not *see* how it
could be remedied ! Mr. Peel ventured to say, in reply to the
greatest of practical lawyers, that he humbly conceived the
evil might be remedied by *abolishing the fees*. We have
heard of another practical man, of the same class, who, on hearing that in Holland no distinction was made between real and
personal property, expressed his extreme surprise at such deplorable barbarism, and wondered how society could hold
together without such a classification. He could form no conception of a state of things, in which the secure possession of
an estate could be conveyed with as little expense or trouble as
the least important article in daily use. Such a " practical
man" is about as competent to judge of the work of codification, or the substitution of any well systematised body of laws
for the incongruous jumble in the administration of which he is
practised, as a well practised hackney-coachman or chairman
would, from his practice, be fitted to judge of a comprehensive

plan of direct and convenient streets, devised by a Sir Christopher Wren for the rebuilding of an old, ill-built, confused city, or even part of a city, with the obscure turns of which, its barbarous names, and the slang and usages of the frequenters, the said practical men were familiar.   Such men are useful, and often meritorious, in their proper places; which are neither in the Legislature, nor, we make bold to say, on the Bench.   Such men may suggest the straightening of an awkward turn; the stopping up of a hole in which they are themselves jolted; or the removal of a wall against which they run their own heads; but the formation of new, plain, and direct roads, and especially any great convenience or magnificent simplicity of combinations, are as much beyond their comprehensions as they are foreign to their habits.   From such minds comprehensive legislation or decisions upon enlarged principles never did and never will proceed. Other similar illustrations will present themselves to every observing person in almost every field of art or science, and not the least frequently in the fields of practical statesmanship.   How rarely is it that the official or practical legislator condescends, in dealing with the subject matter of any legislation in England, to consult the experience even of another of the United Kingdoms, much less the experience of any of the European nations, on the same subject!   When do we see any of the masterpieces of foreign legislation referred to in our Parliament, although they would afford the most valuable instruction?   The report, for example, of Michel St. Fargeau, on the Penal Code, presented to the Constituant Assembly in 1791, and even the debate which then ensued upon it, may be submitted as a contrast to *every* state paper, and to the display of knowledge made on the same subject, during any session of the English Parliament, from the same period to the present day.   The legislation of the great majority of our rulers, who lift their heads aloft above instruction,—who praise their own groping in the dark under the name of practice, and abuse as " theory and speculation" all attempts to act upon extended knowledge and aforethought,—is a scene of continual fumbling and botches; of amendments upon amendments, often producing new evils, and aggravating the evils which they were intended to remedy. The legislation upon prison discipline, upon secondary punishments, and upon the " the licensing systems," might be adduced in illustration of the assertion: The object of the more consummate of these official and practical statesmen would seem to be, not " to commit themselves :" *i. e.* to do nothing ; or to evade difficulties neatly and speciously, and cover with pomp or a bland routine the *dolce far niente* of office ; averting their heads from calamities so long as they are unnoticed, and letting evil principles work themselves out on the community, unless they are forced into notice by clamour. The best of the practical men of routine are those whose pride slumbers, who are not roused to resist amendments proposed by others, and who merely follow as rules of office the old monk's rules of life, *Fungi officio taliter qualiter. Semper benedicite domini priori,* or *Nunquam male loqui de superioribus. Sinere insanum mundum vadere quo vult—nam vult vadere quo vult.* *

The great crime of the class of practical men, is their dishonest dealing with evidence ; shutting their ears to it, and when it is forced upon their perception, depreciating it, conjuring up fictitious obstacles, and exaggerating the force of real ones. When any measure constituting a change is presented to such minds, the question usually asked is not, " Is the evidence in support of it sound and complete ?" but, " What shall I gain or lose by admitting it ? shall I not testify to another's superiority ?" Persons, indeed, who devise measures, and who are not trained in the investigation and application of evidence, commit the faults of omission from over-eagerness or want of skill, or from an extent of ignorance or folly equalling that of the men of mere routine. Nor is it to be overlooked, that in devising measures which, though consisting of many particulars, are well founded in the main principles, the theorist is apt to overlook important details which are familiar to the practical man. Thus it is related, that when one of the great inventors of the machinery which has served as the foundation of so much of the national prosperity had constructed one of his most important and complex machines, in full confidence in the soundness and completeness of the inductions upon

---

* Get through your business in a way or so as to excite no complaint. Always admire and praise everything done by your superiors in office or party, and only see merit in those by whom they are likely to be ousted. Receive your salary quietly, and then get yourself into no troublesome opposition, but let the mad world go on as it will go ; for it always will go as it will go.

which he had formed it, he assembled all his friends to see it start. The power was applied, but lo! the machine could not be got to move. A shrewd practical man who was present declared that he could make the machine work, and would do so provided he received a share of the profits. The inventor was but too happy to assent to anything which would enable him to see the machine work. The practical man, however, would not move until he had the security for a share of the profits signed and sealed. The parties retired to a counting-house to accomplish this; and when he had the document in his possession which secured to him a fortune, he returned to the scene, took from his pocket a piece of chalk, with which he rubbed one roller to prevent the fibres of the cotton from adhering to it, and the vast machine worked completely and successfully. When Winsor, the inventor of the mode of lighting cities, promulgated his plan for a joint stock company with the promise of enormous profits, it was covered with ridicule as wild and visionary; but the plan was in the main sound, excepting that he had inadvertently overlooked as an incidental and minor item the expense of *pipes!*

Whilst some "practical men" adhere closely to their evidence, and coincide with the sound theorist in eschewing the wild hypotheses, or hasty generalizations, miscalled theories, and nevertheless appreciate the conclusions obtained by diligent investigation, and the sagacious comparison of a variety of phenomena; it is to be observed of the greater part of those empirical persons, who laud themselves as practical, that they are of all others the most infected with rash and baseless speculations. If our space permitted we could give many illustrations of the truth of the remark of Dugald Stewart, "that the simplest narrative of the most illiterate observer involves more or less of hypothesis; nay, that in general it will be found, that in proportion to his ignorance the greater is the number of conjectural principles involved in his statements." As, he observes, "a village apothecary (and if possible, in a still greater degree, an experienced nurse) is seldom able to describe the plainest case without employing a phraseology of which every word is a theory," (or an hypothesis,) "whereas a simple and genuine specification of the phenomena which mark a particular disease,—a specification unsophisticated by fancy or preconceived opinions, may be regarded as unequivocal evidence of a mind trained by long and successful study to the most difficult of all arts, that of the faithful interpretation of nature."

On the whole, it may be laid down as a general rule, that unless the mind of a practical man has been trained to habits of generalising beyond the details of his profession, his conclusion as to the effect of any extensive change in his practice is less to be relied upon than that of any other man of equal general intelligence, to whose mind *the same facts* are presented, and who gives them an equal degree of consideration. Yet, it is the evidence of this class of practical men which, in all questions of change and improvement, governs the opinions of our legislators and of a large portion of the public. It is important to have the real value of such evidence better understood ; and for this purpose we have digressed thus far, to avail ourselves of some illustrations presented by the reports before us. If the general observations are found to apply to the evidence of practical men whose avocations are of a more intellectual nature, *à fortiori* will they apply to those engaged in ordinary pursuits.*

---

* The whole subject of the administration of the poor laws is replete with illustrations of pseudo practical statesmanship, and of the states of the practical minds of the country. The new measures are founded on inquiries so much more extensive, and on inductions from facts so much more numerous and various, than it has hitherto been the practice to require for legislative measures, that if any of them fail, the failure may confidently be pronounced to be the fault of those who are charged with their execution. Yet the exposition of the results was hurried, unavoidably perhaps, by the Government, and was therefore deficient in the completeness attainable, had circumstances permitted an extension of the period of the labour being from a few months to a year. We shall submit from this inquiry a few illustrations of the state of mind of the practical men concerned in that branch of administration.

'I have,' says Mr. Chadwick, in his report, 'endeavoured to ascertain from several of the magistrates who are advocates for the allowance system, or for the regulation of wages, in what way the labouring man within their districts expends for his maintenance the sum which they have declared to be the minimum expenditure, to sustain life ? Some of these gentlemen admitted that they did not know ; others stated that they laid it down as a general rule, that a labouring man must have bread and meat ; but whether three or four loaves of bread, whether a pound or a pound and a half of meat, constituted the least quantity requisite as food for a given period, none of them could state. Several promised to make inquiries on the subject, when I asked them how they could safely set aside the decisions of the parish officers, or determine with due precision what was the minimum allowance of money for the pauper's subsistence, unless they knew how many commodities were absolute necessaries for him, and the exact quantity and the price of each.

The practical men whose evidence supported the doctrine that the duration of life has not been extended since the time of the formation of the Northampton tables, were Mr. W. Morgan, the actuary of the Equitable Insurance Company, which is the most wealthy and extensive institution of the kind in Europe ; Mr. W. Glenny, the secretary to numerous benefit societies and insurance companies for the labouring classes ; and Mr. W. Frend, the actuary of the Rock Life Insurance Company. We shall extract some portions of the evidence given by the two latter witnesses, and with only slight observation leave them to the reader's judgment. But the former deserves a more special notice, since his opinions, from the circumstance of his enjoying a more extensive practice than any other man, have obtained a degree of weight that entitles him to the distinction of being presented as the specimen *par excellence* of the " practical man."

Mr. Frend's evidence is to this effect :—

' Do you apprehend that, since the Northampton tables were formed, the value of human life has increased?—No, I do not; there may be a difference in the higher classes, but I cannot say that I conceive the general notion that it is so is correct.

' Whilst complaining of the effects of the beer-shops established under Mr. Goulburn's Act, the same magistrates have frequently stated that habits of drunkenness prevailed with the whole of the labourers within their districts, and that these labourers were accustomed to carouse during one or two days in the week, gambling and indulging in the most vicious habits. Having received evidence that so large a proportion of the agricultural poor-rate is expended in aid of wages, I have been startled by the declarations that the habits of dissipation had become so prevalent. In answer to further inquiries, I have received assurances that the habit is *general;* that there are few, if any, exceptions. I have again asked whether the exceptions are formed of those who received parochial relief, and I have been assured (and satisfactory evidence has been adduced to me), that the agricultural labourers receiving poor's-rates in aid of wages are to be found at the beer-shops as frequently at least as the independent labourers. The questions which have appeared to me naturally to follow are, — Do you consider beer or gin a necessary of life to the paupers? If it be admitted that beer is a necessary of life to the independent labourers, the quantity required for intoxication can hardly be necessary ; ought you not then to ascertain and deduct the amount of money spent in drunken revelry? As it must be presumed that a man pays for the beer he drinks at the beer-shops, (which beer is not deemed absolutely necessary for his subsistence,) is it not clear that you have not arrived at the minimum allowance? If, for example, you order wages to be made up to a man to the amount of nine shillings a week, and you find that he gets drunk one or two days in the week, and that his excess of drink costs him two shillings a week, since he actually lives on seven shillings a week, does he not prove by so living that seven is all that he really requires ?'
' So far as I have been able to examine the answers to the query circu-

' Are the Committee to understand that it is not your opinion, that among any but the higher classes the life of a man of twenty is more valuable than it was, or than it was estimated to be,

---

lated by his Majesty's Commissioners, whether the family of a labouring man in full work could lay by anything? it appears that a great majority of the respondents state positively that the labouring man cannot save anything. About half the respondents from Devonshire make no answer to the query. W. J. Coppard, the minister of Plympton, St. Mary's, says, " *A few* have trifling sums in the savings-bank." The other respondents either express a strong doubt whether anything could be saved by a labouring man, or declare positively that he could lay by nothing; yet we find upwards of 70,000*l.* saved, under all obstacles, by two thousand labourers, or by one out of every ten heads of agricultural labourers' families in this same county.

'The larger proportion of the magistrates, clergymen, and parish officers who are respondents from Berkshire, declare that the labourer could not save; only three or four indicate a belief that he could. Colonel Page, who is one of the trustees of the savings-bank at Newbury, says, " Hard to answer." Yet in the bank of which he was a trustee, were found 593 agricultural labourers depositors of an aggregate of savings to the amount of 6,500*l.*'

'About thirty labourers in the metropolis, when interrogated by the governor of the Cold-Bath Fields House of Correction, stated that they could live on 1*s.* a day. Labourers and others, earning such wages as 2*s.* per day, are found to be depositors in the savings-banks of the metropolis. The following are the statements of some of the respondents (clergymen and gentlemen serving parochial offices in the metropolis) to Queries 35, 36, 37, 38 — What can a family earn, and whether they can live on these earnings and lay by anything?

'The answer from Chiswick states that a family might earn 49*l.* per annum, on which they might live, but could not save. St. Anne and Agnes, and St. Leonard, Foster-lane—family might earn 60*l.*; could not live on it. St. Botolph Without, Aldersgate — family might earn 63*l.* 18*s.* on which they might subsist, but could save nothing. Mile End, New Town, and St. Mary's, Somerest, City of London—family might earn 65*l.* on which they might live, but could not save anything. St. Leonard, Eastcheap — family might earn 78*l.*; could not save, and cannot ascertain whether they could live upon it. St. James's, Westminster—man might earn 78*l.*, besides material assistance from his wife and children; might live on wholesome food, but cannot attempt to say whether they could save. Holy Trinity the Less —family might earn 93*l.*; might live on spare diet; could not save anything. Mr. Baker, the coroner and vestry clerk of St. Anne's, Limehouse, states that a family might earn 100*l.*, on which they could live, but *not* save. Hammersmith—a family might earn 49*l.* 8*s.*, which would give them wholesome food, and they might and *do* save.

'The extract I have given will, perhaps, suffice as a portion of the evidence tending to show the state of information on which rates of wages are determined, and adjudications are made on appeals against the allowances of parish officers. But on the part of those parish officers who come more immediately in contact with the labouring classes, and have the means of obtaining better information to determine as to the absolute necessity of the relief, I commonly found, in the districts where the allowance system prevails, that they were daily acting in the teeth of conclusive evidence, constantly obtruded on their notice. At Newbury, for instance, on examining the books in the presence of the assembled parish officers, I found that they gave relief in aid of wages.

twenty years ago?—If I am asked that as a matter of opinion, it must be matter of opinion merely. I very much suspect, that it is not a whit better: I rather think the calculation comes very near-

---

The officers expressed a decided opinion that it was impossible for labourers of that class to subsist without such assistance as they received from the parish. The following is an extract from my notes of the examination of these same officers:—

" Are those whose names appear in the books as persons receiving relief in aid of wages, all the labourers of this class or of those conditions residing within the town?"—The parish officers declared that they were only as a minority of those in the town. [Colonel Page, who did me the favour to assist me in the inquiry, observed that they did not probably form more than one-tenth of all the labourers in the parish.]

" Do the rest of the labourers receive no higher wages than those who obtain parochial relief?—We believe that their wages are the same."

" Amongst the large class of labourers who do not come for relief, is there not the usual proportion of married men, and many with large families?—Yes, we know there is."

" And yet, working at the same description of work and receiving no higher wages than the others, they maintain their families without asking aid of the parish?—Yes, they do do it, but how they do it we cannot tell. They are above coming to the parish."

" Is not the fact that these independent labourers *do* live without receiving relief in aid of wages, any proof to your minds that others *may* live without rates in aid of wages? Is not the occurrence of the fact before you any evidence of its possibility?"

' To this interrogatory I received no answer; and I passed on to another head of inquiry.'

These, be it observed, are not exemplifications of the states of mind of individuals, but of *classes*, with respect to the plainest operations of which they may be presumed to be capable of judging. The following is an individual exemplification from the evidence given by a practical witness, a farmer and an appraiser of land, produced by the Marquis of Chandos, before the Committee which recently sat to inquire into the causes of agricultural distress. The witness had ascribed the fall of the price of wheat to the reduction of the duty in foreign corn. The witness was asked—

' Do you recollect the alteration of the Corn Laws in 1815?—1815 was the time when it was reduced under Lord Castlereagh, and the prohibition was reduced from 80s. to 70s. It was in 1822 the protecting duty was diminished?—Yes. Do you remember that wheat was very low in 1822?—Yes. Do you remember its rising in 1823, 1824, and 1825?—Yes. Notwithstanding the reduction in the duty?—Yes; I know it *rose* in price.—The reduction in the duty could not very well have produced a *fall* in price, for the price *rose* in the three succeeding years?—I have understood it from the newspapers, that there were ten millions of foreign corn imported into England in one year. Supposing that were to be the fact according to the returns, it would not have tended to depress the market in 1822?—I think it would. Then, if by the Corn Law of 1822, the rate of duty was diminished upon the importation of corn, and the price immediately *rose* for three years succeeding, that reduction of the duty could hardly be said to be the cause of the *fall* in price?—I consider that the extremely low price *was* produced by the amazing quantity of foreign corn brought into the English markets. There was none brought in 1822: there was some brought in in 1819?—I recollect one year in which it was stated there were ten millions worth of foreign corn brought into England, but I do not recollect the year.'

ly to the same point. As to the general measure of human life, that it is not materially altered, no tables whatever can be formed that are accurate ; for our tables end at the age of ninety-six, whereas we know every year that people live beyond an hundred ; therefore it is clear that no tables which human ingenuity can devise come exactly to accuracy ; but it is luckily like the property of the asymptote, it comes near enough for practical purposes.'— *First Report*, p. 87.

We are bound to give the witness credit for sincerity even at the expense of his reputation for capacity ; but had he intended to nonplus the hon. members, he could not have succeeded more completely. They did not put to him another question on this subject.

From Mr. Glenny the Committee received the following testimony :—

' Having yourself constructed tables in a great degree from actual observation, you are confirmed in the opinion that Dr. Price's tables were correct ?—The nearest to correctness.

' Do you not think that health has improved by the improvement of medical science since the time of Dr. Price ?—Not much more in adults, but very much in children.

' Supposing that you have in one district an accurate table of mortality, and also an accurate table of the average of sickness ; that in another district you have the table of mortality only, which I will suppose to differ considerably from the table of mortality in the other district ; do you think, that by constructing a table of sickness in the latter district, bearing the same relation to the sickness table of the former as the mortality table in the second bears to that of the first, you would come to an accurate result ?— No, I do not. I think it would depend so much upon other circumstances ; it would depend so much upon the manufactures. In some trades the mortality is much more severe, and the sickness much lighter ; and I have been much perplexed, in the course of nine years' close observation, by these two results : my proceed-

---

The type of the genus of practical men, as opposed to theorists and innovators, may really be presented ·in a story of some Russian fruit-dealers, who had been accustomed, when they had sold the fruit out of one of the panniers with which their asses were laden, to put stones in the empty pannier to balance the one containing fruit. "My good man," said a gentleman to one of these personages, "would you not save your beast much toil, and yourself some trouble, if, instead of filling the empty pannier with stones, you were simply to divide the apples and put half the contents of the full pannier into the other one ?"—"I do not know how that may be," replied the practical man ; "but this is the way I have always done myself—this is the way my father did, and my grandfather, and my great-grandfather before them, and I won't now call all of them, and myself too, fools by trying any of your new-fangled schemes."

ings for the next five years, I hope, will obtain the results of the various large manufactures of this kingdom, as the only correct means of preparing a correct sickness table.

' In what particular business have you observed the difference between mortality and sickness, that the mortality should be great and the sickness less ?—I have found the gilders very subject to sickness, and I have not found that it materially shortens life.

'What sort of sickness?—Chiefly debility arising from the mercury.

' Do you not include painters ?—Next to gilders, the casters in lead, and workers in lead of all descriptions, are more subject to sickness than to mortality comparatively. They have rheumatic pains ; they have affections in the joints, and many disorders which prevent them periodically from following their business : hence they are turned out of most societies, or rather not admitted.

' Is that the case with painters also ?—I class them among workers of lead of every description. Watchmakers are very apt to be affected in the sight, and they also go into declines, and hang a long time on the funds, frequently without dying at a more early period than other men. Husbandmen are subject to much less sickness, I think, from the returns I have been able to procure, than almost any species of mechanic.

' And do you not think they live longer also ?—I think they do. In London there are an immense number of founderies, where they keep an immense number of men, and there they are subject to be laid on the funds by accident, yet they are not frequently accidents that kill them, so that they are thrown on the superannuated list early.

' Do you not think human life lengthened from the improvement of medical science during the last twenty-five years ?— No, I do not. I think the quantity of sickness lessened, but I do not think life lengthened.—Do you not apprehend that more children are reared ?—Yes, certainly; so much so, that I have been for years trying to form a table to provide something for children during their minority, and I have been comparatively baffled by the difference of life in children within the last twelve or fourteen years, so that I have to go over the whole ground again. I should think the lives of children had increased a fifth, at least from my experience.'—*First Report.*

We shall not stop to examine how far the conclusion of the witness, that life has not lengthened, agrees with his admissions, that, since the Northampton table was formed, the health of adults has advanced a little, and the health of children has been improved very much, so that a greater number are now reared to maturity. With respect to the instances he adduced in support of the paradox, that sickness might increase and mortality yet remain stationary, it did not, perhaps, occur to the Committee to inquire of the witness, whether the classes of debilitated men, whom he mentioned, would be likely to withstand, so well as healthy men, those casual diseases (not incidental to any avocation) to which all classes are exposed.   That men may lose their sight without their general health being materially diminished—that the diminution of life from the effects of injuries which disable a man, and, in some degree, also debilitate his general health, may often be compensated by his exemption as a pensioner from the hard labour, wear and tear, and consequent loss of vitality incidental to his avocation,—no one will dispute ; but that a whole class may be debilitated by sickness without the duration of life amongst them being impaired, is an absurdity.* The operation of general causes of sickness on particular classes, and the diminution of a patient's chances of recovery in proportion to his previous debility, was strikingly illustrated in some returns from the hospitals at Paris, to which we shall hereafter advert.

We now come to Mr. Morgan, whose evidence on this point we shall extract.

'When examined before the Poor-laws Committee in 1817, you stated, that you had no reason to doubt that the tables published in the second volume of your edition of Dr. Price's work were still correct?—I found them correct, and I *do find* them correct.

' Have you any reason to believe that sickness has actually increased ?—Not at all.

' Do you think it has diminished in consequence of the introduction of vaccination ?—Most likely it has ; but the people admitted into these clubs are people from twenty to thirty years of age.

' We were speaking of sickness generally, not as relating to these clubs ?—There may be more in some years than in others.

' Still you have taken it at a lower average ?—Yes, I have.

' You find mortality greater, but not sickness ?—Not sickness.

' Sickness and mortality, both, of course, vary among different classes of people ?—Yes.

' Do you not apprehend that there are some classes in which sickness is more prevalent than in others, but where the lives of individuals are not shorter?—No, I do not think so.

' Are not some places more healthy than others?—They may be ; I know nothing about that.

' Are there not certain trades which afflict individuals with blindness without shortening their lives?—I do not know about that.'—*First Report*, p. 50.

---

* See note *post*, as to the sickness and mortality in gaols.

We shall say nothing as to the value of the testimony of this practical man, who ably and successfully superintends a mighty concern, with a capital of several millions of money, and yet is so ignorant beyond his routine, as not to know that there are some places more healthy than others.   It is to be attributed to the want of skill in the Committee to examine witnesses, and the ignorance of honourable members as to the nature and importance of the points to which they ought to have directed the examination, that more definite answers were not elicited from this witness and others.   But he has explicitly declared, as the result of his own practical experience, which we apprehend was wholly in his society (the Equitable), that Dr. Price's tables are still correct, and therefore that the average duration of life has remained stationary.   Many of our readers, who do not take into account the little exercise of mind which practical men in general bestow on the facts under their own observation, will perhaps be somewhat surprised when we inform them, that from the facts within the experience of this witness, his conclusion has been demonstrated to be extremely erroneous.   It appears, that he has been in the habit of making regular reports to the members of his institution, of the number of persons assured whose names appeared on their books, and of the numbers who died.   Mr. Griffith Davies, the actuary of the Guardian Assurance Office, procured a complete series of these reports, and theorized the facts of the practical man ; that is, " put the whole of the knowledge" which he (according to his reports) "possessed upon the subject into that order and form in which it is most easy to draw from it good practical rules." We have annexed a table, calculated by Dr. Mitchell from the practical man's facts, so theorized by Mr. Davies.   According to the witnesses's evidence, or the Northampton tables, the probable duration of a life already at twenty, is 33.43 years ; according to his facts, when theorized, its duration has extended to 41.05.   A life at thirty, according to his testimony as a practical man, is of 28.27 : according to the result of his reports, it is 33.97 years.   A life of forty, according to Dr. Price, whose tables are stated in the evidence of Mr. Morgan to be still applicable, is 23.08 years in duration: but on this point alone, Mr. Morgan's facts prove them to be inapplicable by four years and a fraction, the value of life having been improved to that extent.   Mr. Babbage and Mr. Gompertz went over nearly the same facts, and, so far as they went, confirmed the correctness of Mr. Davies's theory.

We have considerable presumptive evidence in the superior habits of females, to support the conclusion that the duration of their lives is greater than those of males.   Several men of extensive practice declared, however, that there was no material difference.

The Committee says to Mr. Glenny [*First Report*, p. 41],—

' Then you make no distinction upon the ground of a supposed difference in the value between male and female life ?—No: there are differences of opinion between calculators.   The difference is so small ; there is not a single consideration in the calculation of a table which is not of greater importance than that point.'

Mr. Baily is asked [*Second Report*, p. 27],—

' Do you conceive that it is necessary to have a different rate of payment for males and for females to ensure the same object ?— I should hardly think it worth while to perplex the subject with such a distinction.   Have you paid any attention to the subject ? I have occasionally.   In the valuation of annuities, we generally reckon the females lives worth half a year's purchase more.'

And Mr. Morgan [*Second Report*, p. 45], says,—

' The duration of life, in general, is a little better among females than among males : but, in my opinion, it is not sufficient to render it necessary to compute tables for them.'

These opinions are opposed, not only by the number, and, as we consider, weight, of opinions from other witnesses, but by the evidence of the Swedish tables, which shew the difference between male and female life to be very considerable. New returns were, however, now given to the Committee by Mr. Finlaison, the actuary of the National Debt Office, which established, beyond a doubt, the fact, that great improvement has taken place in the value of life amongst those classes respecting whom the best evidence was previously possessed. He also proved the superiority of the lives of females, as compared with the lives of males, to be very considerable.   When he presented his tables to the Committee in 1825, he stated [*First Report*, p. 44],—*

---

* That those Insurance Companies which do not grant annuities should have been unwilling to admit that the lives of women were on the average longer than those of men, was to be expected, inasmuch as these companies obtained from the few insurances effected on the lives of women the same

'It is now exactly six years ago since I was appointed by Government expressly for the purpose of investigating the true law of mortality which prevails among the people of England at the present time. I say, at the present time, because there has been, as I have discovered, a very extraordinary prolongation of human life in the course of the last hundred years. I also say, in either sex, because it has appeared, from the writings of former authors, that a great difference in the duration of life exists between the two sexes, and that that difference has never been accurately assigned. It was the more necessary to do this from authentic documents, because, heretofore, almost all the known tables are derived from parochial records, which are incapable of affording accurate deductions ; therefore, by the aid of Government, I was enabled to make observations upon the life annuitants of various classes who have been registered as nominees in Tontines, or life annuities properly so called. I made an observation upon nearly twenty-five thousand people in that situation, during a period of more than thirty years, and the consequences resulting from that observation upon each sex will be shewn in a paper, which I beg leave to give in, containing the expectation of life as it is now, and as it was a century ago: the difference is very great upon each sex ; the Committee will find it nearly as three to four. I mean, that the duration of existence now, compared with what it was a century ago, is as four to three in round numbers.'

In addition to the tables constructed upon the basis of the lives of Government annuitants who belong to the higher and middling classes, he calculated the mortality that prevailed during the years 1814 to 1822, amongst 50,682 out-pensioners on the books of Chelsea College, and 20,210 out-pensioners on

---

premiums as if effected on the lives of men. Some companies have, however, been induced by competition to make a distinction, and to advertise lower premiums on the lives of women than on the lives of men. On the other hand, increased sums are of course required for annuities on the lives of women. The Government was at last induced to yield to the evidence adduced by Mr. Finlaison; and in the tables now published, the price of annuities to women is considerably higher than for annuities to men.
In 1829 was printed Mr. Finlaison's report, containing all the elementary facts, of which the results only had been submitted to the Committee. The new tables were put in operation in November 1829. Last year (1835) these tables, and the conclusions of Mr. Griffith Davies and the theorists, have received corroboration from an unexpected quarter. The extensive and important experience of the Equitable Office has been published. At the age of 40, and at every higher age, the duration of life is stated to be just the same as that set forth in the Government tables. Below 40, the mortality is less in the Equitable than amongst the Government nominees. But the apparent reason is, that under 40 the Government observation is formed upon the nominees of the Tontines, enrolled in infancy; and it is alleged that as they grew up to man's estate, they went into tropical climates and into the wars in no small proportion. But the Insurance Office prohibits all this.

the books of Greenwich Hospital. These, he declares, were lives of the worst description. The great majority of them had come in under 45 years of age. They were either persons who had been wounded, or who had lived some time in unhealthy climates, and their claims for other causes than length of service must have been impaired constitutions. Yet the chances of these lives were at every age better than the chances given by the Northampton table, and after 50 as good as those given by the Carlisle tables.

The Committee obtained from Baron Delessert, the founder of the Philanthropic Society at Paris, extracts from the reports of " Les Sociétés de Prévoyance, L'Annuaire, par Le Bureau des Longitudes," and " Les Recherches Statistiques sur la Ville de Paris et le Département de la Seine." The returns thus obtained from France confirm, as far as they go, the theory that the value of life has improved with the improved habits and condition of the people. According to a document which the men of science in France treat as satisfactory evidence, it appears, that the annual deaths in Paris during the " age of Chivalry," (the fourteenth century,) was one in sixteen or seventeen. During the seventeenth century, it was one in twenty-five or twenty-six; and in 1824, it was one in 32·62.* When the other parts of France were added to the capital, the proportion of deaths appeared still farther to have decreased ; and, throughout the whole of France, the deaths during 1781 were one in twenty-nine. During the five years preceding 1825, it was one in thirty-nine. We have not the whole materials before us to enable us to determine accurately, but the total results prove, to the satisfaction of men of science on the other side of the Channel, that the value of life has doubled in France since " le bon vieux tems," and gained nearly one third since the Revolution.

In this state was the evidence submitted before the first Committee in 1825. We have shewn the quality of nearly the whole of the opinions called evidence, adduced to support the

---

* From the table constructed by Dr. Price to exhibit the average mortality in London, [see *Observations on Reversionary Payments,* vol. ii. p. 305, 310,] it appears that during the ten years ending with 1780, one inhabitant out of 19⅔ died annually. Mr. Milne has shown [Art. 755 of his treatise on Assurances], that in the ten years ending with 1810, there died in the metropolis, annually, one person in 34·19.

Northampton tables ; and we have described the nature of the evidence by which they were proved to represent the duration of life too unfavourably. It might be supposed that it could hardly have escaped the most careless and incompetent member of the Committee, that in proportion as the old tables represented the duration of life below the true rate, the public money was improvidently expended in granting annuities ; that is, in contracting, on consideration of the receipt of a given sum, to continue a certain annual payment so long as the grantee should live. It was matter of notoriety that Insurance Companies had grown extremely rich by the use of the old tables in the converse operation—that of assuring lives ; *i. e.* receiving an annuity during the life of an individual, on condition of paying a given sum at his death. It was then sufficiently well known, that these private companies would not grant annuities on the same terms as Government, or on the old tables ; obviously because they discovered that they would be losers by the transaction. These two facts alone made a case for stopping this source of public expenditure until inquiry could be made, and more satisfactory tables formed. The tables, however, now produced, proved beyond a doubt that the public money was expended at an enormous loss in granting annuities. We shall state one or two instances of the ruinous nature of these transactions.

On an average of the last hundred years, the price of three per cent. stock has been between seventy-nine and eighty. At that rate of interest, and the rate of mortality which, according to Mr. Finlaison, actually prevails among the Government annuitants, the annuity which ought to have been allowed on a life of sixty, for every 100*l.* sunk, was 8*l.* 10*s.* 7*d.* [Vide *Appendix to the Report of* 1825, p. 131]: whereas the annuity actually allowed on that age was 10*l.* 6*s.* 3*d.* for each 100*l.* sunk, making an absolute loss to the country of 1*l.* 15*s.* 8*d.* per cent. annually during the remainder of the life which was calculated at fifteen years' duration.—*Ibid. Appendix*, p. 125.

The deferred annuities were granted on still worse terms : for on reference to the rate of interest, and tables of mortality, above alluded to, it may be seen that the value of 1*l.* annuity purchased by a person at the age of forty, but which he is not to begin to receive until the age of fifty, is above eight years' purchase, or, in other words, that on such contingency the Government ought not to have granted above 12*l.* 10*s.* for every 100*l.* sunk ; whereas they gave 15*l.* 8*s.* per cent. making an absolute loss to the public of 2*l.* 18*s.* per cent. during the remainder of the life.

This expenditure, which had gone on for a series of years, was allowed to continue during two years more, though attention was strongly called to the subject.

In consequence of some observations which were made on Mr. Finlaison's tables, he went over the operation of theorizing the whole of his data a second time ; *i. e.* observing exactly the facts, " to make a perfect collection of them ; nothing omitted that is of importance ; nothing included of none ; and to record them in that order and form in which all that is best to be done in practice can be most immediately and certainly perceived." He performed this operation by new methods, and found the results to coincide in nearly every instance.   The extreme difference between the two sets of tables in granting an annuity would be fifteen shillings in the hundred pounds.   The difference between male and female lives he found to be very considerable in every period of life excepting in infancy (under ten years of age), and excepting also in extreme old age ; *e. g.* beyond eighty-five, when no distinction is perceptible in the returns.   He states the general result of the comparison in these terms :—"Supposing a mother were to leave a pension to her son ; the value of such a pension would only be two thirds of a pension left by a father to his daughter—the relative ages of the children and parents being precisely the same.   It follows, therefore," (and here let the reader refer to the testimony of those blind guides, the practical men,) "that any society making no distinction of sex, and granting pensions to widows according to the strict arithmetical result, would inevitably be ruined."— Vide *Second Report*, p. 57.

The Committee, it appears, in their Second Report, came to the conclusion that the evidence appeared "strong and decisive" in favour of tables which gave "an expectation of life higher than the Northampton," and that there was "not even a *primâ facie* case" in favour of the latter.—*Second Report*, p. 4.

Mr. John Naylor, speaking of Mr. Finlaison's table, says,

‘ I am inclined to believe it to be accurate, and for this reason ;

that with reference to the annuities calculated from this table, on male and female lives of course, the mean between male and female annuities would not give the proper annuity for lives in general, but still it would be sufficient for the purpose of comparison; and by comparing such annuities with the Carlisle tables, they are found to agree to a very surprising degree of exactness, especially from ten to fifty years of age. I have compared such annuities with De Parcieux's annuities, and also with Babbage's annuities, and with Davies's annuities, as deduced from what those gentlemen call the experience of the Equitable during the last fifty years; and from ten to fifty years of age the annuities agree with a surprising degree of exactness; and in consequence of the agreement of such annuities with annuities as deduced from the Carlisle tables, I am satisfied that Mr. Finlaison's calculations are correct.'— *Second Report*, p. 35.

Mr. Griffith Davies, and other actuaries, bear testimony to the superior value of Mr. Finlaison's tables to any others of which the public are in possession.

Mr. Naylor, when asked whether or not the rate of mortality had diminished in England, replied,

' I am decidedly of opinion that it has. This opinion is the result of several comparisons of the proportions of deaths to the numbers living at the same places at different times; from which I infer, that independently of the effects of vaccination, the mean duration of life has increased in England during the last fifty years.'—*Second Report*, p. 85.

Mr. Griffith Davies, on this point, gives evidence which we think worthy of particular attention.

' As another corroboration of the increased value of life within the last hundred years,' he says, ' I think, on examination of the different tables, the fruitfulness of women, say from the age of fifteen to fifty, will be found nearly the same at all periods; and, in the greater part, I believe, of the different countries of Europe that we have tables for, prior to the time when Dr. Price wrote, that degree of fruitfulness was scarcely adequate to compensate for the existing mortality; so that he strenuously argued that the population was decreasing in this country; and I believe that, supposing the documents he had to reason upon to be correct, the conclusion he drew was not so erroneous as it has been represented. It is not an increase of the number of births, as compared with the number of bearing women, that has increased the population, but the increased number of children that have been reared from the birth and passed through the several stages of life. In other words, I would observe, that about one hundred years back, if any dependance can be placed upon the registers, the number of annual births did not exceed the number of burials, and, as a consequence, the population could not then have been on the increase. The increase of population since that period must, therefore, be attributed to an increase of fruitfulness of the female sex ; to the effect of immigration ; to a diminution of the rate of mortality; or to two or more of these causes combined. But as far as documentary evidence goes, it does not appear that the number of births has increased in comparison with the number of bearing women ; and it is clear that the increase of population cannot be attributed to immigration, otherwise the number of burials must have increased with the number of births, which is contrary to the fact, as established on indisputable evidence ; the increase of population must, therefore, be entirely attributable to a diminution of the rate of mortality.'—*Second Report*, p. 38.

The relative chances of the duration of life, as determined by the several tables of which we have treated, are thus displayed in the following table.—*See Table* A.

[TABLE A.]

Age.	Northampton	Swedish.		Carlisle.	Equitable.	Government Annuitant	
		Male.	Female.			Male.	Female.
0	25·18	37·82	41·01	38·72		50·16	55·51
1	32·74	46·26	48·60	44·68		50·13	55·59
2	37·79	48·12	50·28	47·55		50·04	55·37
3	39·55	48·84	50·90	49·82		49·80	55·05
4	40·58	49·05	51·15	50·76		49·42	54·65
5	40·84	48·99	51·04	51·25		48·93	54·23
6	41·07	48·80	50·79	51·17		48·36	53·72
7	41·03	48·60	50·38	50·80		47·71	53·15
8	40·79	47·91	49·78	50·24		47·02	52·50
9	40·36	47·30	49·23	49·57		46·30	51·80
10	39·78	46·68	48·55	48·82	48·83	45·57	51·05
11	39·14	45·95	47·83	48·04	48·02	44·83	50·27
12	38·49	45·21	47·09	47·27	47·20	44·07	49·48
13	37·83	44·59	46·00	46·51	46·40	43·31	48·70
14	37·17	43·67	45·51	45·75	45·60	42·53	47·93
15	36·51	42·88	44·72	45·00	44·81	41·75	47·19
16	35·85	42·11	43·95	44·27	44·03	41·01	46·51
17	35·20	41·34	43·18	43·57	43·27	40·29	45·86
18	34·58	40·57	42·73	42·87	42·50	39·61	45·22
19	33·99	39·79	41·62	42·17	41·78	38·98	44·60
20	33·43	39·05	40·90	41·46	41·05	38·39	43·99
21	32·90	38·32	40·05	40·75	40·33	37·83	43·36
22	32·39	37·61	39·16	40·04	39·59	37·34	42·73
23	31·88	36·91	38·66	39·31	38·88	36·87	42·09
24	31·36	36·19	37·91	38·59	38·15	36·89	41·45
25	30·85	35·48	37·17	37·86	37·44	35·90	40·81
26	30·33	34·75	36·43	37·14	36·73	35·41	40·17

[TABLE A. *continued.*]

Age.	Northampton.	Swedish.		Carlisle.	Equitable.	GovernmentAnnuitant	
		Male.	Female.			Male.	Female.
27	29·82	34·68	35·69	36·41	36·02	34·86	39·52
28	29·30	33·30	34·96	35·69	35·23	34·31	38·87
29	28·79	32·57	34·22	35·00	34·65	33·75	38·22
30	28·27	31·85	33·49	34·34	33·97	33·17	37·57
31	27·76	31·12	32·77	33·60	33·30	32·59	36·91
32	27·24	30·39	32·04	33·03	32·64	32·00	36·26
33	26·72	29·66	31·33	32·36	31·98	31·40	35·61
34	26·20	29·07	30·61	31·68	31·32	30·79	34·96
35	25·68	28·20	29·90	31·00	30·66	30·17	34·31
36	25·16	27·48	29·19	30·32	30·00	29·54	33·68
37	24·64	26·75	28·48	29·64	29·35	28·91	33·04
38	24·12	26·03	27·77	28·96	28·70	28·28	32·40
39	23·60	25·32	27·26	28·28	28·05	27·65	31·76
40	23·08	24·62	26·35	27·61	27·39	27·02	31·12
41	22·56	23·93	25·65	26·97	26·74	26·39	30·46
42	22·04	23·24	24·97	26·34	26·08	25·74	29·81
43	21·54	22·56	24·47	25·71	25·40	25·08	29·14
44	21·03	21·87	23·61	25·09	24·75	24·42	28·48
45	20·52	21·18	22·92	24·46	24·09	23·75	27·81
46	20·02	20·51	22·21	23·82	23·44	23·07	27·13
47	19·51	19·84	21·49	23·17	22·72	22·38	26·44
48	19·00	19·18	20·77	22·50	22·12	21·68	25·75
49	18·49	18·53	20·06	21·81	21·47	20·98	25·06
50	17·99	17·90	19·37	21·11	20·72	20·30	24·35
51	17·50	17·30	18·70	20·39	20·20	19·62	23·65
52	17·02	16·72	18·05	19·68	19·59	18·97	22·93
53	16·54	16·14	17·39	18·97	19·00	18·34	22·22
54	16·06	15·55	16·74	18·28	18·37	17·73	21·50
55	15·58	14·97	16·08	17·58	17·88	17·15	20·79
56	15·10	14·37	15·45	16·89	17·27	16·57	20·08
57	14·63	13·80	14·82	16·21	16·71	16·02	19·38
58	14·15	13·25	14·20	15·55	16·15	15·47	18·69
59	13·68	12·70	13·58	14·92	15·60	14·93	18·00
60	13·21	12·17	12·98	14·34	15·02	14·39	17·32
61	12·75	11·66	12·40	13·82	14·50	13·84	16·64
62	12·28	11·15	11·84	13·31	13·96	13·28	15·96
63	11·81	10·64	11·30	12·81	13·42	12·72	15·30
64	11·35	10·11	10·76	12·30	12·88	12·17	14·64
65	10·88	9·60	10·16	11·79	12·36	11·63	14·00
66	10·42	9·11	9·69	11·27	11·82	11·10	13·37
67	9·96	8·61	9·18	10·75	11·33	10·61	12·73
68	9·50	8·14	8·67	10·23	10·81	10·14	12·13
69	9·05	7·68	8·17	9·70	10·32	9·67	11·57
70	8·60	7·25	7·69	9·18	9·83	9·22	10·99

[TABLE A. *continued.*]

Age.	Northampton.	Swedish.		Carlisle.	Equitable.	Government Annuitant	
		Male.	Female			Male.	Female.
71	8·17	6·88	7·25	8·65	9·35	8·79	10·44
72	7·74	6·50	6·85	8·16	8·88	8·37	9·92
73	7·33	6·16	6·47	7·72	8·41	7·96	9·41
74	6·92	5·82	6·11	7·33	7·96	7·54	8·92
75	6·54	5·50	5·78	7·01	7·52	7·12	8·46
76	6·18	5·22	5·39	6·69	7·07	6·69	8·00
77	5·83	4·94	5·10	6·40	6·64	6·23	7·53
78	5·48	4·51	4·80	6·12	6·20	5·78	7·19
79	5·11	4·41	4·50	5·80	5·78	5·35	6·83
80	4·75	4·09	4·22	5·51	5·37	4·94	6·50
81	4·41	3·86	3·98	5·21	4·99	4·55	6·20
82	4·09	3·67	3·77	4·93	4·60	4·18	5·89
83	3·80	3·50	3·55	4·65	4·30	3·82	5·57
84	3·58	3·36	3·40	4·39	4·00	3·46	5·22
85	3·37	3·23	3·23	4·12	3·73	3·12	4·84
86	3·19	3·07	3·16	3·90	3·50	2·81	4·44
87	3·01	2·95	3·01	3·71	3·30	2·53	4·03
88	2·86	2·78	2·83	3·59	3·11	2·31	3·62
89	2·66	2·68	2·57	3·47	2·91	2·12	3·21
90	2·41	2·50	2·26	3·28	2·65	1·95	2·83
91	2·09	2·38	2·06	3·26	2·35	1·83	2·49
92	1·75	2·18	1·83	3·37	2·02	1·65	2·21
93	1·37	1·96	1·75	3·48	1.70	1·49	1·97
94	1·05	1·87	1·72	3·53	1·25	1·34	1·75
95	0·75	1·70	1·70	3·53	1·05	1·13	1·55
96	0·50	1·50	1·50	3·46	0·75	·97	1·32
97		1·00	1·00	3·28		·75	1·12
98				3·07		·50	·94
99				2·77		·00	·75
100				2·28		·0	·50
101				1·79			
102				1·30			
103				0·83			

The results as respects pecuniary provisions against contingencies are thus set forth in the Second Report.—*See Table* B.

[TABLE B.]

	1	2	3	4	5	6	7
	By Dr. Price's table, founded on the register of Birth and Burials at Northampton.	By the first Swedish tables, as published by Dr. Price, for both sexes.	By De Parcieux's tables, founded on the mortality in the French footnotes prior to 1745.	By Mr. Milne's table, founded on the mortality observed at Carlisle.	By Mr. G. Davies's table, founded on the experience of the Equitable Life Assurance Office.*	By Mr. Finlaison's tables, founded on the experience of the Government life annuitants. — According to his first investigation, mentioned in 1825. — Mean of both sexes.	According to his second investigation, mentioned in 1827. — Mean of both sexes.
Of 100,000 persons aged 25, there would be alive at the age of 65 -	34·286	43·137	51·033	51·335	49·330	53·470	53·950
Of 100,000 persons aged 65, there would be alive at the age of 80 -	28·738	25·704	29·879	31·577	37·267	38·655	37·355
Expectation of life at the age of 25 years - - - - - -	30·85	34·58 (a)	37·17	37·86	37·45	38·35	38·52
Expectation of life at the age of 65 years - - - - - -	10·88	10·10 (b)	11·25	11·79	12·35	12·81	12·50
Value of an annuity on a life aged 25, interest being at 4 per cent. -	£15·438	£16·839	£17·420	£17·645	£17·494	£17·534	£17·634
Value of an annuity on a life aged 65, interest being at 4 per cent. -	£7·761	£7·328	£8·039	£8·307	£8·635	£8·896	£8·751
Value of a deferred annuity commencing at 65, to a life now aged 25, interest being at 4 per cent. -	£0·55424	£0·65842	£0·85452	£0·88823	£0·88723	£0·99078	£0·98534

* *Note, by the Committee.*—In all the above tables it is to be observed, that the mortality is deduced from an equal, or nearly an equal, number of each sex, with the single exception of Mr. Davies's table, founded on the experience of the Equitable, in which office, from the practical objects of Life Insurance, it is evident the male sex must have composed the vast majority of lives subjected to mortality. But as it is agreed on all hands, that the duration of life among females exceeds that of males, it follows, that the results of Mr. Davies's table fall materially short of what they would have been, if the facts on which he reasoned had comprehended an equal number of each sex. The tables have not, in all cases, been computed at four and a half per cent., the rate allowed by Government.

(a) Swedish, 2nd table, 35·47; 3rd table, 36·33.

(b) 2nd table, 10·19; 3rd table, 9·93.

Notwithstanding all this evidence, Government still persevered in the wasteful expenditure which we have noticed, and which, at the time when this Committee presented their Report, was proceeding with increasing rapidity. The misapplication has been stated by Mr. Finlaison in terms so clear and forcible, that we shall quote them from the letter which he wrote to Mr. Herries on the 30th of April, 1827. In this letter Mr. Finlaison states,

" 'That unless the tables by which those life annuities are now sold, shall be immediately changed, the Sinking Fund will incur a most enormous loss, which has been for many years increasing, is now advancing at the rate of 8,000*l.* every week, and during the last three months has exceeded 95,000*l.*

" ' That judging by the experience which we now have had for these last eighteen years and a half, of the transactions of the first year of the life-annuity system ; viz. the year ending 31st of August 1809 ; confining the question to that single year, in which only five hundred and forty annuities were granted (in all 58,506*l.* 10*s.* per annum), it appears there are still two hundred and twenty-eight of those annuities payable, to the extent of 23,251*l.* 13*s.* per annum, which, in reference either to numbers or income, is about four tenths of the whole, and some of those will no doubt continue payable for many years to come. In the mean time the account is closed with the annuitants.

" ' They have been paid back as much as would have re-purchased all that they gave, and 10,759*l.* of stock to the bargain ; consequently, as long as they live hereafter, the Sinking Fund sustains a clear additional loss to the extent of the principal and interest of whatever may be hereafter paid to them ; and if this be, at present, the consequence of granting only 58,506*l.* 10*s.* per annum, the loss may easily be imagined which will eventually result from having granted 810,000*l.* per annum (for to that extent the life annuities have since been carried) on the very same erroneous measure of value.

" ' Now I humbly beg leave to represent, that the third and last statement is a mere question of fact which cannot be gainsaid. If doubted, it may instantly be set at rest by the most simple inquiry ; as this much, at least, depends on no valuation of life by any table of mortality whatsoever, nor any other reasoning that is not within the most ordinary apprehension. By a reference either to the Bank or the Auditors of Public Accounts, it will most certainly be affirmed ; and if so, I respectfully submit whether there is not matter for the most serious consideration."

Mr. Finlaison, eight years before, had forced the subject upon the attention of the then chancellor of the Exchequer (Mr. Vansittart), and had submitted to him nearly the same evidence. That statesman contented himself with directing that measures should be taken to form more correct tables (a work of many years), and meanwhile allowed the expenditure to run on. Mr. Finlaison made another effort, in 1823, to obtain from his lordship's successor some attention to the progress of the evil, but only obtained a repetition of the orders previously given him, to proceed in the formation of the tables, while the expenditure was still allowed to go on increasing. In 1825 the evidence we have described was produced and offered to the notice of ministers, but then a " greater degree of correctness was required." A great annual loss was not to be stopped until the extent of the loss was proved to the fraction of a farthing ! Mr. Finlaison again went over his tables, and, as we have already stated, found the extreme difference made in granting an annuity by his several tables would amount to fifteen shillings in the hundred pounds ; and, lastly, after having given evidence before the Committee on Benefit Societies, he tried what was to be done with a new chancellor of the Exchequer. It seems that we are indebted, for the escape from future burthens of the same kind, entirely to the Finance Committee.* Since there appears no sinister interest on the

---

* It might have been expected, that with a set of tables calculated according to a rate of mortalities derived from the experience of the long lives of the government annuitants, the nation would in future have been protected from loss by the sale of annuities. But the vigilance of individuals surpassed that of the department of administration. It was quickly perceived that if persons at a very advanced period of life were selected, who were in a more than usually good state of health, and soundness of constitution, enormous gain might be made. For example ; if the price of stocks were at, from 91½ to 93 ; the price of an annuity of £20 a-year, so long as a person of ninety should live, was £31 19s. 10d. by three half yearly pay-

part of the Government, prompting them to persevere in this system of expenditure, we can only conjecture that it was continued from mere aversion to change, and perhaps from a presumption that nothing valuable could be produced by a clerk with a salary of only five hundred a year, who, for aught that appeared, had never been at either university, written a nonsense verse, or scanned a line of Horace : perhaps it was deemed improper to encourage such suggestions from people of this description, as it might occasionally lead to a notion on their parts of superior aptitude and capacity, which would endanger the proper official subordination, &c. &c.

We shall here advert to another source of extravagant expenditure. Connected with this subject, as part of the means of providing against the casualties of sickness and mortality, are the invaluable institutions of Benefit Societies and Savings' Banks. The commissioners for the management of the National Debt pay four and a half per cent. upon all deposits, whether received from Friendly Societies or Savings' Banks. We are ignorant of any good reason why the public should receive these deposits on other terms than those which would be settled between [1] individual and individual in a common mercantile transaction. Admitting to the full extent the importance of giving encouragement to economical habits, we deny that the payment of bounties is necessary for such a

---

ments, the purchase money would nearly all be got back. But if the man should live until four, five, six or seven half yearly payments were received, the gain to the Proprietor of the annuity would be prodigous, and the loss to the country in the same proportion, great. It is well known that several gentlemen of fortune, and it is said some banks, sent to the most healthy districts and sought out individuals of advanced age who were in a superior state of health and soundness of constitution, and also of long-lived families, and laid out large sums in the purchase of annuities to be received as long as these men should live. The adventurers even carried the speculation so far as to supply the men thus selected with the comforts suitable to their years, and employed medical men to be always ready to assist them in order to keep them alive as long as possible. After the existence of such operations was discovered, one session of parliament was allowed to elapse before the Chancellor of the Exchequer could be persuaded to obtain an act empowering the commissioners to refuse annuities to men of very advanced age. It is stated in justice to Mr. Finlaison that he was one of the foremost, in his endeavours to put a stop to the malpractise.

purpose, or that more is requisite than to extend to the parties that superior accommodation, and greater security for investment, which it is in the power of Government to afford. This we apprehend would form an inducement adequate to every salutary purpose. All that is given as interest, beyond the market-price of money, is simply a premium upon fraud. Not long after the Savings' Banks were brought into operation, the market-interest of money being below four and a half per cent. it was found that investments were made in great numbers by far different persons from those for whose benefit the institution was intended. Instead of reducing the rate of interest to the level of the market, and thereby taking away the motive to the commission of fraud, the legislature enacted, that no more than 200*l*. should be received from one person: that no person should make investments of monies at two or more banks, on pain of forfeiting the additional sum beyond a total of 200*l*. so invested, &c. &c. But it is only requisite to know the amount of the bounty which four and a half per cent. at the market-price of money, did then, and does now, afford, to be satisfied that these enactments are constantly evaded. When these institutions make a deposit of their savings in the hands of the commissioners for the management of the National Debt, the latter purchase stock with it in the market. The present price, eighty-six and three-quarters, will yield 3*l*. 9*s*. 2*d*. per cent. interest; and as they allow to the depositor interest at 4*l*. 11*s*. 8*d*. per cent. the public are losing at the rate of 1*l*. 2*s*. 1*d*. upon every hundred pounds received: they lose in addition all the expenses of management. When a depositor can thus obtain for each 100*l*. deposited, as much interest as 131*l*. 19*s*. 7*d*. laid out in stock at eighty-six and three-quarters would bring in the market, even though subject to the risk of depression, it needs excite no surprise that these deposits amount to the enormous sum of upwards of sixteen millions of money. It is notorious that, in consequence of these inducements, the legislative enactments are set at defiance by persons who, besides their own deposits, make fraudulent investments in the names of the various members of their families, their relations, or their friends. Thus skilfully do our legislators attempt to cultivate good habits among one portion of the community, and succeed in promoting bad habits among another !*

Before we quit the subject of the expenditure of public money with respect to these contingencies, we shall offer another specimen of the description of legislation which we may expect from those who transact the public business by way of an elegant amusement.

The Committee (the chairman of which was T. Peregrine Courtenay, Esq. one of the new administration) requested several actuaries, and amongst others Mr. Griffith Davies, to investigate the sufficiency of certain tables, and to state whether they considered the payment required upon them adequate for a society consisting chiefly of persons of the lower orders,' and having the privilege of investing its funds at four and a half per cent. Mr. Davies declared the scale of contributions inadequate to provide for the annuities proposed, because he did not believe that such societies could make four and a half per cent. compound interest upon their money. But we will give the Committee's account of his objection, as well as their answer, in their own words :

' Mr. Davies's opinion is unfavourable upon two grounds : first, he states that the rate assumed will not in practice be obtained at compound interest ; secondly, he thinks that an allowance ought

---

* The interest on deposits was subsequently reduced. The reduction has been followed, as was anticipated, by a withdrawal of the larger deposits ; the deficiency having been supplied, and the increased total amount (now approaching to twenty millions of money) having been formed, by the increase of the smaller deposits. The interest at the present time somewhat exceeds the interest derivable from the funds. The whole arrangements of these institutions appear to us to be susceptible of considerable improvements to adapt them to the wants and conveniences of the labouring classes. The Annuity Societies, the formation of which have been introduced by the present Government, are excellent institutions ; but why should the annuities be restricted to twenty pounds per annum ? why should not the convenience of obtaining Government annuities be to an amount adapted even to the middle classes, upon terms to defray the expense of the machinery ? The new Loan Societies are also useful institutions ; but why should not the functions of Annuity Societies, and Loan Societies, and others, be exercised by the trustees and paid officers of the Savings' Banks ?—Fair security being given to our friend Mr. Tidd Pratt : the Central Board, sole of these institutions, whose zeal for the welfare of the labouring classes is somewhat recompensed by the multiplication of fees consequent on the multiplication of such institutions, should not suffer by the consolidation. It would be a wonder-working arrangement, if the interests of all public officers were as well adjusted to beneficent ends.

to be made in consideration of the annuity being paid weekly, whereby there is a loss of interest.

' Your Committee are disposed to overrule these objections, because they apprehend that the arrangement of the debenture does insure to Friendly Societies, doing business upon a large scale, the means of realising compound interest on very nearly the whole of their funds ; and the other gentlemen who have approved of the Dorsetshire tables appear to have taken into consideration the weekly payment of the allowance.'—*Second Report*, p. 8.

It appears from the last clause of the Committee's answer, that it would have been too much to expect of honourable gentlemen to take upon themselves the trouble of examining the not very difficult question whether there really was a loss of interest by paying the annuity weekly. It was easier to rely upon such testimony as happened to be given them. The answer contained in the other clause of the paragraph might have been given more plainly in these words : " Yes, four and a half per cent. can be obtained by these societies, because it can be given, and shall be given, from the public money :" the question whether such an employment of the public money is advantageous being one upon which they were not called to concern themselves.

We must, before we quit the subject of the management of the expenditure, connected with the contingencies of mortality and sickness, pay Mr. Morgan the compliment of a valedictory notice, and bestow a few remarks on his new pamphlet, which is intended as a defence of the conduct of his society, against those who have impugned its management, and its rates of insurance. In this pamphlet, and also in his answers given to the Committee of the House of Commons subsequently to the publication of the new tables, he eminently displays the vicious habit of mind to which we have adverted, as characteristic of the majority of practical men ; namely, obduracy to the reception of new evidence—indifference to the truth. This is a vice with which most men are more or less tainted ; but the practical men of his genius are distinguished by its mischievous excess. When the Committee ask him his opinion respecting the tables framed by Mr. Finlaison, he says, " I have no opinion at all of them, I do not think favourably of them ;" but assigns no reasons for thinking unfavourably of them.   In his pamphlet he holds this language : " Of those absurd opinions which have been lately entertained respecting the improved health and greater longevity of the human race, I feel no disposition to enter into the discussion" [very likely, discussion being, to his interests, dangerous].   " They do not appear to be supported by any documents of the least credit or authority" [! !], "and I have only to express a hope that they may never be suffered to mislead this society" [*i. e.* to reduce its exorbitant charges to the public]. " From its first establishment, I know of but one instance of a person's dying at the advanced age of ninety-four, and not above three or four instances of persons dying at the advanced age of ninety ; and the whole number of nonagenarians now existing does not exceed seven or eight.   As far, therefore, as the *Equitable experience* avails, this new doctrine has no foundation." Future returns may be expected to exhibit a greater number of nonagenarians, but the new doctrine is, that fewer people die in the earlier stages of existence, that more attain a vigorous maturity ; not that more live beyond the extreme period he mentions, at which, it may have been observed, most of the tables approximate.   The fears of persons like Mr. Morgan cause them to exaggerate and misrepresent new opinions, and we expect to hear it proclaimed in derision, " That the philosophers have discovered we are to live as long as Methuselah, that sickness is banished from the earth, and the Millennium is at hand."   We do not, however, impute to this gentleman any wilful misrepresentation ; we believe that he is himself misled by his interests. Had he not been under the most extraordinary infatuation, he would scarcely have published a document such as is contained in this pamphlet, which furnishes a piece of the most striking confirmatory evidence the " new doctrine" could require.   He actually sets forth [p. 41], as the one source remaining, from which his society derives its chief security and success, " the higher probabilities of life among its members, than those given in the table, from which its premiums are computed."   " But," he says, " even the benefits derived from this source have their limit."   " In a society composed entirely of young lives, selected from the general mass of mankind, the rate of mortality will necessarily be lower than in a table including lives of all descriptions.* In a more advanced period of its existence, the effect of this selection will gradually lessen, till, in process of time, the society will become like any other community, and subject to the ordinary laws of mortality:" meaning, we suppose, to inform us, that they will not live for ever. " This is particularly exemplified in the following table of the decrements of life in the society during the last twelve years." The second column of this table represents the number of polices for the several ages; the third column shows the proportion of insurers who actually died; the fourth column exhibits the number who " should have died," had the Northampton table been correct.

Age.	No.	Died.	Should have died.
20 to 30	4,720	29	68
30 „ 40	15,951	106	243
40 „ 50	27,072	201	506
50 „ 60	23,307	339	545
60 „ 70	14,705	426	502
70 „ 80	5,056	289	290
80 „ 95	701	99	95

" Here," he says, " we see the probabilities of life in the society, which so far exceed those in the Northampton table in the earlier ages, continually approaching to them at a more advanced age, till, at last, arriving at an age at which no new members are admitted, they become nearly equal, and afford a striking proof of the accuracy of that table" !!!

The difference between the number who actually died, and the number " who should have died," on the one hand, shows the risks which individuals who insure upon rates founded on the Northampton table pay for beyond those they encounter; and, on the other hand, it exhibits the loss which Government has occasioned to the public by the use of that table to

* If our readers will refer to the tables of mortality we have given, and compare the experience of the Equitable Society with the Swedish table, they may estimate the effect of selection in presenting diminished chances of mortality, and give Mr. Morgan credit for it; and they will then perceive how considerably his own table of decrements yet makes against the Northampton table, on the experience of the great majority of lives under 70.

form its rules for granting annuities. It is declared, for instance, on this table of decrements, that where sixty-eight should have died, had the Northampton table been now applicable, only twenty-nine have died; consequently, if these parties, instead of being insured, had been Government annuitants, the public would have been burthened with thirty-nine annuities beyond the number calculated upon. We may say more than thirty-nine, because the lives of annuitants are better than those of insurers; because it is rare that an individual purchases an annuity who does not believe himself to be in good health, and of sound constitution, to enable him to enjoy it for a long period. Annuitants are also, in most cases, relieved from the painful anxiety which generally attends the pursuit of a livelihood, and more or less diminishes the duration of life amongst large classes.

More complete and satisfactory evidence of the improvement in the value of life among the classes whose condition and habits have improved, could not well be obtained. But still the lives of Government annuitants, and the navy and army pensioners, are to be considered as select lives, and we are left to conjecture how far they may, or may not, be applicable to determine the chances of mortality among other classes. The Northampton, the Swedish, the Carlisle, the Equitable, and the Government tables, differing as they do considerably, have each their advocates, as being most applicable to govern societies for insuring the labouring classes of the community. We are inclined to agree with the conclusion of Dr. Mitchell in favour of the Swedish tables, as being probably the best adapted to represent the chances of mortality amongst the labouring classes. We question whether the Chelsea and Greenwich out-pensioners are to be considered, relatively to others of the labouring classes, lives of the " very worst" description. " Many of these men," he observes, " had no doubt suffered in their constitutions from service in foreign climes, and some from severe wounds; but, on the other hand, we are to recollect that the men who enter the army are admitted, not as the sticking-bills of the recruiting serjeants express it, for good character and education, but for good stamina and vigorous constitutions: so that, taking one chance against another, we may expect the lives of the Chelsea and Greenwich out-pensioners to be better than those of the ordinary mechanics and labourers of the United Kingdom. Now the chances of the pensioners of Chelsea College are at any age better than those of the Northampton tables ; and, after fifty, are as good as those of the Carlisle tables." The Carlisle correspond very closely, as may be perceived, with the Equitable tables, and the Equitable tables are founded on very select lives. Therefore the Carlisle and the Government tables, in all probability, present too favourable a rate for the classes who form Benefit Societies ; and the Swedish are the most applicable, as giving the probabilities of the life more favourable than the Northampton, and less favourable than the Carlisle, tables.

The mean chances between classes who differ widely in their circumstances, or the averages formed from the mortality which obtains in large classes, are obviously inapplicable for the safe guidance of any but institutions of great magnitude. The desideratum is to ascertain in what degree mortality is influenced by particular trades and avocations, and by the circumstances under which various classes have been placed. It is only in Paris that the collection of any satisfactory information of this kind has been attempted even. M. Villermé made a comparison of two arrondissements of that capital ; of the first arrondissement, which contains the largest proportion of wealthy people, and the twelfth, which contains the greatest proportion of poor people. The total difference is such, that when fifty people die in the first arrondissement, one hundred die in the twelfth. There is one birth annually for more than every thirty-two inhabitants of the first arrondissement, and one in twenty-six of the twelfth, and yet there are not more children from the age of 0 to 5 years in the last than in the first ; a proof that the poor bring forth more children than the rich, but preserve fewer. From a paper compiled by the same gentleman from the registers of the hospitals at Paris, it is made to appear that disease is not more frequent among the poor than among the rich or middling classes ; but it is more frequently fatal to the former than to the latter, and the gradations of wealth, or the means of providing comforts, (and we may add, more prudent and temperate management,) may be almost taken as the scale of mortality. Thus, in the higher classes of workmen, such as jewellers, printers, and compositors, who enter the hospital, one in eleven dies; whilst among the shoe-makers or brick-makers, one in seven is the average mortality; of the stone-masons, one in six; of the common labourers, one in five; and of the poorest classes of all, the porters and rag-merchants, one in four: amongst the soldiers, who are in more favourable circumstances, not one in twenty; a fact which corroborates the observation of Dr. Mitchell, that the lives of our soldiers are better than those of the average of artisans. Our soldiers are in general better lodged and fed than those of the French army: we may infer, therefore, that their lives are better. The baleful effects of poverty were most perceptible in the greater mortality among the aged and the very young.

M. Villermé has also made some highly valuable researches to ascertain the amount of mortality in the whole of the prisons in Paris. He has proved that the average annual mortality in prisons is about one in twenty-three; and from this fact, comparing it with the average mortality in France, he concludes, that to be sent to prison one year in that country is equivalent to a deprivation of about twenty years of life. This would by no means apply to imprisonment in this country, where prisoners are often better lodged and fed than the classes out of prison from whom they are taken. It would be worth while, however, to make a similar inquiry, in order to determine the average mortality which prevails amongst the various classes of prisoners, that, from the results, the effects of various modes of punishment might be ascertained. Such an inquiry should be extended to the prisons for debtors, and we have no doubt that the facts elucidated would startle the public. Will any Howard, any Villermé, in this country ever investigate the average mortality among the suitors in Chancery? Having witnessed individual instances of the ravages of its long, anxious, and tormenting process on the health of suitors, and seen a suit attended with more deadly effects than a fever, we seriously believe that the amount of the deprivation of life among the victims of that detestable Court would almost be found equal to the average loss of life in any hospital in the metropolis.

Little was done, compared with what the Committee might by a small expenditure of labour have effected, to procure information similar to that obtained in Paris by M. Villermé.

They contented themselves with idly observing in the first report, " It must be owned that no extensive information has hitherto been collected as to the duration of life among the lower orders ; and it is obvious that neither experience drawn from the higher and middling classes, nor results taken from the army, or from the London hospitals, can be depended upon in reference to the general mass of the manufacturing population."

Mr. Finlaison stated to the Committee [*Appendix to the First Report*, p. 138], that " materials exist, however, which may be furnished with facility for estimating the sickness now actually prevailing among the labouring classes to a degree probably of very considerable accuracy. There is in the Navy Pay-office a pay-list received annually from each of the seven dock-yards, containing the age of every workman, artificer, or labourer in those great establishments, the amount of his wages or earnings in the year, and the number of days in which he received no wages by reason of sickness, the fact of such sickness being always verified by the public medical officer. I have not been permitted to avail myself of this document extra-officially, else I would now have submitted the result to your honourable Committee." On a cursory view of the document, he found the amount of sickness among those under fifty to coincide very closely with the average of sickness reported by the Highland Society. He suggested that further returns should be made, and other materials for the formation of tables collected, from the various dock-yards, and from every regiment in the service. He was permitted to inspect some returns made to the Adjutant-general's Office respecting the sickness prevalent in the army, which appeared to be thrice the average amount found by the Highland Society to prevail among the members of Benefit Societies in Scotland. As, however, it is well known that soldiers, during peace, live better than the majority of workmen, there must be much imposition practised to make the amount of sickness appear, on these returns, to be so considerable in the army. The best, and almost the only data we have to judge of the probable amount of sickness among the labouring classes in Great Britain, are, the returns obtained by the exertions of the excellent society to which we have just alluded. This society procured returns from seventy-nine Benefit Societies situate in sixteen counties of Scotland. These returns were made up from the books kept during various periods, in some instances extending from 1750 to 1821. The aggregate number of members on the books of the respective societies was, 104,218. The first table ever formed to exhibit the probable annual sickness which a labouring man will sustain through life, is to be found in an able report drawn up by Mr. Oliphant for the society. The results stated are, that a working man will experience in a year, at

Years of Age.	Sickness.	Years of Age.	Sickness.
21	4 days	66	$5\frac{4}{10}$ weeks
46	1 week	67	$6\frac{6}{10}$ weeks
57	2 weeks	68	8 weeks
63	3 weeks	69	9 weeks
65	$4\frac{4}{10}$ weeks	70	10 weeks

The proportion, after that period, goes on increasing rapidly, at a rate that puts the individual beyond the means of assurance possessed by any of these institutions. The society endeavoured to ascertain, also, the different degrees of intensity to be expected in this sickness; and they state, as their nearest approximation, that, of ten weeks of sickness amongst persons of all ages under seventy, two may be assumed as bedfast sickness,—five as walking, three as permanent sickness.

In addition to the returns which Mr. Finlaison suggested, others, no doubt, might have been obtained from the East India Company, of the amount of sickness which prevails among the great number of workmen whom they employ. Other public bodies, the Dock Companies for instance, probably keep exact accounts of the time during which the labourers whom they have in their service are absent in consequence of sickness; and from these and other such sources, highly valuable information might have been collected by the Committee; but it seems they did not think it a matter worthy of any trouble, since we do not find in the Second Report any of the returns suggested by Mr. Finlaison.* They took the easiest course, and adopted, on specu-

---

* Messrs. Tooke, Chadwick, and Dr. Southwood Smith, the Commissioners constituting the Central Board of the Commission appointed to inquire into

lation, a set of tables grounded upon an estimate of sickness considerably higher than that which results from the inquiries of the Highland Society. We would recommend to the philanthropy of private individuals, or to the industry of similiar societies in England, the task of obtaining correct returns of the nature and extent of the sickness which prevails among various classes of our artisans, who might with no great difficulty be brought to keep correct accounts of the facts which it is desirable to collect. If the sickness consequent upon different sets of circumstances were accurately recorded, the operation of causes which cannot now be clearly detected in single instances would be pointed out for removal ; as, in the numerous cases where classes of workmen

---

the effects of labour in factories upon the general condition of the operative classes, obtained as a means of comparison, from the Directors of the East India Company, returns for ten years of the experience of the labourers in their service. The number of these labourers was at the commencement of the period of the service, 2461.

As the most accurate account had been kept, and a sum of one shilling and sixpence had been paid to every man during sickness, the most exact return was obtained. The result, as calculated from this return, was as follows :—

Age.	Average duration of sickness per annum for every man employed.	Average duration of sickness per annum for every man sick.
	Days and decimal parts.	Days and decimal parts.
16 to 21	4·02	13·96
21 to 26	5·40	17·22
26 to 31	4·49	20·18
31 to 36	4·55	21·44
36 to 41	5·57	23·84
41 to 46	5·18	22·83
46 to 51	5·43	23·59
51 to 56	6·80	28·61
56 to 61	7·21	28·28
61 to 66	10·24	31·25
66 to 71	9·93	26·89
71 to 76	10·60	29·67
76 to 81	12·67	38·88

This experience of the labourers of the East India Company agrees as far as the age of 41 with that of the Societies of which account was taken by the Highland Society of Scotland, and is rather more favourable from 41 to 51. After that it is much more favourable, which is readily accounted for from the circumstance that the East India Company pensioned off all the men who had become invalid, and no account was kept of their sickness. It may appear surprising that the experience of a body of men living in London should be as favourable as that of the societies chiefly composed of persons living in rural districts. The causes are explained in the evidence of Mr.

sustain unnecessary injury to their health from want of precaution, and from methods of working which admit of change.
Returns displaying, as they must do if collected properly, the
consequences of vicious peculiarities and habits, would effect
more in the way of reformation with the old, and of prevention
with the young, than the most inflammatory preaching that
could be brought to bear upon them. The utility of such
returns would be greatly augmented if they were accompanied
by accounts of the wages received contemporaneously by each
class, and the prices of their most common food, together with
every material change in any of the circumstances affecting their
condition*.

Lewis Leese, jun. The men were in the first instance select, nearly as much
so as recruits going into the army; care was taken also to give men who became infirm such labour as they could perform without severe exertion : but,
above all, they had the benefit of medical advice without any expense ; and
being thereby induced to make early application, disease was cut short at
once on its first appearance. All persons who employ large bodies of people
would at once study their own interest, and exert the most useful benevolence, by imitating the East India Company, in providing medical relief
to their people.

The following is a comparison of the other chief existing Sickness Tables :

Age.	Mean duration of sickness per annum, in weeks and decimals of a week.			Ratio of mean annual sickness in the English societies to that in the Scotch so- cieties, the lat- ter being taken as one.
	According to Dr. Price's hypothesis.	According to the Highland Society in 104,218 cases.	According to the Diffusion Society in 24,323 cases.	
20	. . .	. . .	740	. . .
21	. . .	575	793	1·37913
25	. . .	585	762	1·30256
30	. . .	621	832	1·33977
32	1·0887	641	887	1·38378
35	1·1550	675	964	1·42815
40	1·2488	758	1·160	1·53034
45	1·4449	962	1·327	1·37942
50	1·6842	1·361	1·726	1·28618
55	1·9022	1·821	2·443	1·34157
60	2·2448	2·346	3·154	1·34442
65	2·7255	4·400	5·498	1·24955
70	3·4482	10·701	11·685	1·09195

* Mr. Chadwick, in his Report as a Commissioner of Enquiry into the
administration of the Poor Laws, suggests that it is only by means of careful
and extensive collections of facts or statistics that medical science can be
rapidly advanced. He states, ' It appeared to me, (and some of the best-

The last departments of the subject to which the space allotted to us permits us to allude, are the probable prolificness of marriages, and the mortality to which the children produced

---

informed medical men whom I have examined in the course of these enquiries assented to the conclusion,) that the medical inductions from the observation of individual cases, or from the small number of cases of the same class, which usually come within the range of the practice of the most eminent practitioners, complicated as most medical cases are with idiosyncrasies, afford scarcely any, or at the best but doubtful results or indications; and that it is only from the most extended collections of facts, *in which the disturbing causes are merged in the most general effect*, that the general principle can be displayed with the certainty requisite for safe action. Take, for example, the medical doctrines with relation to the diet of different classes of people.

'I have shewn that the difference in the quantities of food consumed by agricultural labourers and artizans when procured in return for their labour, as compared with the allowances which persons obtain by becoming inmates of workhouses, prisoners in our gaols, convicted thieves, or transported felons, are as follows:

As agricultural labourers - - - -	122
As artizans (of the highest wages) - -	140
As paupers - - - - - -	150
As soldiers - - - - - -	168
As prisoners in gaols - - - - -	217
As convicts on board the hulks - - -	239
As transported felons or convicts - - -	330

ounces weekly of solid food.

The proportions of the dietaries in bulk of the five last classes are proved by the official returns.

'In some cases a healthy labourer who has to provide for himself will eat about 136 ounces of solid food weekly; but it is rare that an independent labourer's family consumes more than 122 ounces of solid food per head weekly.

'This has been proved by detailed enquiries, such as those already recited, made of agricultural labourers in different parts of the country, as to their actual consumption, by detailed enquiries made of shopkeepers, as to the quantities of provisions they are accustomed to sell to the families of independent labourers of various classes; by the fact that when from the wages of the independent labourer who maintains a wife and an average family are deducted house-rent, the cost of clothing, and other expenses of maintenance, enough will not be left for the purchase of a diet for the family so high as would be received by them if they were to become criminals; also by the fact, that when such labourers and their families become paupers, and are received into the workhouse, they generally declare that the diet received even there is much better than they have been accustomed to procure for themselves as independent labourers. And it may be added, that the paupers who become criminals and inmates of prisons declare that the diet which they obtain in prisons is still superior to that which they obtain in workhouses.' (See the evidence of the paupers stated in p. 257 of the "Selections from the Reports, &c.")

'These dietaries of the last five classes are prescribed, with medical sanction, in gaols in the same town and in the same county; and for similar classes of prisoners,—dietaries varying to the extent of one being double the amount of the other are prescribed by the medical officers. These variations

from them are liable, information essential for endowments and for providing for marriages and families. The attention of the Committee was much occupied on these topics, yet but little in-

---

are marked by variations in the health of the prisoners. The like discrepancies in diet are observable in the dietaries prescribed by medical men to the inmates of workhouses within the same district. And on examination I have found that the ordinary observation of one or two prisons, or of one or two workhouses, which is the usual extent of experience of a medical man, does not suffice for the establishment of any conclusion (which can be termed accurate) as to whether a given amount of sickness in such places is the effect solely of a certain quantity or quality of diet, it not being allowable to make *experiments*, although such experiments might be safely made with different diets upon the same classes of prisoners.

' The agricultural labourers of this country are on the whole a strong body of men. Notwithstanding many defects in their modes of life, as to the other essentials of life—simple and sufficient diet, warmth of clothing and lodging, and ventilation, including a circulation of air which is warm as well as pure, they are, comparatively to other labourers, a healthy class. That the agricultural labourers are on the whole more healthy than the preceding generation of labourers, is proved by the encreased duration of life amongst them as shewn by the mortuary registers.

' This being so, the question presented itself, whether an encreased amount of food to those who had less labour,—namely, paupers and prisoners,—was requisite to maintain a fair average degree of health amongst them. The dietaries of this class appeared, however, to have been prescribed without reference to any standard.

' The governors of several of the workhouses where the paupers were allowed a high diet stated to me that the change of diet on the first entrance of paupers into the house sometimes proved too much for them, and " carried them off." From the statements made by medical men, it appeared that in such houses acute disease was often rife and fatal. The number of these statements with reference to large classes of persons appeared to me to establish the conclusion that the heavier diets are amongst the least healthy; but inasmuch as no account that I could find is ever kept of the sickness prevalent at any of the workhouses, I was unable to obtain any precise results on the subject.

' On further enquiry, I found, however, that a general account of the sickness and mortality which occurs in each gaol throughout the country is annually returned to His Majesty's Secretary of State for the Home Department, in compliance with the regulations of the Gaol Act. Upon an examination of these returns, I found frequent instances where the average amount of sickness bore a proportion to the amount of diet. Where the diet was encreased in point of quantity on account of the prisoners being subjected to hard labour, there the sickness also encreased. These results led me to a further examination of the subject.

' There are returns sent annually from 128 gaols and prisons in England and Wales; and on an examination of the returns for three years, 1830, 1831, and 1832, it appears that the total number of *commitments* averages no less than 97,279. The total number of *persons* in the gaols at *any one time* appears to be about 25,000. The average number of persons sick each year is 9,044, or 9½ per cent. on the whole number of commitments.

formation of value was elicited from any of the witnesses, except from Dr. Granville, a physician and accoucheur of very extensive practice, connected with several public institutions. We know

---

' The deaths each year average 247, or 1 in 394 on the whole number of commitments.

' The cost of maintaining the prisoners varies from 1s. 2d. to 5s. and even 7s. per week; but the average cost is 2s. 6d. per week.

' Of the 128 returns, 27 do not serve the inquiry as to diets, either because they are so deficient that a correct calculation cannot be made from them, or because in the prisons to which they relate money is paid to the prisoners in lieu of food. On examining the 104 more complete returns, it will be found that the general results closely correspond with those already indicated by the particular instances above quoted. Thus, taking of the 104 returns, the 20 gaols where the expense and quantity of the diet are the lowest, the 20 where the expense and quantity of the diet are the highest, and the 20 where they are intermediate, the results appear as follow :—

	Cost per week.		Ounces of solid food per week.	Sick per cent.	Deaths.
	s.	d.			
Twenty lowest diets	1	10½	188	3	1 in 622
Twenty intermediate diets	2	4¼	213	18	1 in 320
Twenty highest diets	3	2	218	23½	1 in 266

' With a view to determine whether any new results could be obtained from the remaining 41 diets, I divided them into the 21 diets of the lowest cost, and the 20 diets of the highest cost. In these instances it appeared that the 21 gaols with the diets of the lowest cost were, from the circumstance of their being chiefly in rural districts, where the provisions are the cheapest, the gaols where the diets were the heaviest. It appears as a concomitant that in these gaols the amount of the mortality was also the greatest. The following are the results :—

	Cost weekly.		Ounces of solid food weekly.	Sick per cent. annually.	Deaths annually.
	s.	d.			
Twenty-one lowest cost but highest quantity	2	5	257	11½	1 in 277
Twenty highest cost but lowest quantity -	3	0½	238	11¼	1 in 351

' There is nothing set forth in the face of these returns as to the localities, and nothing in the circumstances of any of the prisoners to mark the predominant cause, other than the invariable connexion of heavy and light diets with the comparatively high and low rates of sickness and mortality.

nothing of this gentleman beyond the evidence given in the report; but his attention to this subject appears to have been highly meritorious.   His opportunities for observation were very

---

' In the returns of the 20 gaols of the lowest cost, will be found several of the larger gaols of the metropolis, such as Newgate, Clerkenwell, Horsemonger-lane; crowded gaols, in which the prisoners remain for shorter periods than in the gaols of the agricultural districts.   From this circumstance it might be inferred that the diminished amount of sickness in those gaols is attributable chiefly to the shorter periods of confinement of the prisoners; but this inference is rebutted by the facts, that the sickness consequent on any change of diet takes place at the commencement of the confinement, or within shorter periods than those during which the average of the prisoners remain in the gaols in question; and that the health of the prisoners is proportionately good in other gaols, where the average periods of confinement are long, but where the diet is simple and the cost is low.   It is to be observed also, that this objection does not apply to the intermediate diets compared with the highest diets; there being, as will be seen in a subjoined table, no material differences in the periods of detention between the prisoners of the two classes.   It is further to be observed, that in the gaols where the cost of maintaining the prisoners has been reduced, the sickness of the prisoners has in no recent instance been increased, but has in general been diminished.

' Dr. Julius, who is the commissioner appointed by the King of Prussia to examine the prisons in the Prussian dominions, and who is now on a tour for the examination of the prison discipline of other nations, informs me that the dietaries of the prisons in Prussia, which consisted chiefly of bread, formerly varied from 16 ounces to 32 ounces daily.   Attention was recently attracted to the subject, as he believed, in consequence of the discussions on diet contained in our published Reports under this commission.   Returns of the dietaries were required to be forwarded to a central office; and in consequence of the discrepancies observed in them, an ordinance was issued in the spring of last year, fixing the allowance of bread at 22 ounces daily, or 154 ounces weekly, in every prison throughout the kingdom.   The change of diets was made gradually; but the medical superintendents report favourably of it so far as it has proceeded.

The returns of the sickness and mortality prevalent in the same gaols during the years 1834 and 1835, making allowances for the variation of the food from change of management, corroborate the conclusions derivable from the returns of the previous years.   The summary of the returns for the years last mentioned is as follows :

Dietaries.	Weekly cost per head.	No. of oz. of solid food per head per week.	Number of sick per cent.	Number of deaths.
	s. d.			
20 lowest dietaries......	1 10	187½	3¾	1 in 736
20 intermediate dietaries	2 3	222	20	1 in 326
20 full dietaries........	2 4½	254	21¼	1 in 334

considerable. The number of cases which came before him professionally were numerous. With reference to women, the number of cases were, at the Westminster Dispensary, during

In the higher class of dietaries, where it appears that the proportion of meat has been diminished and the vegetable food increased, there the amount of sickness has also been reduced. The bulk of the intermediate dietaries has been increased: the sickness also has been increased. The returns of the effects of the diets in the forty-one remaining gaols, during the same years, are also confirmatory of the same conclusion.

Dietaries.	Weekly cost per head.	No. of oz. of solid food per head per week.	Number of sick per cent.	Number of deaths.
	s. *d.*			
21 lowest cost	2 1¾	259	15¼	1 in 336
20 highest cost	2 4	232	11½	1 i 409

It will be observed, that in the 20 gaols where the cost of maintaining the prisoners is the highest, there has been a like reduction in the amount of food, (which is shown somewhat in the reduction of the price,) followed by a reduction in the amount of sickness. I submitted the tables to Mr. W. Farr, the surgeon and medical statist, who has combined the facts differently. The above results were obtained from the number of the committals to other gaols. He has deduced the subjoined results from the numbers in the gaol at the time of making the returns, on the supposition that these furnish an approximation to the mean population of the three classes of prisoners.

5 Years, 1830-4.	Prisoners committed.	In gaols at time of return.	Attacks of sickness.	Deaths.	Mean time of detention.	Annual attacks of sickness in a mean population of 100.
20 gaols of lowest dietaries ..	164,714	15,173	6,127	243	34	40·4
20 gaols of intermediate dietaries	63,440	12,398	11,550	188	70	93·15
20 gaols full dietaries	39,717	7,932	8,937	137	73	112·7
60 gaols	267,871	35,503	26,614	568	48·4	75·0

According to this mode of obtaining the results, it appears that the attacks of sickness increase progressively with the increase of the dietaries. The mortality varies very little; but it is the highest where the diet is full.

' I might venture to assume from these facts, at least, that the sickness is increased as the quantity of food is increased; and at all events, that the

seven years and one quarter, 7,060 ; at the Benevolent Institution, during three years, 2,755 cases ; and at both these institutions, with respect to children, 9,000 ;—while at the Royal

---

lowest actual dietaries have no deteriorating influence on the health of the prisoners.

' I submit these results, however, as establishing a case for further inquiry. I do not deny the existence of any countervailing facts, though I am aware of none.   In general I should rely more confidently on the examinations of the particulars than upon deductions solely from an array of statistics or columns of figures, and would act upon no such deductions unless confirmed upon an examination of the particulars to which the figures refer : for most statistics consist of accumulations of items or units, each of which items or units represents but one of a *train* of particulars which cannot be represented by means of figures ; and as those items are well or ill chosen, (which can only be determined by an examination of the whole of the particulars,) so are the results indicated likely to be sound or unsound.   This I have had occasion to exemplify more fully elsewhere.   I may mention however as illustrations, that in the course of the inquiry into the labour in factories, a return was presented to us of the number of surgical cases of factory operatives taken to the Manchester Infirmary.   The return was presented in support of an inference as to the injurious effects of the employment in factories, and if received as presented it was certainly a strong piece of evidence ; but on inquiry into the particulars of each item in the return, or case enumerated, it appeared that the greater proportion of the cases were of injuries received in drunken quarrels, or from accidents in the streets or elsewhere ; and that only a small proportion of the whole were cases of injuries received within the factories.   Each item in this return represented only the fact that an operative had been treated in the infirmary ; but that fact or particular, was only one of a train of other particulars, comprehending the essential ones, as to the mode in which the injury had been received, whether by his own fault or the negligence of his employers.   So in the statistics of crime : the columns of figures representing the numbers of persons tried or convicted have been implicitly received by the public and the legislature as representing the amount of crime committed ; whereas a statistical return of the number of fish caught in the Thames might be received in like manner as a correct measure of the number of fish in the river ; or the acts of prey in which the fish, like the depredator, were caught, might be taken as evidence of the number of acts of prey which they had committed, or as evidence of the number of acts of prey committed by the whole of the fish at large.   On investigation, it is found that in some districts, where a judge may receive white gloves from the absence of prisoners, crime riots ; there being no pursuit, and consequently no apprehensions or committals, nothing in the display of statistics showing criminality ; whilst in other districts, where a newly-appointed police opens an active pursuit and brings numerous offenders to justice, the prevalent conclusion is, that crime is on the increase, and *cum hoc ergo propter hoc,* the police has been the cause. A short time ago an allowance of the expenses of prosecutions was made in one county to constables by the magistrates assaulted in the execution of their duty.   Forthwith the statistical returns showed so great an increase of the crimes (*i. e.* of prosecutions), that it appeared that scarcely a warrant could be served without exciting resistance to lawful authority, and that there was an end to all order.   So when an extra allowance of expenses was made for prosecutions for attempts to commit rape, the crimes (*i. e.* the prosecutions) increased so considerably, that the worthy magistrates on the bench

Infirmary for Sick Children, no less than 5,640 cases came before him ;—giving a general total of 24,450 cases for observation. He submitted the register of a considerable number of these

---

were lost in speculations as to the cause of the *avatara* of lust which had come upon the county.

'Where the whole of the particulars of each case suggest, or upon full examination establish a conclusion, then statistical returns are useful and necessary to test the soundness of the conclusions, and to measure the extent of the operation of the causes indicated. I have found statistics—that is, statistics confirmed by inquiry into the particulars of the case—more useful as tests and measures than as indicia of general principles, or of the prevalence of general causes. Their public importance for these purposes is yet but little appreciated.

'Recurring to the returns with relation to the various dietaries for the ears first named, I submit the following facts to illustrate the extent of the evil :—

'Taking the highest average of food, the food of an agricultural labourer's family, at 130 ounces of solid food per head per week, we find that the gaol allowance is about 180 ounces per head per week, or 50 ounces more than the labourer obtains weekly per head for his family. A conception of the aggregate excess of allowance in point of quantity may be formed by considering that the 25,000 thieves, and other prisoners constantly in the gaols, consume 50 ounces per week more than is obtained by each of a labourer's family, or in the aggregate upwards of 1,800 tons of food more than the same number of agricultural labourers obtain in a year in return for their honest labour. 2,400 horses would be required to draw the excess in quantity, (allowing each horse a load of 1,500 weight,) and it would maintain 8,300 agricultural labourers one year.

'The excess in cost of money may be determined by the consideration, that if the whole of the prisoners in England were placed upon the low and more healthy diet at the cost of 1s. 10*d*. per head per week, the annual saving would be 43,336*l*. 6*s*. 8*d*. But if the whole of the prisoners were placed upon the simple and healthy diet of such prisons as those of Manchester and Coventry at a cost of about 1s. 3*d*. per head, the saving in diet only would amount to the annual sum of 81,250*l*.

'To the cost in money to the public must be added the serious cost in sickness and mortality to the prisoners, amongst whom it must not be forgotten that considerable numbers are confined for offences comparatively slight.

'The average of the sickness which is the concomitant of the lowest diets being 3¼ per cent., it would seem to follow that the excess of sickness beyond that rate is the effect of the profuse diets, and consequently (the total number of sick being 9,044 instead of 3,161 annually, at 3¼ per cent. on 97,279,) it follows that an average of 5,882 prisoners are every year made sick in consequence of the profuse diets.

'The average of the mortality which is the concomitant of the lowest and most healthy diets being only 1 in 635, and the total average of deaths being 247 annually, (instead of 153 at the lowest average,) it follows that 94 prisoners are annually sacrificed by the operation of the higher dietaries.

'This mortality is exclusive of the mortality by the agency of the executioner ; the average number of criminals executed being, even during those years, 58 annually.

'In illustration of this difference, it may be stated, that in the year 1830,

'The deaths by the executioner were 46.

'By apparent excess in the supply of food, 96.

cases to the Committee. The "practical men" who were his predecessors at these institutions had merely troubled themselves to ascertain the name and age of the patient, whether she had produced a boy or a girl, and what was the date of its birth. Dr. Granville observes,

' As my attention had been frequently directed to the statistical questions of the increase of population among the poor, I thought that the public institutions I belonged to might be made available in obtaining the information to which I have just alluded, and I therefore established these analytical registers, in which, under particular heads, and in separate columns, I enter the information that the mother gives me.'

' It must still be recollected that a large proportion of the prisoners amongst whom this sickness and death falls are untried, and that many of them would probably be discharged as innocent, and many of them are confined on sentences of a few days' or a few weeks imprisonment. Whilst it appears that prisoners may be maintained in a state of health with no more than $3\frac{1}{4}$ per cent. of sickness, and a mortality of 1 in 635, what can be said if no efforts are made for the discontinuance of a system, in which a prisoner, in addition to his sentence, is in fact subjected to a forced lottery, in which 23 lots out of every hundred entail a fit of sickness, and amidst every 266 there is one fatal ticket—a sentence of death?

' As the lowest diets are in point of quantity so much above the diets with which the independent labourers are contented, it was scarcely to be expected that any variation in the re-commitments would be found to accompany the variations in the amounts of the diets. It will, however, be found, that whilst in the ten prisons where the cost of maintenance averages 3s. $7\frac{1}{2}d$. per head per week the numbers re-committed average $6\frac{1}{2}$ per cent. per year, the numbers re-committed to the gaols where the cost of maintenance is 1s. $8\frac{1}{2}d$. per head per week is $4\frac{1}{2}$ per cent.

' Supposing, as I see no reason to doubt, that these results should be confirmed by a more close scrutiny, I would submit the facts in illustration of the importance of a central control. By means of an institution of that nature, it appears to be practicable to bring to a focus such evidence of the results of past experience as may serve for the future guidance of the general and local administrators of the law, and in some degree serve as checks against neglect to take the measures which the evidence may indicate. Had the evidence from which the conclusions above recited are deduced been presented to the attention of a determinate person, or set of persons, who were specially charged with the duty of supervising the establishments and with the power of regulating them, they could scarcely avoid taking measures to put a stop to the waste of life, health, and money which the existing modes of administration occasion. There appears to me to be no ground for any imputation of mismanagement imputable from these facts to the magistrates who are charged with the superintendence of the prisons in question. Their own and adjacent jurisdictions rarely supply them with any standards of comparison. *A priori*, the highest allowance appears scanty for the maintenance of an adult; and, in fact, in the greater proportion of cases the dietaries are determined by the surgeon or medical officer of the establishment. Nor is blame imputable to those officers, as they cannot be censured for not acting

For this purpose the Doctor put a variety of questions, to ascertain the earliest age at which women of the poorer classes marry,—the number of children they produce in a given period, —how many of those children may be expected to die within a given period, and of what diseases,—at what period of life married women among the labouring classes are the most prolific, —at what time they cease to bear children,—what is the influence of the occupations of the parents on the health of the offspring,—what is the effect of locality, under the head of resi-

---

upon evidence which could not, for the reasons stated, be present to their minds.

' I would observe, however, that on strict principle, neither criminals nor paupers can be entitled to or can be safely allowed as high a degree of comfort as the lowest of the labouring classes. And had the average of ordinary sickness attendant upon the reduced scale of diet been greater instead of less, it may be submitted that the reduced diet ought, notwithstanding, to be enforced. It is highly satisfactory, however, to perceive from the evidence cited, and from other evidence to which it were unnecessary to advert, that to the health as well as to the morals the restriction to a simple vegetable diet is equally beneficial. By those good persons whose hearts are larger than their heads,—who, under the disastrously ambiguous word " poor," confound the independent labourers with the dependant paupers—who can see only, the real or imagined privation before them—whose sympathies are boundless for the prisoner, be he robber or murderer—whose eyes see not, whose hearts therefore rue not, the sufferings of the honest who have been robbed, or of the relations of those who have been murdered ;—by these well-meaning persons, as well as by those who profit by profusion and by misrepresentation, the display of the effects of the management, for which they are in some measure responsible, and the suggestion of the necessity of an alteration of the ordinary diets, will doubtless be received as a suggestion for a reduction of the diets and comforts of the labouring classes. A strict administration in all these cases, it will be found, only affects the comforts of the labouring classes, in the way of augmentation. The independent labourers, to whom the degrading appellation of " poor men " is applied by their intended friends but real enemies, are as much entitled to the widest range of comforts which their means will enable them to obtain, as the rich men. But I do not see how it can be reconciled to any sound principle of administration, that either paupers or felons should enjoy heavy dietaries with meat, whilst to a large proportion of the people of the three kingdoms even bread is a luxury. " But why always the dearest grain? why white bread for the worst class of population — namely, felons—whilst soldiers live well on brown bread? Why always, and at all events, bread ? Is bread everywhere a necessary article? I may ask in the words of a late eminent philanthropist? ' The bulk of the people in Scotland live on oatmeal; the labouring population of Ireland live not even on brown bread, but on potatoes. Are the Irish a puny race ?—Has the arm of the Highlander been found weak in war?—Is the lesson to be held out to the great bulk of the population, that the food with which *they* are content is not good enough for indolent able-bodied paupers, or even for felons?' "

dence, among the poor,—besides a number of other questions on medical as well as statistical points of inquiry, the answers to which he registers in the manner he has described. He submitted to the Committee the registered cases of 876 women, for the truth of whose statements he possessed the most satisfactory securities ; but in all other respects they were taken indifferently. The following table, derived from their answers as to the age at which they respectively married, is the first ever constructed to exhibit to females the advance and decline of their chances of marriage at various ages, and is deserving of the study of spinsters. Of the 876 females there were married,

			Years of Age.					Years of Age.
11	.	.	at 13	22	.	.	at	28
16	.	.	,, 15	17	.	.	,,	29
43	.	.	,, 16	9	.	.	,,	30
45	.	.	,, 17	7	.	.	,,	31
76	.	.	,, 18	5	.	.	,,	32
115	.	.	,, 19	7	.	.	,,	33
118	.	.	,, 20	5	.	.	,,	34
86	.	.	,, 21	2	.	.	,,	35
85	.	.	,, 22	0	.	.	,,	36
59	.	.	,, 23	2	.	.	,,	37
53	.	.	,, 24	0	.	.	,,	38
36	.	.	,, 25	1	.	.	,,	39
24	.	.	,, 26	3	.	.	,,	41
28	.	.	,, 27					

It is to be borne in mind that the females whose relative ages at the time of their marriage are above exhibited, were all of the middle lower classes. Among an equal number from the higher classes we should not probably find so many as 195, or more than one-fifth, married under the age of 19 ; or so few as one-sixteenth part after 28 ; or only one-thirtieth part after 30. From these 876 marriages there had been, previously to the then existing pregnancies, 4,621 pregnancies ; of which number 655 had miscarried ; 176 were still-born ; and 2,914 children were born alive. Thus there may be said to have been 3,966 births, or an average of 4½ to each marriage. Of these 1675 children survived. He had no means of ascertaining what proportion the marriages which were unproductive bore to those which were productive. Mr. Malthus gives 4½ as the average number of children produced from each marriage. Dr. Granville found, that, during the whole time at which these women continued to bear children, they had each two children in about four years. Considerable exertion was bestowed by the Doctor to determine what effect the age at which a woman married had on the number of children she produced. He observes,

' It is a curious fact, that if a woman marries at twenty-one or twenty-two, and is placed under precisely similar circumstances for the following fifteen years as women at fourteen, fifteen, and sixteen marrying at that age may be supposed to be under, she will produce the same number of children as the latter would, though the party marry seven or eight years later : and the reason is this, that those who marry very young cease either sooner, or go a great number of years without children. When they arrive at twenty or twenty-five years of age, they will stop till about thirty, and begin again : whereas, the age of maturity at which a woman is most prolific appears to be about twenty ; and there seems to be no stoppage, except disease steps in,—going on regularly every two years, or, if she do not suckle, every year, until she arrives at forty or forty-two years of age, which is the usual period for it to terminate.'—*Second Report*, p. 42.

He found that the permanent ordinary state of health of the father, as well as of the mother of a child, had a greater influence on its health than was commonly suspected. The witness had made greater progress in the collection, than in the operation of theorizing his facts ; and on several points he abstained from stating his conclusions to the Committee, as he did not consider that he had yet attained the requisite degree of completeness to warrant him in promulgating them.[*]

---

[*] Some additional information of the fecundity of women, and of the period of time from child to child, was obtained in 1833, from returns made to the Factory Commission, the results of which are worked out in Dr. Mitchell's Report.

In Catrine, in Ayrshire, out of 110 married women who had worked in the factory in their youth, there were 42 who were 45 years of age and upwards, and therefore may be presumed to have been past child-bearing. They had had amongst them 316 children, being on the average 7·52 each. The average period from child to child, according to the experience of these 110 women, was 2 years and 24 weeks, or 128 weeks.

In the same village, of 109 married women who had never worked in any factory, were 58 who had attained the age of 45 and upwards. They had borne amongst them 460 children, being on the average 7·92 each. The period from child to child of these 109 women was 2 years and 31 weeks, or 135 weeks.

At

The Committee gave more than usual attention to a scheme set on foot for the purpose of inducing unmarried men to pay a certain sum annually, on condition that every child resulting from any marriage he might subsequently contract, should, when it attained a certain age, be entitled to a certain sum of money, or a certain annuity. On the practicability of this scheme Dr. Mitchell observes,

' It is not likely that single men will be induced to pay down a sum of money, or to contribute annually for such a contingency. And if ever any considerable number of single men in this country should become so prudent as to do so, it may be questioned whether, with so much prudence, we should have so many marriages as at present; and we may expect that, in that case, the amount of population, now so overwhelming, would be reduced to so healthy a state as to raise the price of labour, and enable a man to support his family without such assistance. It is, perhaps, unnecessary to occupy time to show this scheme to be undesirable in its effects, as it does not appear likely ever to be carried into practice.'

The data were found insufficient for the establishment of any safe theories on the subject. As an instance of the ruinous extremes to which practical men are carried when they have no sound theories for their safe guidance, we may mention the cir-

---

At Deanston, in Perthshire, 23 women, who had been married each 16 years and upwards, had had amongst them 170 children, or 7·9-23 each. The average period from child to child was 119 weeks. Some returns were obtained from Staffordshire; but of these there were only 17 who had attained 45 years and upwards. They had had amongst them 92 children, being on the average 5·7-17 each. Of the 130 women, the average period from child to child was 2 years and 26 weeks, or 130 weeks.

The experience of these 17 women falls far short of the fecundity of the 123 in Catrine and Deanston ; and it is to be regretted that the short period allowed to that extensive inquiry (two months) did not enable the commissioners to collect returns sufficiently extensive to give an average which might be depended upon. According to the experience of the 123 females, the fecundity of a female who has been in the marriage state sufficiently long for its complete developement is on the average very nearly 8.

As to the effect on the number of children resulting from the age at which the females married, the returns from Catrine showed that the greatest number of children was borne from women marrying at 18, and gradually decreased according to the advance in age of the mother, though not much so, for women of any age below 25 ; but women marrying after 30 had on the average considerably fewer children than women marrying ten years earlier. There were, however, individual exceptions.

cumstance, that a case was submitted by the Committee to Mr. Morgan, to determine the allowance that should be made on an assurance for each child produced from any marriage. He declared that 5*l.* a year might be given to each child. The very same case was submitted to Mr. Francis Bailey, and he answered, that 19*l.* 15*s.* a year might be allowed for each child.

We have now adverted to the chief subjects relative to population and the duration of life on which the Committee made inquiries. These subjects begin to excite some degree of interest, and we have been compelled to go over the whole very imperfectly, that we might not be too late to give whatever aid may be in our power to any discussions which might take place on the formation of more equitable provision against the contingencies of sickness and mortality amongst those classes who are yet sufficiently independent and virtuous to desire to live only on the fruits of their own honest industry. The evidence contained in both Reports is highly deserving perusal, as showing how much remains to be accomplished on almost every point. Dr. Mitchell's treatise comprises the substance of the information relative to the provisions against casualties of sickness and mortality, put into a shape to render it available to the labouring classes. He has interspersed the facts with useful suggestions, of which they stand in great need, for the most prudent investment of their money. It is well known that, hitherto, works on such subjects have in general been profitable nearly in the inverse proportion to their utility: and, therefore, when we find them written for the use of those classes, and published, as we learn this is, at the author's own expense, we are bound to hail them as the results of unusual benevolence.

Mr. Milne, who, since the days of Dr. Price, has written most extensively and ably on these subjects, in explaining to the Committee why he had not accomplished some investigations of scientific importance, made some observations which sufficiently account for the little progress made in this and several other departments of knowledge. He states :—

' Subjects founded on general calculations such as I have made require a great deal of attention; and when all that has been done, the author must publish them at his own expense, and I am satisfied they will never pay him interest on the money they cost to make them. What I have done, I have done with great ardour; but the sale of such works is so confined that it will not pay, and I do not think that a man's success in life is promoted by the publication of them. But I beg to make a further remark. Such calculations enable those who pay attention to them, to make estimates of the value of property depending upon the contingencies of human life; they consequently have occasionally cases laid before them, for which they receive fees, and those fees afford them some compensation for the trouble and time they expend upon them. But these societies, when they apply in that way, cannot afford to remunerate them, although there is a great deal more trouble than in other cases.'

These observations set forth a ground of extenuation applicable to the best of the practical men of science. We remember hearing, that on the occasion of a trial in the Court of King's Bench, when the case turned upon an important principle of medical science, which appeared to be unsettled in the minds of the most eminent medical men who were examined as witnesses, one of them was asked whether it was not extremely important to all sufferers by the malady, and to the public at large, that the principle in question should be settled? " True, it was so," replied the witness; " it was most important that it should be settled." " Then why," asked the counsel examining, " was it allowed to remain unsettled ?" " Because there was no payment; there were no fees to be got as remuneration for the labour of settling it," was the reply of the medical professor, who might have retorted the question with relation to the opprobrious deficiencies in the whole field of the art and science of which his questioner was a professor. In this view even of their own interests we believe these practical men are to a considerable extent mistaken; for conspicuous improvements in practice leading to fame and profit can only be based on improvements on sound principle or on sound theory. But in many cases the toil of elaborating sound general principles, which can only be accomplished by careful examinations and inductions from particulars, is great, and the results are rarely appreciated with justice. The toil detracts from the reputation for attention to the arts and particulars of every-day routine, on which professional success mainly depends: it gains no fees; " success in life is not promoted" by it. The consequences of this neglect of sound general principles are not presented to the attention of the classes possessing the means of employing their leisure in liberal pursuits, otherwise we might expect their cultivation ; for there is, perhaps, no other country in which such strong benevolent sympathies, or such ardent desires to render disinterested service to the labouring population within their immediate neighbourhoods, pervade the wealthier classes. The misdirection of these sympathies, and their operation in inconsiderate charities and the profuse expenditure of the poor's-rates, have formed the most potent means of retarding the improvement of the labouring population ; and it seems to us that the wealthy have yet to learn what are the means by which they may render the best services ; which means, we conceive, will be found to be, in acting with the labouring classes rather than for them ; in enabling them to act for themselves, by provident institutions, securely based on sound knowledge of the nature of that of which we have treated. The promotion of such knowledge appears to be the province of endowed public bodies, or of the government in cases beyond the reach of private individuals. But it has not hitherto been the habit of practical statesmen to take the initiative, in measures which are "abstract" from any clamour, —which yield no immediate popularity and appear singular or enthusiastic, and "are not called for" as conducive to any immediate party objects, and which present the difficulty of gaining over those numerous votes of the representatives of the ignorance and prejudices of the country. And where, for the advancement of knowledge, the government, has stepped out of what is called by men of routine, its direct way, — its steps have too frequently been in the way of needless profusion and mismanagement. Take for example the Record Commission, instituted, we suppose, for the promotion of historical knowledge. Half a million of money, probably, has been expended in printing and methodising the records, without having brought to light any entertaining facts worth a thousandth part of the sum expended, or having even rendered the records more accessible for the pursuit of whatever useful information they may contain. A small proportion of the money thus misapplied would, if well directed, have sufficed to obtain all the data desirable to be deduced from the past experience of the casualties of sickness

and mortality.* We venture to repeat that it behoves a government intent upon its higher duties, to set to the uninstruct-
ed multitude an example of forethought in searching out, pre-

---

* The Bill for the Registration of Marriages, Births, and Deaths, now
pending, appears to us to have been "called for" in a narrow sectarian spirit,
and to be opposed by several persons in a spirit even more narrow and bigoted. The business of a civil local registration for all the purposes to which
it might be made subservient, will be found to be one of the highest importance, and to have been settled in a manner only excusable as the commencement of a change which the prevalent ignorance would not allow to
be more comprehensive and complete. The representatives of the dissenting bodies and the high church party, to whom the discussion is given up,
appear to assume that the business of the registration of the occurrence of
certain facts,—is their business exclusively, and involved in their respective ceremonies; as if all religious ceremonies, even as essentials of contracts, or as the foundation of civil rights, might not have been kept perfectly distinct from the business of registration? The objects to be attained
by registration, in the prevention of litigation by the pre-appointment of
evidence, are but slightly adverted to, whilst the numerous and more important uses are entirely overlooked by both parties : namely,—the registration
of the causes of disease, with a view to devising remedies ;—the determination of the salubrity of places in different situations, with a view to individual
settlements and public establishments ;—the determination of comparative degrees of salubrity as between occupation and occupation in places differently
circumstanced, in order that persons willing to engage in insalubrious occupations may be the more effectually enabled to obtain adequate provision for their sufferings in respect of health ;—the collection of data for
calculating the rate of mortality, and giving safety to the immense mass of
property insured ; enabling every one to employ his money to the most advantage, whether for his own benefit, or for the benefit of persons dear to
him, and that without the impression of loss to any one else ;—the obtainment
of the means of ascertaining the progress of population at different periods,
and under different circumstances ; directing the attention of the government
and the public to the extent and effects of calamities and casualties, and the
prevention of undue interments, and concealed murder, or deaths from culpa-
ble heedlessness. Nor is any allusion made to the wants to be supplied by
a system of local registration, for notarial and various judicial purposes, in
the preservation of deeds and evidence of private and public contracts ; with
relation to which wants England is, of all European nations, barbarously
deficient in due provision. The opponents of the measure are "content,"
as were the Russian apple-merchants, with their practice, and as wise-
ly express their scorn of what they call philosophy. The preceding
evidence with relation to the effects of various diets, indicating by an easy
alteration the relief of thousands from the infliction of sickness, and the
saving of deaths by the hundred, is but a fragment of the evidence which
might be adduced of other important and extensive results, obtainable by
means of sound information on such topics as those to which we have adverted. The Bill for the Registration of Births and Deaths, as originally
proposed, provided a tolerably fair tentative machinery : with this exception,
that the foundation of these registries was not made, as we think it should be,
on certificates from the medical men who last attended the deceased; and, in
the case of births, from the accoucheurs, midwives, or other persons who aid

paring, and enforcing all the various means which conduce to the exercise of the virtues of frugality and forethought in modes by which pain is to the greatest extent avoided and mitigated, and the sum of public enjoyment increased.

---

the deliveries ; the preparation and due depositing of such certificates entitling the medical practitioner to a small fee and the omission incurring a penalty, and the falsification subjecting the offender to heavy punishment as a serious crime. The parties thus preparing the certificates would thus be the principal witnesses in the nearest degree cognizant of the facts. A system of registration will scarcely be complete, which depends for the requisite information chiefly on the success of the registrars in seeking it out, or on the parties bringing it, even though the performance of the duty be enforced by a penalty. As a general rule, such duties may be expected to be the best performed by the persons who are accustomed to attend the most frequently to the class of events to which the duties relate. In cases of death, the relations of the deceased can scarcely be expected to attend to such incidents in the midst of calamity, and to them more important arrangements of private interest. Certificates by the medical attendants should not of course exclude professional care in the process of the registration of the more important medical facts. The efforts made by the contending parties to dispense with the machinery of the new unions will, we are apprehensive, be found to be wasteful and mischievous in their effects, as they are blind and bigoted in intention. But notwithstanding the defective state of the measure, we trust that the Registrar General will be enabled to obtain several of the important objects of a good registration.

THE END.

Means of Preventing Abuses

Thoughts on the Means of Preventing Abuses in Life Assurance Offices
(London: C. Whittingham, 1835)

This pamphlet, published outside London, reflects continuing concerns about the practices of the burgeoning life offices. The debate continued for at least another twenty years and indicates both the uncertainty and the differences of opinion about the proper conduct of the business. It is probable that the provincial life offices were rather more cautious than some of the London offices, which were by now fiercely competing against each other. This may be evident in the views expressed here.

THOUGHTS,

&c.

THOUGH the Legislature has thought proper, with what degree of wisdom or propriety I shall not here discuss, to reject the Bill which was introduced last year, for the Registration of Deeds affecting real Estates, yet there remains one class of documents, the enrolment or registration of which, is wholly free from the objections which were successfully urged against the measure introduced by Mr. William Brougham, and which, I submit, being in a great degree, if not wholly, of a public nature, are above all others the proper objects of legislative interference and arrangement. I allude to deeds establishing joint stock companies and partnerships, other than those which are strictly of a private nature. Companies which are open to the public, and the

shares in which are transferable without the
consent of each person interested in the partnership, stand on a ground very different from
mere voluntary associations for the purpose
of prosecuting a trade or manufacture.   In
the latter, several persons are joined together
in order that the different partners may super-
intend the different branches of the trade ;
each person is in general an active agent in
his own particular department, or should he
merely furnish a portion of the capital, as
sometimes is the case, yet the whole state and
circumstances of the firm are open to his inspection and subject to his control, and should
any undue preponderance be obtained by any
member, it is open to a remedy by the instant
interference of the rest.   Partnerships like
these are strictly private concerns, and with
them the legislature has no right to interfere ;
but the case is widely altered when we consider joint stock companies, where the property of the company at large is under the
delegated control of a committee of management or a board of directors.   There the
general body of proprietors take no active
part in the business of the society, shares

there are considered more in the nature of funds, or stocks (producing, indeed, a greater interest than the government securities,) and as long as the members receive a tolerable good interest for their money, they trouble themselves but little about the management of the company's concerns. Hence joint stock companies are liable to fall by degrees under the control of a few individuals constituting the managing body, and though a legal right remains in the body of subscribers or shareholders at large, to inquire into the state and prospects of the society, yet the difficulty and expense of proceeding, the danger of failure owing to technical difficulties, and the small interest or share of each individual member, are apt to deter persons from taking effective measures to penetrate into the secrets of the directory, and to induce them often to acquiesce in evils which, though probable, are uncertain and distant, sooner than expose themselves to the vexation, hazard, and odium of a suit in equity. On these grounds I contend that it is competent for the legislature to interfere with joint stock companies, even with those now in existence, to the extent of

requiring the deeds by which they are established to be enrolled, and public and effectual notice to be annually given of a meeting
of the proprietors at large, to receive reports
of the actual circumstances of the association.
There is one species of association to which
I contend these observations apply with very
considerable force, inasmuch as they are,
without exception, the most useful institutions
of civilized life, in whose well being and good
management society at large is most deeply
interested, and whose failure must be productive of the most serious and lamentable
consequences, not only to persons now in
existence, but even to a future generation,
and would be most deeply felt by those who
have no means whatever of interfering to prevent them.   I mean societies for the purpose
of effecting insurances on lives. These, above
all other companies or associations, are public
in their nature and object, while their extreme
utility should obtain from them the greatest
and most tender care and protection from the
legislature. It is of the very highest public
importance that these societies, on which the
happiness of families, particularly those of

persons engaged in professional pursuits, so greatly depend, should be conducted on sound and philosophical principles and with the strictest integrity. It is not sufficient to say, that no man need insure in any one office unless he please, and that competition will ensure good management. Competition among life societies, as has been hinted, I think by Sir John Herschel, may be carried to excess, and the desire of obtaining public patronage, by holding out the temptation of superior economy, may induce the managers of these offices to undertake more than they can perform. The remedy of this, however, must be found in the good sense, prudence, and caution of the insurer, it would be absurd to think of restricting competition. It is however the positive duty of government to prevent, as far as possible, the existence of an ill-conducted, unsound institution. On the same ground that frauds are punished by the law, that the penalties of felony are annexed to forgery, in order that the sanction of criminal justice may step in in aid of individual prudence, on the very same ground, it would be highly wrong to permit the existence of an office improperly conducted, which in fact would be nothing more than an extensive, organized, deliberate engine for the perpetration of fraud the most insidious, and the omission of laws to prevent is almost tantamount to an actual permission or sufferance. If any society exist in this country whose affairs are improperly conducted, that society is a public nuisance, leading to consequences the most dangerous, and, at all events, by general regulations, by which the possibility of the existence of such evils would be prevented, increased confidence would be produced, and greater security given to all institutions of the kind. It happens unfortunately, moreover, that insurance societies in their origin and nature are, above all other joint stock companies, liable to be mismanaged, and to fall into the hands of one or two members or officers, more active and enterprising than the rest, for the simple reason that immediate profit or advantage is not expected from them; the gain is not to the contributor, but to his children or representatives. From their very nature, several years must elapse before considerable demands begin to be made upon them.

Contributions will steadily pour in for some time without any drain to countervail them, and yet in this very season of apparent prosperity the seeds of dissolution and decay may be sown. The general body of insurers expect no profit or emolument from their contributions; their attention, therefore, is not subject to be excited like that of contributors to other joint stock companies, by the scantiness or delay of a dividend, and thus a degree of apathy is likely to be generated, which may cause the management of affairs to fall into the hand of those who ought to be merely ministerial, and the watchful attention which is requisite to secure good conduct even in the best of servants and officers, to be lulled to sleep; and when once caution is set at rest on the one side, and cupidity excited on the other (and the very possession of wealth even as a trust has no small tendency to excite it), it is an easy matter to devise means to obtain, unsuspected and unobserved, a far greater authority and influence than can be, under any circumstances, wholesome or desirable. Besides, those who have longest contributed to the funds of the society, and

have the greatest stake in it, are the least
likely to interfere. Though they may know
that an explosion must come sooner or later,
yet it may not occur during their life, nor
until their representatives have received the
amount for which they are insured. They
therefore will endeavour to hush matters up,
that the evil day may be deferred as long as
possible. I will proceed to illustrate my argument by a case by no means impossible or
even improbable. Let us suppose a society
to have been instituted some twenty or thirty
years ago, on fair and equitable principles,
with an efficient board of directors, with a
deed of trust duly executed (but which under
the existing law will not be public), and the
contents of which will therefore be known to
few, and of course, if abuses prevail, will be
carefully concealed, with officers of good reputation. Up to the present time but few demands
will have been made upon it, the incomings
would exceed the outgoings ; and as all things
appeared to go on prosperously, little anxiety
would exist as to its solvency. Perhaps no
stated periods might be provided by the trust
deed for meetings of the insurers, or no method

of giving public notice of them might be prescribed. In this case the officers of the society
might by degrees become possessed of something beyond what was originally intended.
As the board of directors, who would in the
first instance have been men probably past the
middle age, died off, no steps might be taken
to replace them, or too great deference being
paid to the recommendation of an active officer,
his friends or connexions, or humble depen-
dents, might by degrees be introduced, and he
might assume, under the shelter of an osten-
sible but inefficient board, the entire control
and management of the society. The name of
the most insignificant fiddler or farmer, with
the addition of esquire tacked on at its tail,
would look well at a distance. Perhaps even
the number required by the trust deed might
be dispensed with, and the board of directors
be reduced to two or three mere men of straw,
whose names might not even be announced to
the public, who might be dazzled with a list
of titled patrons and trustees. Nay, persons
might actually be held out as trustees who were
not so. If public inquiry or suspicion should
make it desirable to fill up the list and restore

it to its original number, men who have received obligations from the master hand that might thus direct the concern, or who from good will and friendship might be desirous of obliging him, might consent to become members, forgetful of the heavy responsibility they would incur, should they not at once put an end to the irregularities they would in fact be intended to perpetuate. They might perhaps be announced to the public without any legal appointment whatever. The evils to be apprehended from a state of things like this, and this state of things is perhaps not entirely imaginary, are too manifest to require to be urged. But let us concede pecuniary integrity, and suppose that the importance and power to be gained by the control and management of a great monied institution are all that is sought for, yet even here a temptation is begotten to compromise the interests of the society and to oblige private friends or political partizans, by loans on insecure real or even on personal securities, and thus the interests of the society may, in spite of the strictest uprightness and honesty, be seriously compromised. The prevention of these evils is easily effected.

Let all deeds, even those of existing societies, be enrolled at length, so as to be easily accessible to the public; let public meetings be annually called, and widely circulated notices given at proper intervals in the London Gazette and other papers both general and local; let the emoluments of the officers be publicly announced; and let means be furnished for remedying existing defects by statement of the circumstances, and by application to Chancery or some other court. Perhaps even, it should be made penal to publish or retain the names of persons as trustees, who have never actually been such, or who have withdrawn themselves; and no public act of the society should be valid, unless sanctioned by a majority of the whole body of directors required by the deed of settlement. From societies properly constituted I anticipate no opposition, and resistance to a public measure like this, may be considered as a criterion by which to judge of their soundness and integrity. Nor is this principle new, either in this country or elsewhere. We have interfered by statute to prevent the abuses and frauds which existed in Friendly Societies, and what are

Societies for Life Insurances but an extended species of the same thing. In the United States, private banks are compelled to publish their accounts, that improper credit may not be given. Our legislature in renewing the charter of the Bank of England has required publicity. When we are told that publicity may shake confidence and credit, I reply that credit obtained by concealment is in its nature fraudulent, and instead of beneficial is pernicious in the extreme. Fairness and open dealing are the true and wholesome sources of legitimate credit; and when I see an institution which dreads scrutiny, and whose proceedings are conducted with secrecy and mystery, I need no argument to convince me of its rottenness.

To these evils, in the existing state of things, societies are liable which in their origin were respectable, fair establishments, really possessing the capital they announced to the public. All societies, however, are not equally reputable; there may be some which were at first set going by needy adventurous persons, tacked on perhaps to other institutions already flourishing, and under the auspices, apparently, of wealthy individuals of known fortune and respectability, whose names are considered by the public as a guarantee and security for the undertakings and liabilities of the society. Whereas nothing can be farther from the truth. Were any danger incurred, we should not find men of fortune quite so ready to lend their names to swell the lists we see announced in the newspapers. Directors or managers wilfully or by neglect sanctioning a breach of trust, or an improper investment of the funds, may make themselves responsible; but the Policies of an Insurance Office pledge only the funds of the society, and not the persons or property of the members; and this is a fact to which the attention of the public ought to be most seriously directed. It thus appears that societies of this kind may be established and go on for some time with apparent prosperity, though they really possess little or no capital; and while their income, which ought to be carefully secured to provide for future demands, may all the while be frittered away in improper and unfair dividends or bonuses, extravagant allowances, and preposterous rates of commission, or advanced on improvident and insecure loans to the friends and adherents of the officers.

As new institutions are continually spring-
ing up, it is highly desirable that some
regulation should be made to prevent these
evils for the future. As this would be entirely prospective, no objection can be raised
against it on the score of interference with
private property, and on the grounds of public
policy I submit that Parliament is competent
to interfere even with institutions already in
existence, and to institute an inquiry into
the actual state of their funds and liabilities.
It may be objected, that before endeavouring
to put the Legislature in motion, I ought to
show the actual existence of some of the evils,
the possibility of which I have pointed out;
but however great existing evils may be, the
danger of announcing publicly even notorious
abuses is too great to be incurred by an
individual. It is not improbable that parliamentary inquiry would disclose ample
grounds for interference.

FINIS.

de Morgan,
An Essay on Probabilities

Augustus de Morgan, Chapter VIII 'On the Application of Probabilities to Life Contingencies', Chapter XI, 'On the Nature of the Contract of Insurance, and on the Risks of Insurance Offices in General', Chapter XII 'On the Adjustment of the Interests of the Different Members in an Insurance Office', Chapter XIII 'Miscellaneous Subjects Connected with Insurance, etc.', *An Essay on Probabilities and on their Application to Life Contingencies and Insurance Offices* (1838)
Anon., 'Review of Augustus de Morgan', *The Quarterly Review*, vol. CXXVIII (1839), pp. 285–307

Augustus de Morgan (1806–71) was a mathematician and logician. At the age of twenty-two he became Professor of Mathematics at the new University College, London. His contributions to mathematics were broad and substantial, including areas such as mathematical logic, mathematical induction, and algebra.

This volume, first published in the series *The Cabinet Cyclopedia*, attempts to apply the scientific principles of probability to the practice of insurance at a time when there was much consideration of the basis of the assurance of life. Morgan joins the debate about the Equitable Society, which had been criticised for its conservatism. He saw the Equitable as a unique institution whose methods had been forced upon it historically, and felt that other societies could be more flexible in their practices. He uses the opportunity to put forward his ideas on a range of matters concerning the insurance business.

CHAPTER VIII.

ON THE APPLICATION OF PROBABILITIES TO LIFE CONTINGENCIES.

WHEN questions connected with life contingencies were first considered, it was regarded as most deliberate gambling to be in any way concerned in buying or selling such articles as annuities, or any interests depending upon them. Before we can well enter upon the question of the truth or falsehood of the preceding notion, it will be necessary to ask what laws the duration of human life follows, and whether it follow any laws at all? Take two separate hundreds of persons, each aged twenty, is there any reason to conclude that the united lives of all the first hundred will make an amount of years nearly equal to that of the second?

In order to try this point, I shall take another question, yet more unfavourable to the result which I wish to establish. In 100 persons all aged twenty, we know that there is but a very slight chance that any given one of them shall reach the age of eighty; and we may consider it a certainty (or of an extremely high probability), that none of them will see the age of a hundred and twenty. We will consider it therefore as given, that no one shall live to the last-mentioned age, and we will even suppose that all ages of death between 20 and 120 are equally probable. This of course very much increases our chance of fluctuation : but even with this supposition it is not very great.

Let us suppose a lottery in which there are counters marked with every possible number or fraction intermediate between 0 and E: so that the drawing may have any mark whatsoever. If then we draw out 100 counters, the least possible amount of drawings will be 0, the greatest 100 times E: and if all drawings be equally probable, we have no reason to suppose that our amount will exceed 50 times E, which does not equally apply in favour of its falling short of that quantity. That we shall have exactly 50 times E, is an event of which the chance is infinitely small : but that the amount shall lie between limits which are tolerably near 50 times E, is very probable.

PROBLEM.   Let there be counters, in equal numbers, with every possible mark between 0 and E.   What is the probability that the average of n drawings shall not differ from the half of E, one way or the other, by more than k.

RULE.   Multiply k by the square root of six times n, and divide the product by E.   Call the quotient t; then the value of H (Table I.) is the probability required.

EXAMPLE.   In 600 drawings, each of which may be any thing between 0 and 100, required the probability that the average of all the drawings shall lie between $50 + 5$ and $50 - 5$.

$n = 600, E = 100, k = 5$; the square root of 6 times 600 is 60, and 5 times 60 divided by 100 is 3.   The first table does not contain values of t higher than 2: an event being almost certain, or of a very high probability when t is equal to 2.   Table II., however, furnishes us with an extension of Table I. ; the K opposite to any value of t in that table being always nearly the H which belongs to half that value of t.   Consequently, the H belonging to t = 3, is the K belonging to t = 6.   But the second table only goes to t = 5; in which case K is ·999.   It is then more than 999 to 1 that the average of the 600 drawings is within the limits specified.   If we take $k = 1$, in which case t = ·6, we find it is 3 to 2 that the average is contained between 49 and 51.

If then there were 600 infants born, and if it were the law of human life that any individual is as likely to die at one age as another, for any age not exceeding 100 years, even then, and with so much more scope for fluctuation than is actually found, it would be more than 999 to 1 against the average life of the 600 infants exceeding 55, or falling short of 45 years ; and more than 3 to 2 that the same average should fall between 49 and 51 years. If such be the case, it is obvious that the chances of fluctuation are much diminished by the superior chances of death happening at some periods of life rather than at others ; as well as by the smaller limits of human life, which need not for any practical purpose be supposed to extend as far as one hundred years.

To suppose that the duration of human life is regulated by *no* laws, would be to make an assumption of a most monstrous character, *à priori*, and most evidently false. For it is a law, were it the only one, that no individual shall attain the age of 200 years. So much is known to all; but to those who consider the subject more closely, by the aid of recorded facts, it may be made as evident as the existence of a limit to human life, that the casualties of mortality are distributed among mankind in so uniform a manner, that the average existence of a thousand infants will differ very little from that of another thousand born in the same country and station of life. It is true that differences of race, climate, manner of living, &c., &c., produce marked effects upon the duration of life ; which is no more than might be expected : but it is equally true that the notorious *individual* uncertainty of life cannot be discovered in the results of observations made upon masses of individuals.

There are various results of observation, which are called *tables of mortality*, which differ only in the methods of presenting the same sets of facts. Firstly, we have what may be called tables of the numbers living. These show, for a given number born, how many attain each year of age. Thus, in the Carlisle table, opposite to 0 and 50, we find 10,000 and 4397, indicating that, according to observations made at Carlisle, the proportion of those born to those who saw their fiftieth birthday, was that of 10,000 to 4397. Again, opposite to 60, we find 3643, meaning, that of 4397 persons aged 50, 3643 attain the age of 60. Secondly, we have tables of *yearly decrements*, in which the same number of per-

sons are supposed to be alive at every age, and the proportion who die in the next year is set down in the table.
Thus in the government annuity tables, opposite to 50
and 60, we find 161 and 315, meaning that, according
to the observations from which these tables were constructed, of 10,000 persons aged 50, 161 died before
completing the next year of life; and of 10,000 persons
aged 60, 315 died before attaining the age of 61.
Thirdly, we have tables of *mean duration* of life (commonly called expectation of life), which show the average
number of years enjoyed by individuals of every age.
This, in another variety of the Carlisle tables, opposite
to 50 and 60, we find 21·11 and 14·34 ; meaning that,
according to these tables, persons aged fifty live, one
with another, 21·11 years more, and persons aged 60,
14·34 years more.

Until observations of human mortality become more
extensive and correct, I prefer the tables of mean
duration to all others.   The events of single years are
subject to considerable error, and generally present
such varieties of fluctuation, that it has become usual to
take some arbitrary and purely hypothetical mode of
introducing regularity.   This practice cannot be too
strongly condemned, since the tables thereby lose some
of their value as representations of physical facts,
without any advantage ultimately gained.   For if by
using the raw result of experiments, tables of annuities
were rendered unequal and irregular, it would be as
easy, and much more safe, to apply the arbitrary method
of correction to the money results themselves, than to
introduce it at a previous stage of the process.   It is
not, however, a matter of much consequence as to the
annuities, &c., deduced from the tables: and as yet, the
rudeness of the original observations renders the effect
of any such alteration not so great as the probable
errors of the observations themselves.

The mean duration of life is approximately calculated
as follows.   Suppose (taking an instance from the Carlisle tables) that 75 persons are alive at the age of 92,

of whom are left at the successive birthdays, 54, 40, 30, 23, 18, 14, 11, 9, 7, 5, 3, 1, 0.   Consequently, in their 93d year, 54 persons enjoy a complete year of life, and 21 die, whom we may suppose, one with another, to live through half the year, and 54 years and 21 half years make $64\frac{1}{2}$ years, which is the total life of 75 persons for that year.   Proceeding in this way, we find that there are,

in the 93d	year 54 + $\frac{1}{2}$ of 21 years.
94th	40 + $\frac{1}{2}$ of 14
95th	30 + $\frac{1}{2}$ of 10
96th	23 + $\frac{1}{2}$ of 7
97th	18 + $\frac{1}{2}$ of 5
98th	14 + $\frac{1}{2}$ of 4
99th	11 + $\frac{1}{2}$ of 3
100th	9 + $\frac{1}{2}$ of 2
101st	7 + $\frac{1}{2}$ of 2
102d	5 + $\frac{1}{2}$ of 2
103d	3 + $\frac{1}{2}$ of 2
104th	1 + $\frac{1}{2}$ of 2
105th	0 + $\frac{1}{2}$ of 1

Total, 215 + $\frac{1}{2}$ of 75

Hence 75 individuals, aged 92, enjoy 215 + $\frac{1}{2}$ of 75 years, and each has, one with another, the 75th part of this, or 3·37 years.

RULE.   To find the mean duration of life from a table of the living at every age out of a given number born, add together the numbers in the table for all the ages above the given age, divide by the number at the given age, and add half a year to the result.

The preceding rule is mathematically incorrect, being only an approximation to the truth, even supposing the tables perfectly correct.   The error of computation may be found, nearly, as follows.   Divide the number who die in the year next following the given age by twelve times the number in the table at that age, and diminish the result of the preceding rule by the quotient. Thus, in the instance before us, 21 divided by 12 times 75 is ·02, so that 3·35 is nearer the truth.   This error, however, is immaterial for practical purposes.

A more important question is that of the degree of confidence which may be placed in tables of mean duration, the errors of observation being supposed to be as likely to be positive as negative. In order to estimate this, we must compute the mean square of the duration of life; that is, multiplying the time which each individual lives by itself, we must add the results together and divide by the whole number of individuals. To make a rough approximation to this in the case before us, remember that

21 individuals live $\frac{1}{2}$ a year	$\frac{1}{2} \times \frac{1}{2} = \frac{1}{4}$ giving	$\frac{21}{4}$
14 ——	$\frac{3}{2}$ —	$\frac{3}{2} \times \frac{3}{2} = \frac{9}{4}$ —	$\frac{126}{4}$
10 ——	$\frac{5}{2}$ —	$\frac{5}{2} \times \frac{5}{2} = \frac{25}{4}$ —	$\frac{250}{4}$
7 ——	$\frac{7}{2}$ —	$\frac{7}{2} \times \frac{7}{2} = \frac{49}{4}$ —	$\frac{243}{4}$
5 ——	$\frac{9}{2}$ —	$\frac{9}{2} \times \frac{9}{2} = \frac{81}{4}$ —	$\frac{405}{4}$
4 ——	$\frac{11}{2}$ —	$\frac{11}{2} \times \frac{11}{2} = \frac{121}{4}$ —	$\frac{484}{4}$
3 ——	$\frac{13}{2}$ —	$\frac{13}{2} \times \frac{13}{2} = \frac{169}{4}$ —	$\frac{507}{4}$
2 ——	$\frac{15}{2}$ —	$\frac{15}{2} \times \frac{15}{2} = \frac{225}{4}$ —	$\frac{450}{4}$
2 ——	$\frac{17}{2}$ —	$\frac{17}{2} \times \frac{17}{2} = \frac{289}{4}$ —	$\frac{578}{4}$
2 ——	$\frac{19}{2}$ —	$\frac{19}{2} \times \frac{19}{2} = \frac{361}{4}$ —	$\frac{722}{4}$
2 ——	$\frac{21}{2}$ —	$\frac{21}{2} \times \frac{21}{2} = \frac{441}{4}$ —	$\frac{882}{4}$
2 ——	$\frac{23}{2}$ —	$\frac{23}{2} \times \frac{23}{2} = \frac{529}{4}$ —	$\frac{1058}{4}$
1 ——	$\frac{25}{2}$ —	$\frac{25}{2} \times \frac{25}{2} = \frac{625}{4}$ —	$\frac{625}{4}$
75	(Average square 21·5)		$\frac{6451}{4}$

RULE. From the mean square of the duration of life at any age, subtract the square of the mean duration at that age: divide the difference by the number of lives of the given age from which the table was made, and extract the square root of the quotient. Take four tenths (more correctly ·39894), of this square root, which gives the mean risk of error, and ·67 of the square root gives the probable error.

Suppose that in the case before us, the number of lives aged 92 was 40 *, from which the preceding table was made. We have then,

* This is nearly the number of lives at that age among those from which the Carlisle table was formed, but the arbitrary help introduced from other tables at the older ages, on account of presumed insufficiency of data, makes the result of this example of no greater value than a numerical instance arbitrarily chosen.

Mean square of durations   21·5
Square of 3·37, the mean duration 11·36
                                  ————
$$40)10·14$$
$$·254 \quad \sqrt{·254} = ·504$$

·504 × ·67 = ·33 of a year, the probable error.

The same process may be applied to any other case, and the result of the whole is, that observation of a number of lives which is not very great, will be sufficient to give the mean duration of life with considerable approach to exactness. This is confirmed by the results of various tables, from which it appears that when the individuals composing an observation are of the same country, and under the same general circumstances, the results of such tables come very near to each other.

The reader who desires to know the history of tables of mortality should consult the articles MORTALITY and ANNUITIES in the new edition of the Encyclopædia Britannica, both from the accurate pen of Mr. Milne, the author of the Carlisle tables. I cannot, in this work, pretend to give more than a slight summary of results connected with life contingencies, such as may guide the reader who understands the main points of the theory of probabilities to safe conclusions.

From some tables made from observations at Breslau, De Moivre concluded that the following hypothesis, namely, that of 86 persons born one dies every year till all are extinct, would very nearly represent the mortality of the greater part of life, and that its errors would nearly compensate one another in the calculation of annuities. The Northampton tables of Dr. Price, which have been used by most of the insurance offices, very nearly represent this hypothesis at all the middle ages. But both give much too large a mortality for the circumstances of the last half century, as is proved by all the tables which have been lately constructed. The greater part of the difference, I have no doubt, is due to the real improvement of life which has taken place, from the introduction of vaccination, more temperate habits of life *, better medical assistance, and greater cleanliness in towns. We may now state, as a much nearer approximation to the mortality of the middle classes, that from the age of 15 to that of 65, the *average* may be represented as follows : — of 100 persons aged 15, one dies every year till the age of 65. But the mean duration of life will serve to give a more precise idea, and a simple rule may be given, which will, for rough purposes, represent the Carlisle table between the ages of 10 and 60. Of persons aged 10 years, the average remaining life is 49 years, with a diminution of 7 years for every 10 years elapsed; thus of persons aged 20 years, the average remaining life is 49–7 or 42 years ; at 30 years of age, 35 years. The following list of tables will be followed by some notice of each.

---

* I must be understood, here, as speaking particularly of the middle classes, in English towns and cities. Most of the tables have a majority of this class, and there is not any very precise information on the mortality of the labouring classes, or in the inhabitants of the country as distinguished from those in towns. With regard to the point on which this note is written, all old persons remember the time when what we should now call hard drinking was almost universal.

Years of age.	De Moivre's hypothesis.	Northampton.	Amicable.	Carlisle.	Equitable.	Government, males.	Government, females.	Years of age.
0	43	25·2	– –	38·7	– –	– –	– –	0
5	40·5	40·8	– –	51·3	– –	48·9	54·2	5
10	38	39·8	– –	48·8	48·3	45·6	51·1	10
15	35·5	36·5	– –	45·0	45·0	41·8	47·2	15
20	33	33·4	36·6	41·5	41·7	38·4	44·0	20
25	30·5	30·9	34·1	37·9	38·1	35·9	40·8	25
30	28	28·3	31·1	34·3	34·5	33·2	37·6	30
35	25·5	25·7	27·7	31·0	30·9	30·2	34·3	35
40	23	23·1	24·4	27·6	27·4	27·0	31·1	40
45	20·5	20·5	21·1	24·5	23·9	23·8	27·8	45
50	18	18·0	17·9	21·1	20·4	20·3	24·4	50
55	15·5	15·6	15:1	17·6	17·0	17·2	20·8	55
60	13	13·2	12·5	14·3	13·9	14·4	17·3	60
65	10·5	10·9	9·9	11·8	11·1	11·6	14·0	65
70	8	8·6	7·8	9·2	8·7	9·2	11.0	70
75	5·5	6·5	6·2	7·0	6·6	7·1	8·5	75
80	3	4·8	5·0	5·5	4·8	4·9	6·5	80
85	0·5	3·4	4·0	4·1	3·4	3·1	4·8	85
90	– –	2·4	2·9	3·3	2·6	2·0	2·8	90
95	– –	0·8	1·4	3·5	1·1	1·2	1·6	95
100	– –		·· –	2·3	– –	– –	– –	100

1. *De Moivre's hypothesis* was suggested by Halley's Breslau tables, made from observations of the mortality of that town in the years 1687—1691. It confessedly errs considerably at the beginning and end of life.

2. The *Northampton* tables were constructed by Dr. Price from the mortality of that town, in the years 1741—1780, the numbers of male and female deaths being very nearly equal. These tables were, and are, almost universally used by the assurance offices, and are those by which legacy duties are estimated in the act of parliament, 36 Geo. III. cap. 52.

3. The *Amicable Society*'s table was formed some years ago by Mr. Finlaison, at the suggestion of that gentleman and myself to the directors, and as a means of furnishing information upon points * as to which they had consulted us. The Amicable society was founded in 1705, and the table is formed from the experience of more than half the subsequent period ending in 1831.

4. The *Carlisle* table, formed by Mr. Milne from the observations of Dr. Heysham upon the mortality of that town, in the years 1779—1787. They are to be considered the best existing tables of healthy life which have been constructed in England. The relative proportions of the sexes are 9 females to 8 males.

5. The *Equitable* table (published by the Equitable society in 1834) gives the results of the experience of that society from 1762 to 1829. The total number or deaths recorded is upwards of 5000.

6. The *Government* tables (male and female life separately). These tables were constructed by Mr. Finlaison, actuary of the national debt office, from various tontines, &c., of which the records are in the possession of the government. Each table contains about 5000

---

* In mentioning this subject, I may be allowed to state my full approval of the plan subsequently adopted by the society, and my conviction that the errors of their ancient system have entirely disappeared.

The mean durations above given were computed by myself, from the tables of decrements circulated by the directors among the members.

deaths. These are the tables on which the commis_
sioners for the reduction of the national debt grant life
annuities in lieu of stock.

I will now add some deductions made by myself
from the tables contained in the *Recherches sur la
Reproduction*, &c., &c. Brussels, 1832, by M. Que_
telet and Smits; republished in the treatise *Sur l'Homme*,
&c. of the former. They are founded upon the
statistical returns of the whole of Belgium, made in
three successive years, and distinguish not only the
sexes but the residences of the parties, whether in
towns or in the country. The middle table is the
general average of the whole country, whether male or
female, in town or country.

Age.	Towns.		Both.	Country.		Age.
	Males.	Females.	Both.	Males.	Females.	
0	29·2	33·3	32·2	32·0	32·9	0
5	45·0	47·1	45·7	46·1	44·8	5
10	42·9	45·0	43·9	44·4	42·9	10
15	39·0	41·3	40·5	41·2	40·0	15
20	35·4	38·0	37.3	38·1	37·0	20
25	33·1	35·0	34·7	35·7	34·2	25
30	30·4	32·1	32·0	33·0	31·5	30
35	27·5	29·2	28·9	29·7	28·7	35
40	24·4	26·5	25·8	26·0	25·9	40
45	21·5	23·3	22·7	22·5	23·2	45
50	18·3	20·1	19·5	19·1	20·0	50
55	15·5	17·1	16·4	16·2	16·9	55
60	12 8	14·0	13·4	13·3	13·7	60
65	10·4	11·2	10·8	10·6	10·9	65
70	8·2	8·6	8·4	8·2	8·5	70
75	6·3	6·6	6·4	6·3	6·5	75
80	4·8	5·1	5·0	5·0	5·1	80
85	3·7	4·0	3.8	3·8	3·8	85
90	2·9	3·0	3·1	3·1	3·2	90
95	1·8	2·0	2·1	2·2	1·9	95
100	0·0	0·5	1·3	0 5	0·5	100

Most tables in which the sexes are distinguished unite in presenting this result, that female life is materially better than male life. But this fact is much more distinctly apparent in towns than in the country, and in the Belgian tables the phenomenon is reversed, so that while female life is decidedly better than male life in the towns, it is not so good in the country. Mr. Milne has remarked that in Stockholm the difference between male and female mortality was three times as large a per centage of the whole as it was in all Sweden. The probable reason for this discordance is the different employment of women in town and country; all the tables yet constructed which distinguish the sexes, and include rural life, having been made from a great preponderance of the working classes. The only tables which separate the sexes, and which are formed from the middle classes, are those of Mr. Finlaison; and here the difference is greatest of all.

This consideration is very material in comparing the tables which I have given. If a table of male life should fall short of one of female life, all other circumstances remaining the same, it is no more than we might expect; while at the same time the true proportions of male and female life, as well as the manner in which they depend on local or other circumstances, are very imperfectly known. But if a table of male life only should present the same results as one of mixed lives, we are then sure that the former represents a longer duration of existence. For instance, the table of the Equitable insurance office, which is almost entirely composed of males, is almost identical with the Carlisle table in which there are more females than males. This shows that the select male lives of the office are much better than the *male* lives of the Carlisle table: but that the male lives of the office, constantly recruited as they have been with selected lives of all ages, are *no better* than the mixed lives of the Carlisle table. Similarly, the males of the Amicable table are very much better than those of the Northampton table. The male and female lives of the latter are nearly equal in number; the former is almost entirely founded upon male lives : while the former, with its male lives only, gives a longer duration of life than the latter. For old lives, however, the Northampton table gives a some_ what longer duration than the Amicable. This is only one fact out of many which show that the Northampton table, while it gives much too great a mortality to the younger class of lives, errs in the other extreme as to the older. Of thirty-five tables, made in different countries and at different times, and including all of any celebrity which had appeared before 1830, I find that the Northampton table is the eighth from the lowest at the ages of 10—25, and the tenth from the highest at the age of 65. The same may be said of De Moivre's hypothesis, which the Northampton table closely follows.

The Northampton and Amicable tables are decidedly older as to the period at which their members lived, than the Carlisle and Equitable. Life is shorter in the former pair than in the latter, while both of the former agree in presenting the older lives comparatively better than the younger ones, as compared with the latter pair. By the Northampton table, the duration at 65 years is about a third part of that at 25; while the same proportion is decidedly less in the same ages of the Carlisle table : a similar result appears in the Amicable and Equitable tables. I remember remarking the same phenomenon in the results of a comparison of the lives of naval officers. There can be little doubt that the reason is as follows : in circumstances which create a large mortality at the younger ages, all the feeble constitutions are prevented from attaining old age, so that the lives which really arrive at advanced years are the remains of the very best lives. I saw the ocur_ rence of the same disproportion in the lives of officers of the Anglo-Indian army; in which, however, it was probably increased by the residence of many of the officers in question in England during the latter years of their lives.

The Equitable society has the character of having been much more careful in the selection of its lives than was the Amicable society during the earlier part of its existence. This, together with the gradual improvement of human life, serves to explain the very great difference between the results of their experience. The latter years of the Amicable society do not exihibit any very decided difference of the sort.

The state in which we stand with respect to tables of human life is singular, considering the enormous amounts which daily pass from hand to hand in the purchase of life interests. I may have occasion to speak more at length on this subject in the sequel: in the mean time let the reader observe the difference between the various tables, and remember that each has its votaries. If the late Mr. Morgan (whose name stands very high as an authority on such matters) had been requested to state the value of an annuity on the life of a female aged 40, and the same for a male of the same age, he would have replied that there was no material difference between male and female life, and that both belong to a class whose average existence is 23 years ; and he would accordingly have used the Northampton tables of annuities. At the national debt office, it would have been answered by Mr. Finlaison that the male and female life are two very distinct cases, and that the two different classes to which they belong have severally the average lives of 27 and 31 years. That such differences should exist, is a proof of insufficiency of information upon the subject: a want which nothing but the government can supply, but which no government ever will attempt to supply until increasing knowledge among the community at large creates an influential body of remonstrants.

Having given a table of mean durations, it is easy to find the proportion who die in one of the intermediate periods, on the supposition that the deaths are equally distributed through the period. This supposition is not actually true, though for a long course of ages the amount of mortality does not vary much from year to year. The main feature of De Moivre's hypothesis, equal decrements, appears in some measure at the adult and middle ages of life in all tables. I do not, however, know of any observations in which the numbers dying at every age are large enough to produce much confidence in the details of the tables of decrements, though the fluctuations may compensate each other in the determination of the mean durations of life. Tables which agree in the latter point may differ materially as to the former. As an instance, I give the following comparison of the Carlisle and Equitable tables, which agree more closely than any others in their mean durations. The first column shows the common age of 10,000 persons, the second and third the number who die in the following year in the Carlisle (C.) and Equitable (E.) tables.

A.	C.	E.	A.	C.	E.	A.	C.	E.	A.	C.	E.
10	45	72	35	103	92	60	335	315	85	1753	2210
15	62	75	40	130	110	65	411	428	90	2606	2686
20	71	73	45	148	127	70	516	639	95	2333	5566
25	73	76	50	134	150	75	955	931			
30	101	81	55	179	208	80	1217	1329			

According to the Carlisle table, of 10,000 persons aged 30, 101 die before attaining the next birthday; while one fifth less die in the Equitable table. And yet, one with another, the average lives of two sets of 10,000 do not differ by more than their 170th part. I now compare the actual tables of decrements, writing opposite to each age the survivors of 10,000 births who attain that age. (A, age ; C, Carlisle ; E, Equitable.)

A.	C.	E.	A.	C.	E.	A.	C.	E.
0	10,000		35	5362	5292	70	2401	2310
5	6797		40	5075	5034	75	1675	1572
10	6460	6460	45	4727	4751	80	953	898
15	6300	6192	50	4397	4441	85	445	354
20	6090	5956	55	4073	4069	90	142	86
25	5879	5733	60	3643	3588	95	30	21
30	5642	5524	65	3018	3002	100	9	

In the Equitable table, 5000 persons are supposed, each aged 10 years; this I have altered to 6460, to make the two tables agree at their outset.

The successive quinquennial decrements of the Carlisle table from the age of 20 are 211, 237, 280, 287, 348, 330, 324, 430, &c. If these deaths be supposed to take place at equal or nearly equal intervals during the five years,—if, in fact, we may suppose each of the individuals who die in a period to enjoy, one with another, half that period of existence,— we may ascertain the law of mortality from the table of mean durations in the following manner.

RULE. To the mean duration at the end of the period add the term elapsed and subtract the mean duration at the beginning; divide by the smaller duration increased by half the term, and the quotient is the fraction which expresses the proportion dying during the term. For example : the mean durations of life at 25 and 30 in the Carlisle table are 37·9 and 34·3; and 34·3 + 5 — 37·9 is 1·4; which, divided by 34·3 + 2·5 or 36·8, gives $\frac{1·4}{36·8}$ or $\frac{7}{184}$; so that of 184 persons aged 25, 7 die before attaining 30 years. In the table, we have $\frac{237}{3879}$, while $\frac{7}{184}$ is about $\frac{224}{3879}$.

If we were to take any table now existing on English lives, and ask, (as in p. 92.), what is the probability that a large number of lives, say 1000, should drop nearly in the same manner as those from which the table was formed, we should find the resulting chance not strong enough to make it prudent to risk much money in such contingencies. Nevertheless, the application of this theory to pecuniary risks has always been in a more forward state than the physical theory of human life. The reasons will be explained when we come to treat on the grounds of the confidence to which a contingency office is entitled. In the mean while, supposing a table to represent perfectly the average of a large number of the lives of the class to which an individual belongs, I proceed to show the method of using such a table

Persons who are desirous of using tables of life on a larger scale, are referred to the standard works of Messrs. Morgan, Baily, and Milne, on life insurance. In the present work I assume that it will be sufficient to be within two years and a half of any age which may be named, and I have given the several tables for intervals of five years. The extremes which are used by actuaries generally being contained in the Carlisle and Northampton tables, and having given the former, I now add the latter. The first column contains the age, the second the table of decrements, the third the number out of 10,000 who die in one year after completing the age in the first column.

Age.			Age.			Age.		
0	10,000		35	3487	187	70	1056	649
5	5356		40	3116	209	75	713	962
10	4864	92	45	2784	240	80	402	1343
15	4648	92	50	2449	284	85	159	2204
20	4399	140	55	2098	335	90	89	2609
25	4080	158	60	1747	402	95	3	7500
30	3759	171	65	1399	490			

Supposing the tables perfectly accurate, the following simple questions will show the nature of the first steps which occur in their application. The Carlisle tables are used throughout.

Question 1. What is the chance that an individual aged 35 will live to the age of 50? Of 5362 persons aged 35, 4397 live to be 50; hence the chance in question is $\frac{4397}{5362}$ or ·82. Answer, 41 to 9 for the event.

Question 2. What is the chance that A aged 45 and B aged 50, shall both be alive in ten years? The chance for A, by the last question, is $\frac{4049}{4397}$, or ·862 and that for B $\frac{3643}{4397}$ or ·829; the product of these (p. 43.), or ·715, is the chance required. Again, the chances of A and B dying during the ten years are 1 — ·862 and 1 — ·829, or ·138 and ·171; whence,

	The chance is
That both shall live	·862 × ·829
That A shall live and B die	·862 × ·171
That A shall die and B live	·138 × ·829
That both shall die	·138 × ·171

Question 3. What is the chance that A aged 25, shall die between the ages of 60 and 65? Of 5879 persons aged 25, 3643—3018 or 625, die between the ages of 60 and 65; hence $\frac{625}{5879}$ is the chance required.

Questions of this kind are readily solved, the only impediment being the arithmetical operation. It frequently happens, however, that the probability of one individual surviving another is required, which though an even chance when the individuals are of the same age, is a matter of considerable calculation when one is older than the other. Suppose, for example, that the chance of A (aged 25) surviving B (aged 30) is required. The *survivorship*, as it is called, meaning the period during which A lives after the death of B, may begin in any one year of A's age. For each year the probability of the survivorship beginning in that year must be calculated. To make this calculation for one individual year, say that in which A is between 49 and 50, two cases must be considered: either B may die between 54 and 55, and A may attain 50 complete years (of which the chance may be found as in the preceding questions), or both may die in the same year (that is A between 49 and 50, and B between 54 and 55), but B may die first. If the chance of both dying in that year be, say, ·012, it is sufficiently correct to consider the half of this chance, or ·006, as being that which expresses the chance of A's survivorship both beginning and ending in that year: a supposition which is quite correct only when the deaths of the year are equally distributed through it. The result of this calculation is arranged in tables, of which I here give a brief abstract.

Older.	Younger.	Northampton.	Carlisle.	Older.	Younger.	Northampton.	Carlisle.
15	5	·447	·400	80	50	·136	·093
20	10	·415	·383	85	55	·113	·094
25	15	·420	·381	90	60	·097	·113
30	20	·423	·375	95	65	·037	·147
35	25	·417	·372	45	5	·252	·177
40	30	·409	·366	50	10	·206	·146
45	35	·402	·360	55	15	·201	·135
50	40	·394	·350	60	20	·193	·119
55	45	·385	·329	65	25	·172	·110
60	50	·376	·315	70	30	·148	·097
65	55	·360	·323	75	35	·124	·081
70	60	·339	·322	80	40	·102	·075
75	65	·317	·303	85	45	·082	·059
80	70	·300	·320	90	50	·069	·052
85	75	·292	·332	95	55	·025	·078
90	80	·302	·329	55	5	·195	·125
95	85	·161	·462	60	10	·144	·091
25	5	·377	.307	65	15	·136	·085
30	10	·344	·283	70	20	·125	.071
35	15	·345	·279	75	25	·103	·061
40	20	·343	·270	80	30	·082	·056
45	25	·331	·263	85	35	·064	·046
50	30	·317	·251	90	40	·051	·044
55	35	·303	·231	95	45	·018	·049
60	40	·288	·212	65	5	·143	·086
65	45	·269	·194	70	10	·087	·054
70	50	·246	·177	75	15	·078	·048
75	55	·218	·177	80	20	·069	·040
80	60	·159	·190	85	25	·053	·034
85	65	·166	·174	90	30	·041	·033
90	70	·157	·191	95	35	·014	·039
95	75	·072	·300	75	5	·098	·057
35	5	·314	·235	80	10	·044	·028
40	10	·273	·207	85	15	·037	·024
45	15	·271	·202	90	20	·035	·012
50	20	·265	·189	95	25	·012	·029
55	25	·249	·174	85	5	·063	·040
60	30	·230	·158	90	10	·022	·017
65	35	·209	·143	95	15	·007	·023
70	40	·186	·126	95	5	·021	·036
75	45	·160	·104				

The quantity found in this table is the probability of an elder life surviving the younger. The difference of ages differs in the various compartments of the table ; in the first it is ten years, in the second twenty years, and so on. The two results accompanying each pair of ages are those of the Northampton and Carlisle tables. Thus, according to the Northampton table, the chance of a life of sixty surviving one of thirty is ·23 ; that of the younger surviving the elder is therefore 1 — ·23 or ·77. According to the Carlisle table, the same chances are ·158 and ·842.

Almost universally, the Northampton table gives a greater chance of the elder life beating the younger than the Carlisle. This is a consequence of that undue degree of comparative goodness which the former table gives to older lives, and to which I have already adverted.

If De Moivre's hypothesis were correct, it would be sufficient to divide the mean duration of B's life by twice that of A, and the result would be the chance which B has of surviving A, B being the elder of the two lives. This process, applied to the Northampton table, will give results very near the truth, when neither of the lives is very young. The same rule would give comparatively but a very rough guess at the result of the Carlisle table. If, however, the chance be calculated which the younger life possesses of dying in the average term of the elder, the result will be an approximation to the probability of the elder surviving the younger, when neither of the lives is very young, and when their ages are not nearly equal. Thus, the mean duration of a life of 50 being 21 years, and the chance of a life of 30 years surviving 21 years being ·769, the chance of the same life not surviving 21 years is ·231 ; while in the table, the chance of a life of 50 surviving one of 30 is ·251.

I shall, in the next chapter, consider the application of the tables to pecuniary questions, and shall now proceed to point out the connexion between a table of mortality and one of population.

The whole number of persons inhabiting any country is in continual state of increase from births and immigration, and of decrease from deaths and emigration. There are few countries in which immigration and emigration produce any serious effect upon the population, and, in times of very moderate quiet and prosperity, the births always exceed the deaths : so that, generally speaking, the number of people alive in a given country is yearly augmented by the excess of the births over the deaths. If accurate registers of births and deaths (with the ages at death) were kept for a a century and a half, accompanied, if need were, by a register of incomers and outgoers, with their ages, the community would be in possession of a complete history of its statistical changes, from which the law of mortality might be deduced, and its fluctuations noted, if any.

Again, if in any one year a complete census were made, registering the age of every individual, and if the deaths which took place in the 365 days next following the day of the census were noted, the law of mortality could be deduced. In such a case, the numbers of the living at every age would be so large that the proportion of deaths among them in a single year could be safely depended on for pointing out, with great nearness, the law which regulates the mortality of large masses of people.

No such statistical means exist in this country, partly from the defective manner in which the censuses of population are made, partly from the circumstance of the registries of births and deaths having been, almost up to the time of writing this work, connected with the religious ceremonies of the established church, which has had the effect of excluding many dissenters from registration. In the absence of all specific information, recourse was had to the registers of burials, which are usually accompanied by a statement of the age of the parties, though without any sufficient guarantee for the accuracy of the information. The hypothesis upon which alone registers of burials will give a correct law of mortality, requires that one of two alternatives should exist : either a permanent law of mortality, with a knowledge of the population in every year, and of the number of emigrants and immigrants, with their ages ; or a stationary population, with the same number of births and of deaths in each year, and a permanent law of mortality. This latter supposition is never exactly true ; but, as many societies have made a near approach to it, and as many tables have been constructed by its means, it will be worth while to explain the consequences of the supposition.

If the Carlisle law of mortality remained in uninterupted operation for a century, and if 10,000 infants were born alive in every year, the time would come when the number of the living at any age in that table would express the number alive at that age in the society in question. Thus the number of persons aged 25 would be the 5879 survivors of those who were born 25 years ago ; and the number of the living at every age and upwards would be found by multiplying the number alive at that age by the mean duration of life in the table in p. 166. If, then, the law of mortality of such a society were required, it would be found written in the burial registers of any one year. For the numbers of births and deaths being equal, there would be found for each year 10,000 burials ; which, if the law of mortality were permanent, would be found distributed among the different ages according to the table. Hence the number, out of 10,000 born, who attain a given age, would be found by adding the number buried after that age.

But let us now suppose a population uniformly increasing from year to year, say at the rate of 2 per cent. per annum ; such a population would double itself in 35 years ; and the younger lives would always exist in a greater proportion to the older ones than would be indicated by a correct table of mortality. The burials at the younger of two ages would therefore occur in too large a proportion to those at the older. Suppose, for instance, that 350 deaths take place at the age of 40—41, and 1200 at the age of 5—6; we are not therefore to conclude, that out of 10,000 individuals born, the deaths at 40 and 5 would be as 350 to 1200: for since the population doubles itself in 35 years, those who now die aged 5, are part of twice as great a number of such lives as were of the same age 35 years ago: consequently, of the set from whom 350 died at the age of 40, 600 died at the age of 5. If, then, a table were constructed from burials alone, without paying any attention to the rate of increase of the population, the older lives would appear too good of their kind; that is, relatively to the younger ones of the same society. This, as already observed, is the case in the Northampton table; whereas, in the formation of the Carlisle table, proper attention was paid to the variation in question. The difference is very perceptible in comparing each of these tables with that of the insurance office which it most resembles. At 25 years of age, the mean duration of the Northampton table is 30·9, and that of the Amicable 34·1. If the proportions of the mean durations remained nearly the same, (as generally happens,) then the Amicable table at 60 giving 12·5, the Northampton table should give 11·4; instead of which it gives 13·2.

The preceding supposes, that while the population changes, the law of mortality remains stationary. It is very unlikely that such should be the case; and observation, so far as it goes, tends to confirm the *à priori* suspicion. When provisions are cheap, or wages high,—when, in fact, it is easy to maintain a family,—marriages are more frequent, and are contracted at earlier ages. The same abundance of nourishment which tends to production, also tends to preservation, both of parents and children; the consequence of which is, that a rapid increase of population is often accompanied by a diminution of the proportionate mortality.   On the other hand, and from contrary causes, a diminution of the rate of population may be attended by an increase of the mortality.

As this work does not profess to enter further into statistics than is necessary to exemplify the principles of the theory of probabilities, I shall here close what I have to say on the rate of mortality, considered independently of the most important pecuniary applications. The next chapter will point out in what way money calculations are made.

CHAPTER XI.

ON THE NATURE OF THE CONTRACT OF INSURANCE, AND ON THE RISKS OF INSURANCE OFFICES IN GENERAL.

In laying down the following considerations, I think it right to state most explicitly, that I intend no direct reflection upon any office now in existence, or whose establishment is contemplated.   In a set of societies so numerous and varied as those in question, there must be details in one and another, of which any individual, who turns his attention to the subject, must disapprove ; but the studied exclusion of the name of every office whatsoever will, I hope, be taken as earnest of my desire to confine myself to the enabling other persons to discover the grounds of censure, without directing their attention to the quarter in which they are to be found.   I have not much fear that any part of this chapter could have been misconstrued into allusion ; and perhaps even the present disclaimer may have no other effect than to make some imagine that there must be more meaning somewhere than is openly expressed.   Leaving such lovers of mystery to their search, I proceed to the subject before me.

The avowed levellers in politics, a rare and scanty sect among educated persons, would have an argument of some force, from considerations of general expediency, if it could not be shown that any attempt to equalise property would be attended with a vast diminution of the fund itself, so that the great majority *

---

* The only great alteration of property which is likely to be agitated, is the question of the national debt, the entire abolition of which is not without its advocates.   This enormous sum, as it appears, is really little more than one year's income of the country, and perhaps not so much, if all the colonies be considered.   The honesty of a sponge not being considered, there would still remain this question :—Would the ultimate loss occasioned by the subversion of such a debt, amount to a year's income of the country ? If so, there would be no gain arising from the abolition of the debt.

would really have even less than they now possess, and also less facilities of increasing their stock. The differences of talent and of life would still remain, constantly working towards a restoration of the ancient inequalities, in which they would almost instantaneously show their power. A division of property, to be permanent, must be accompanied by a division of intellect, a division of manual skill, and a division of life; nor would the sum of the parts make up the whole in any one of the four, *except the last*. A law which should tax the property of all who live beyond a certain time of life, to provide an addition to the maintenance of the widows and children of those who die before it, would not be so utterly impracticable, nor so pernicious, as an attempt at equalization of fortune, intellect, or skill. Such a law would, however, fail in its operation, by the mere difficulty of arranging its enormous details, the frauds to which it would give rise, and the temptation to idleness which it would hold out to the young. A small community, consisting of members of known honesty, living under a government in which they reposed entire confidence, and possessing sufficient inducements not to relax in their exertions, by the certainty of a provision for their families, might live under such a law : and such communities actually do exist, under the name of insurance companies.

If a large number of persons, all of the same income and prospects, and all certain of the same duration of life, were to choose a common bank in which to deposit their savings, each laying by a given proportion of his income, it is obvious that each would receive the same sum as the rest at his decease ; but, if the lives were of unequal and uncertain duration, this result would no longer be produced. It might, however, be attained by a covenant, that all sums paid in should remain till all were dead, and then be equally divided among the executors of the parties. Such a bank might be called an equalization office, and it would present the first approximation towards an insurance office such as those which at present exist.

As yet we have not mentioned the interest of money. Suppose the equalization office to pay no interest; and suppose all the lives to be 20 years of age, such as are described in the Carlisle tables, the average duration of which is $41\frac{1}{2}$ years.   If, then, every person pay 1*l.* per annum, each will ultimately receive $41\frac{1}{2}l.$, which is the mere compensation of the inequality of life.   Such persons would enter into a mutual covenant, by which those who live beyond the average term would divide the surplus of their savings among those who fall short of it.

Probably, if the following question were put to all those whose lives are now insured, What is the *advantage* which you derive from investing your surplus income in an insurance office? more than half would reply, The *certainty* of my executors receiving a sum at my death, were that to take place to-morrow.   This is but half an answer; for not only does the office undertake the equalization of life, as above described, but also the *return of the sums invested, with compound interest.*

No one can form an accurate idea of such an establishment, who does not consider it as a savings bank, yielding interest, and interest upon interest.   This is the reason why an office which charges for its insurance more than it is worth, as an insurance, may nevertheless put its contributors in a better position than they could have held if there had been no such institution.   To make this clear, let us consider the working of a simple investment office.   A large number of individuals subscribe a sum, which they intrust to an individual or a company to employ, yielding them the return at some fixed, but distant, period.   Let each share be 100*l.* The best thing which an individual could do with such a small sum, so as to have perfect security for its return, would be to invest it in the funds, at $3\frac{1}{2}$ per cent.   He might also invest the interest, and thus obtain compound interest: but it is not easy for an individual to do this. Unless he provide an agent to draw the dividends immediately on their becoming due, various circumstances will happen to prevent the immediate investment of the interest. It is not at all an unfair calculation to suppose that, upon each half yearly dividend a month will be lost, so that nominal compound interest for 42 years will only be really for 35 years. A single pound, therefore, laid up by a man of 20, and improved for the average term of his life, at $3\frac{1}{2}$ per cent., would only become $3\frac{1}{3}l.$; while, in the hands of a person who lost no time, it would become $4\frac{1}{4}l.$, or nearly a pound more. On the other hand, a company, or a skilful individual who can command large sums of money, can always make the best interest which the market will afford. The funds, from the security of their tenure, and the conveniences which they offer, will always, in ordinary times, represent the lowest rate of interest which money will yield. Other investments, which offer better interest, are generally only accessible to those who can command considerable sums, and are frequently attended with risk; so that it requires knowledge to distinguish between the sound and the unsound. A company, employing the whole time of a person or persons skilled in money matters, and having continual large investments to make, can realise not only more interest, but so much more, that there shall remain a surplus worth considering, after the skill employed has been paid for. It is not assuming too much to say that, all expenses paid, they can command $3\frac{1}{2}$ per cent. compound interest. More than this, they can obtain such interest without any delay in investing the interest. The process is extremely simple: it is not difficult to ascertain what sum should lie permanently at the banker's, in order to meet current expenses, so that the banker has general directions to buy stock as soon as the balance in his hands exceeds that sum; and all cash received is paid into the bank at the close of each day. Suppose it should happen that ten individuals paid 100*l.* into the office on account of life insurance premiums, in the same hour in which the executors of a deceased contributor received a claim of 100*l.* The hundred pounds, which, in the theory of the process, should be sold out, or otherwise set free, to meet the claim, is in its practice supplied by the new premiums, so that the premiums of those contributors are making interest from the hour in which they are paid. But there is always an unemployed sum lying at the banker's. This is true; but the interest of that sum is the salary of an officer of the institution, namely, the banker himself. All such expenses paid, I believe it may be stated, with correctness, that an investment office can net $3\frac{1}{2}$ per cent. compound interest. Hence 1*l.*, improved during the average life of an individual aged 20 years, would become $4\frac{1}{4}l.$

The institution we have hitherto described is simply an office for the investment of premiums and the equalization of results : it becomes an insurance office when it undertakes to pay a fixed sum for a fixed premium, at the end of a given time after the decease of the party. It then begins to incur a risk of a twofold character : in the first place, the lives which it undertakes to insure may not die, one with another, in or near the same manner as those from which the tables were constructed ; in the second place, the rate of interest, upon which it calculates the premiums, may be higher than it is afterwards able to obtain. According to the Carlisle table, the premium which should now be paid to insure 100*l.* upon the life of an individual aged 20, is one pound seven shillings, or 1·32*l.*, at *four* per cent. According to the Northampton table, and at *three* per cent., the same premium should be 2·2*l.* Taking the first premium, and assuming its table, the office will not be sure of avoiding loss, until the party has lived 35 years; by which time the premiums, with their accumulated interest, will have passed 100*l.* It is a little more than 2 to 1 that a life of such an age shall live beyond 32 years after the contract. Taking the premium of the Northampton table, the party must live 28 years before the office can gain by him ; and it is about 10 to

7 that he will outlive this term. We have now to ask, What are the principles which should guide the office in the determination of its premiums, it being remembered that there is an absolute security required, and that the remote chance of bankruptcy, which is almost essential to the ordinary run of commercial affairs, is not to be encountered?

The basis of the tables is the observation of the lives of a comparatively small number of individuals; it being well known that the value of life varies considerably in passing from one class of society to another. Now, we have seen (page 91.) that we cannot depend upon a law of probability, derived from a limited number of instances, with the same degree of confidence, as upon one which we know to exist *à priori*. If we were sure beforehand that the great average of life in England was according to the Northampton, or any other table, we might rely upon such a document as being extremely likely to exhibit, with small fluctuations, the future course of the lives of the two thousand or ten thousand persons insured in any given office. Let such a table be assumed, and let the premiums be so calculated, that it shall be a thousand to one against any ruinous amount of fluctuation, taking the law of the tables as that which will certainly prevail in the long run. Then return from the hypothesis to the truth, and, taking the number of lives from which the table was actually formed, say 5000, suppose another 5000 persons to have commenced an insurance office. The degree of fluctuation within which it was 1000 to 1 that the future results should be contained, is now larger than before, in the proportion of the square root of 2 to 1, or in that of 14 to 10, nearly. Larger premiums would then be required to make ruinous fluctuation as unlikely as upon the preceding supposition. These considerations, which may easily be reduced to calculation by the rules in chapters IV. and V., will serve to show that there may be danger in the assumption of any table formed from experience; and they ought to operate powerfully as a caution against lightly admitting a change of premiums, on the authority of any small number of facts. But more particularly should they be attended to in the formation of new varieties of contingency offices, the chances of which have not yet stood the test of experience.

But there are reasons why the premiums of an insurance office need not be so high as the very limited number of data in their tables might seem to require. If the fluctuations from the average, which are within the most cautious definition of reasonable probability, were all to be encountered at once, or might be encountered at once, it is difficult to say what premiums should be considered as too high. But this cannot be the case, unless, indeed, a pestilence should single out the members of an insurance office, or an earthquake should, by one extraordinary event, swallow them all up in the place where, by a most remarkable coincidence, they were all assembled together. Such extreme cases are not worth consideration; and we may take the chances of life and death as distributed over a large number of years. In the meanwhile the surplus fund increases at compound interest; and the problem is, not whether a given number of lives will, on the whole, drop so much before the predicted time that a given fund will be destroyed, but whether this can happen so fast, that it will outrun the increase of the fund at compound interest. If, indeed, there were compound mortality to set against compound interest; that is, if the number of deaths must become larger from year to year, or if the rate of mortality were increasing, the fear of such a result might be entertained; but all experience is on the other side, and tends to show that the value of life is increasing, instead of decreasing.

The tables of an insurance office must be considered as collections of limited data, the premiums deduced from which are increased by a percentage, to meet the possible fluctuations of mortality. As soon as these tables are formed, and the directors have published their proposals, an *insurance* office is created, with all these fundamental characters already described, and which are but ill represented by the term. The word *insurance* or *assurance* has given rise to some wrong notions, and it will be worth while to examine the nature of the contract.

A and Co. engage with B that, in consideration of 1*l.* a year, paid by him during his life, they will pay 20*l.* to his representatives as soon as he shall be dead. Both parties run a risk ; A and Co. that of having to pay B more than they receive ; B, that of paying more than will at his death produce 20*l.* But the risk of the office is of immediate loss, and that of B, of deferred loss : that of the former is also continually lessening, and that of the latter increasing ; until, should B live long enough, both risks become certainties. If the in_surance be only for a term of years, B runs the risk of losing his premiums altogether.

The office does not inquire what reason B may have for insuring his own life or that of another person, nor do any possible contingencies, except those of life, affect the office calculations. We cannot, therefore, be too much surprised at the ignorance shown by that judge* who declared that life insurance † was of its own nature a contract of indemnity ; that is to say, if, by any lucky chance, B can be proved to have accomplished the object for which he insured by other means, he has ro claim upon the office. The circumstances are as follows ; and the absurd conclusion is law, and would be practice, if the insurance offices had not re-fused to acknowledge the decision, or protect themselves by the precedent. A and Co. covenanted with B to pay 500*l.*, if C should die within the term of seven years next ensuing, in consideration of the usual pre-mium. C did die within the term ; and A and Co., in

---

* Godsall *v.* Boldero. See the report of the case in Mr. Babbage's " 'Comparitive View of Institutions for the Assurance of Lives."

† He might have said that the law would refuse to consider an assurance in any other light ; but he was palpably wrong in asserting that the con-tract, as understood by the parties, was merely one of indemnity.

answer to a claim of 500*l.*, replied, that the intention of B in insuring the life of C, was to obtain security for the payment of a debt of 500*l.*, due by C to B, which debt had been already paid by C's executors: consequently they owed nothing to B.   An action was brought by B, and defended by A and Co. on the above plea ; and a special case being made, the point was decided by the court of King's Bench against the plaintiffs ; thereby establishing the principle, that life insurance is a thing similar to fire or ship insurance ; namely, a contract of indemnity, to be fulfilled with allowance for salvage.

The defendants' case rested upon the asserted nature of the contract, and the statute 14 Geo. III. c. 48., which enacts, that " no greater sum shall be recovered from the insurers than the amount or value of the interest of the insured in such life."   The act does not state at what time this interest is to be reckoned, but the plaintiffs contended that the time of death was the meaning of the statute ; the defendants averred, and the court decided, that the time of bringing the action was to be understood.   The plaintiffs contended that the debt was not the object of insurance, but the life of the insured ; the court decided, that " This action is, in point of law, founded upon a supposed damnification of the plaintiffs, occasioned by the death, existing and continuing to exist at the time of the action brought ; and, being so founded, it follows, of course, that if, before the action was brought, the damage which was at first supposed likely to result to the creditor were wholly obviated and prevented by the payment of his debt, the foundation of any action on his part, on the ground of such insurance, fails."   This sentence contains nothing but very good sense, and, no doubt, very good law : but the application of it was accompanied by a mistake as to the nature of the damnification which the plaintiffs had sustained.   The counsel on both sides, the court, the insurance office, and the plaintiffs themselves, showed a very partial knowledge of the nature of the contract; and I make no doubt, that almost every person who heard it agreed with the court, however much they might impugn the decision on other grounds, that the damage* to the creditor " was wholly obviated and prevented by the payment of his debt."

In order to show that such was not the case, we must suppose that an exactly similar transaction had taken place before any insurance office existed. How this could have been may not be apparent, if we take the notion which the law formerly entertained of such an office; namely, that it is a species of gambling house: but if we prefer to consider it as a savings bank, with an equalization system (page 238.), which is unquestionably the correct notion, we may return to the circumstances which the case would have presented had there been no insurance. C, a person whose credit has become doubtful, is indebted to B to an amount which B could not afford to lose; consequently, B, knowing that his chance of payment is precarious, resolves to diminish his expenses, hoping by economy to restore to his family the sum which he may have lost by his engagements with C. He collects, accordingly, a small fund, which he places with his banker, avowing the purpose of its collection. In the mean time C dies, and some friends pay off his debts, and that due to B among the rest. The latter having now no further occasion for such economy, draws upon his banker for the amount, and is answered, that, since the purpose of the saving was fulfilled by the payment of C's debt, he, B, has no further claim upon his own money. An action is brought, and the courts decide that the banker is right, and that B, having really attained his object in one way, has no right of property in the proceeds of another attempt to serve the same purpose.

* The defendants paid into court a sum somewhat less than the amoun of the premiums they had received from the plaintiffs, doubtless as a precaution, in case the court or jury should think the premiums ought to have been returned.

The only distinction between the case just put and that which actually occurred is, that the banker was a person who gained his profits by receiving such savings during a contingent term, and guaranteeing a fixed sum ; standing the loss, if there were any, and paying himself for it out of the gain which would accrue in another instance: the premium having been calculated so as to insure a moral certainty of profit upon the average of similar cases. It is not pretended, on either side, that the chance of indemnification at the hands of C's executors was made to lessen the consideration paid by B for the guarantee; and the legal iniquity of the decision may, I think, be made clear, as follows : —

It will hardly be disputed, firstly, that the legislature is the judge of what shall constitute valuable consideration ; and, secondly, that a consideration which is expressly allowed to be, good in a statute, should be admitted as such in the decisions of the courts. Now, the contract of insurance, be it gambling, or be it not, rests entirely upon the permission given by the law to consider a high chance of a small sum as good consideration for a low chance of a large sum. If I now pay 2*l*. of premium for 100*l*., in case I should die in a year, and if my executors can maintain an action for 100*l*., it must be because the law sanctions the notion that 2*l*., nearly certain, may, with consent of parties, be considered as an actual equivalent for a distant chance of 100*l*., as much so as one weight of silver for another of bread, or food, clothing, and wages for personal service. It is true that the same law, fearing certain reputed immoral practices, to which the power of making a particular bargain offers temptations, may limit the circumstances under which it will permit such bargains to be made ; but this is equally true in regard to the other sort of contracts mentioned : indeed, there is no sort of bargain which is not under regulation. The law, then, allows risks, and permits unequal chances to be compensated by giving odds ; the courts declare that, after the cast shall have been made, and one of the parties shall have stood *his* risk, which turns out in his favour, the other party shall receive an *ex post facto* release from the conditions of his bargain, because circumstances afterwards arise, which, had they existed* at the time of making the bargain, would have made it illegal. The several principles on which the decision was founded, well carried out, as they say in parliament, would require that the previous contracts of a man who becomes insane should be null and void ; that the meat which a man buys for his dinner should be returnable to the butcher under the cost†, if a friend should invite him in the mean time ; and, in the case before us, supposing that C should have outlived the term, and his debt were paid, as before, then B might have brought his action against the office, for the return of the premiums ; alleging that, as it turned out, the office would have been indemnified, and, therefore, should be considered as having run no risk.

But, said the judge, the damage was "wholly" obviated and prevented by the payment of the debt. To try this point, let us make a debtor and creditor account of the whole transaction. The following is the way in which it will stand.

Cr.	Dr.
£500 worth of goods furnished to C.	£500 paid by C's executors.
Certain small premiums paid to an insurance office, with imminent risk of their entire loss; such premiums, multiplied by the risk of loss, as in chapter V., being good legal consideration for a remote chance of gaining £500, and so considered by both parties.	Those same premiums returned by the office, instead of £500.

* This is admitting more than is absolutely necessary ; for, unless there were mathematical certainty that a third party would step in and pay C's debts, it is difficult to see how B's insurable interest would cease.

† The sum paid into court by the insurance office, was less than the amount of the premiums : but the plaintiffs waived that point.

The advantage of the moral security which a contract of insurance gives is obvious in the transaction which led to this decision ; namely, the insurance of the life of a creditor by a debtor at his own expense. Commercially speaking, such a transaction is literally this: C owes 500*l.* to B, who, doubting his chance of payment if the debtor should die, buys 500*l.* from a third person, and makes believe that it is the 500*l.* which C owes him. Morally speaking, it is the determination of B to retrench his own expenditure, as soon as he finds that a part of his property consists in bad debts. This the office enables him to do in a manner which will make the retrenchment proportional to the necessity for it. In the mean time, it is much to be wished that the law of life insurance were settled upon a fixed basis, which should proceed upon such a definition of the contract as has been here explained, and not on the notions which have been drawn from a supposed analogy between it and the insurance of a ship or a house. The effect of the present state of the law is, that the offices have no law except that of honour, which, though it more than suffices for the protection of the insured, yet may at any time involve the offices in the necessity of paying really questionable policies, without having the means of submitting to open examination the point on which they wish to resist. Policies of insurance are sold daily to persons who have no interest in the lives of the insured parties, on the faith of the good conduct of the offices. If an office were to resist the payment of a policy so transferred, say on the ground of fraudulent representation, the parties so resisted might give out that the opposition of the office arose out of an intention to cover themselves by the present letter of the law. Neither could such a case be carried into court without proof that the plaintiffs possessed that insurable interest in the life of the deceased which the law requires.

The nature of the contract, both in law and usage, having been laid down, we must next ask what are the means which the offices employ to reduce the risk so as to render themselves safe against fluctuation. The state of opinion upon this matter is somewhat unsettled; one party advocating the practice of approaching near to the line which separates security from insecurity; another insisting upon what appears to the first a most superfluous degree of caution. Without expressing an opinion, I will describe the various risks, and the method of avoiding them which has usually prevailed.

1. The insecurity of data, that is, of existing tables of mortality. This divides itself into two parts; that relating to the young and middle aged, and that relating to old lives. With regard to the first, the data might probably be obtained in sufficient numbers to justify a considerable degree of confidence in them as to the chances of a single life, or even of a considerable number; but when the number of lives is to be as great as the number of persons who may choose to offer themselves, the considerations in Chapter IV., again adverted to in page 242, present themselves in force. I am not aware that any writer on the subject in this country has formally taken into consideration the uncertainty of tables, arising from their limited numbers, except Mr. Lubbock, who has made use of (Cambridge *Phil. Trans.*, and Treatise on Probability *Lib. Usef. Know.*) the correction which the probability of living a given number of years should receive on that account. But, considering the probable errors of the data, this correction is small, and the question how far an office proceeding upon such data can deal with the public to any amount is yet in its infancy, though the necessity for its consideration is approaching, and it is one of vital importance to the interests of the middle and lower classes.

The constructor of tables of mortality draws a number of balls from an urn which contains an infinite number, and, having sorted them into red, blue, black, &c., presents them to the world as a necessary representation (or very nearly so) of the proportions in which those colours are scattered throughout the whole urn. He commits an error which is in all probability very small, and which has hitherto been carefully guarded in the deduction of office results. But there is a much more important question behind. Suppose the calculator had undoubtedly succeeded in exhibiting the real law of mortality, and that it were quite certain the next hundred million inhabitants of Great Britain would die in the manner pointed out in a table. In such a case, many will say, the office may charge the real premiums deduced from the table, with a very slight addition for expenses of management. They may leave the fluctuations to take care of themselves, and trust in the long run. This assertion I now proceed to discuss.

If the banker of a gaming-table were to follow the same plan, that is, if he were to stake against all comers with only just enough of advantage to cover expenses, he would infallibly be ruined at last. It might not be in this year nor the next, nor in this century nor the next; but ruined at some time or other he must be (see page 110, and also Appendix I.). If the case of the office managers were precisely analogous to that of the bankers of the gaming-table, I would repeat with as much confidence of the former what I have said of the latter. But, in the first place, the fluctuations of mortality are not, by very much, so great as those which take place in the assortment of cards, nor even so great as those which take place in harvests, in the price of provisions, &c. This is much in favour of the insurance office; but who can say *how much?*.

In the second place, the fluctuations of mortality have of themselves a tendency to create opposite fluctuations. Thus, a very sickly season carries off the weak, and deprives the succeeding years of those who were most likely to have died; causing, therefore, a season of remarkable health. This is a very important item in the theory of the fluctuations of mortality, and there is nothing similar to it in the case of the gaming house. It reduces annual fluctuation itself to a species of regularity, and is, perhaps, the sufficient reason for the slightness of the total fluctuations.

In the third place, with a merchant or a banker, the liability to a demand and the demand itself come so nearly upon one another, that real insolvency and bankruptcy are never far asunder. When credit cannot be sustained by monthly, and even daily, proofs of substance, it takes its departure altogether : but it is not necessarily so with an insurance office, of whose existence it is the essence to be always receiving consideration for bills which, one with another, have a long time to run. Such an establishment, as will presently more distinctly appear, may be in reality *insolvent* many years before the symptoms of *bankruptcy* come on. As no large concern of the kind has hitherto failed, it is difficult to say how they would finally come on : but this much is certain, that an insurance office which could really pay only ten shillings in the pound might, by introducing a better system, or by mere force of circumstances, not only recover its ground, but ultimately become exceedingly profitable. But I throw this part of the argument (though it shows a strong principle of vitality inherent in the constitution of such offices) out of the question ; for, surely, no sane and honest person would trifle with important matters so far as to assert that the possibility of temporary insolvency, to be redeemed by the chapter of accidents, or prudence, when it was wanted, should enter into the deliberate calculations on which men should be invited to stake the subsistence of their children.

If the last contingency be rejected, that is, if it be held absolutely necessary to calculate on permanent solvency, both real and apparent, then I assert that there is not sufficient ground to gainsay the conclusion, that any insurance office charging only *real** premiums (increased for expenses of management) must inevitably have its phases of solvency and insolvency, at the very best. Begin by considering the office as identical in principles with the gaming house, and beat down the

---

* By real premiums I mean those which only cover the risks of life.

certainty of ruin which is thus known to exist, if they play upon equality of chance, by allowing for the first two of the three preceding considerations. There must still remain more risk than it is safe to face of insolvency, either temporary or permanent. And though, in consequence of the smallness of the portion which the office risks upon one hazard, a very small mathematical advantage might be sufficient, yet, so long as the necessity for such an advantage exists, and its absolute amount is unknown, so long must an office guard itself by requiring, in the first instance, a sensible addition to the real premiums.

With regard to the old lives, there is an additional ground of insecurity. Not only are the probable errors of the tables exceedingly large with respect to them, but, from the smallness of the number which will enter an office, there will be a liability to great fluctuations in the results of transactions with them. The first circumstance would prevent the second from becoming ruinous, but at a risk of loss to the capital invested by younger lives : it is usual, therefore, to exclude all lives above a certain age from entering the office, upon the principle that no risks are to be taken of which the numerical amount is not well understood, and of which the number is not large enough to secure an average. But, since the tables of old lives are only a very unsatisfactory approximation, and since the premiums payable by young lives depend in part on the chances of those lives becoming very old, how does it happen that the insecurity of the latter part of the tables does not affect the premiums throughout? It *does* affect them, but not sensibly, for the following reason. If, assuming the Northampton table, we suppose a person aged 40 to insure his life, we see that the portion of the present value of his insurance which depends upon his dying in his 85th year is very small, on two accounts : firstly, because the chance of his living to the age of 84 is very small; and, secondly, because the present value of a sum to be received

45 years hence is small, compared with that of a sum now due, or receivable soon.   This last consideration works as follows:—When a percentage comes to be added to the whole present value or to the premium deducible from it, for the security of the office, that percentage being made upon a much larger sum than the present value just mentioned, a very trifling deduction from the whole additional sum will cover a very serious mistake in the mortality of the older years.   For example, in the Northampton tables, the chance of 40 living to 85 is about $\frac{1}{20}$, and the present value of 1*l.* due in 45 years is about 5*s.* at 3 per cent.   From this it follows that 100*l.*, to be paid if a person aged 40 dies after 85, cannot be worth so much as 1·25*l.*   But the present value of the whole insurance is 53·8*l.* ; and if this be the real value, and 10 per cent. be added for security, then 5·38*l.* is added; so that if 1·25*l.* were considered as added solely for the chances after 85 years, it follows that we might consider ourselves as having allowed for not being able to calculate the chances on old lives within one half, and as having added 8 per cent. to the whole present value besides.   Thus, it appears that our comparatively little knowledge of old life, though not unimportant, yet can be made to be of less importance than might have been expected by one who has not considered the matter.   Of course, the preceding reasoning must be considered only as addressed to a person to whom, for any thing he sees to the contrary, it is of as much consequence to know the *entire* law of mortality in the insurance of young lives as of old ones.

There is one use of the table of old lives, by which an insurance office might make its existence very problematical, to use a gentle term ; namely, by inverting the order of security, and selling *guaranteed** benefits, which are to increase with the age of the party, and to be accumulated solely out of his premiums.   To take

* This, of course, does not apply to divisions of profit *gained*, but to contracts for sums to be accumulated after the date of the engagement.

an extreme case, suppose an office should name a premium for which it would undertake to pay 100*l.*, if the party dies in the subsequent year ; 200*l.* if he dies in the second subsequent year ; 300*l.* if he dies in the third ; and so on. In this case, every fluctuation which bears the appearance of lengthened life, were it only to amount to deferring one death for a single year, would be a new claim of 100*l.* upon the office. The fluctuations which are observable in the very old lives, would become matters of extreme importance ; and though, assuming a given table fairly to represent the average, premiums might be calculated which should be sufficient in the long run, yet there is no possibility of saying what capital might become necessary to meet the fluctuations of half a century. Such an attempt as the preceding can be compared to nothing but gambling, and its stability to nothing but that of a ship running before the wind, with all the heavy cargo lashed to the topgallant mast. Other cases might be mentioned, which should partake of the same species of danger in a less degree ; but every attempt to *guarantee* increased benefits with increasing life should be looked at with caution, as being of its own nature the addition of risks in which the errors of the unsafe part of the tables are, or may be, multiplied into importance. There is an opposite plan, which I am not aware has been tried, but which I should strongly recommend to any new insurance office, as being of a safe character, and also meeting the views under which many insure their lives. It is that of insuring *decreasing* sums, upon either fixed or decreasing premiums. Many persons are so situated, that they will be able to provide for their families if they live a few years. To provide for the hazardous period, they are under the necessity either of insuring for their whole lives, that is, of buying more insurance than they want ; or of insuring for a fixed term of years, which does not meet several contingencies ; or of making complicated survivorship insurances. But, if a person so circumstanced found, by

estimation of his income, that he should want 5000*l.* if
he died in one year, 4800*l.* if he died in the second,
and so on, it would be desirable that he should be able
to insure for these several sums, contingently upon his
dying in any of the several years to which they are
made to belong. Various modifications of this scheme
might be proposed, all having this difference from the
usual plans, in that the latter enable a person to make
a provision for his family, while the former would only
supply the deficiencies which his death would leave in
the proceeds derived from other sources. In an appendix (on the value of increasing annuities) will be
found the method of calculating the present values of
such insurances.

2. The possible fluctuations of the rate of interest.
These may be either general and national fluctuations,
or alterations in the value of the property held by the
office. The former cannot be guarded against or predicted; and, as the rate of interest has been slowly
falling for centuries, there is some reason to suppose
that this depreciation of money may continue. But
this gradual sinking of the rate of interest may be only
partly dependent upon the fall of profits, and part may
be due to the increase of security. I question whether
the political economist has found the historical materials
for determining this most important element; namely,
the extremes of interest at which loans were contracted
in the different periods of our history. The legal
maximum of interest, at the beginning of the reign of
James I., was 10 per cent., and at the end of the century, 6 per cent. But, at the beginning of the century,
land was commonly bought at 20 years' purchase, and
never at less than 16 years' purchase; while at the end
of the century it was still at 20 years' purchase. No
method of proving such a point is better than the
examination of the works on interest which appeared
during the century. If, then, we suppose, with Adam
Smith, and I believe with most others, that the changes
in the legal maximum of interest followed, and did not

precede, those of the market, there is good ground for imagining that the diminution of the rate of interest between borrower and lender (from 10 to 4 per cent.) has arisen more from the increase of security than from any other cause. If such be the case, there is strong presumption that the fall is near its end. But, if the preceding surmise should not be well founded, and if (as was the case in Holland during a part of the last century) the rate of interest should fall until government can borrow at 2 per cent., and others at 3 per cent., the change may happen in a manner which will seriously affect the insurance offices, unless it should come about so gradually that they will have *time* to introduce new premiums for incomers, and *surplus* to meet the claims of those to whom they are already engaged. It is, in the meanwhile, a question well worth the attention of those connected with them, what the causes have been which have determined the rate of interest, and the rapidity and amount of its variations.

The offices depend for the existence of their present system upon the national debt; and they are differently situated from the government which owes the debt, in that the engagements of the latter are all maxima, while theirs are minima. If the rate of interest should really fall, the government will have the means of reducing the interest of the debt, never to rise again; while the offices have, in fact, guaranteed to their existing customers a rate per cent., which is never to fall during their lives. The rate assumed by the offices should, therefore, never be above that at which the government can borrow.

With respect to the second reason for a variation in the rate of interest, as experienced by the office, namely, a depreciation in its own property, such an establishment, not being allowed to run the usual risks of mercantile life, should not deal in any but the most secure investments, and those which depend on the personal security of others should be altogether avoided. The only point which it is incumbent to mention, in addition to general cautions, is a mistake to which such offices are subject in the valuation of their property; namely, the estimation of different items by their reputed worth, or by the price which was given for them, instead of the actual income which they produce. We shall see the effect of such a mistake in considering the proper method of inquiring into the state of their affairs.

The precedent are the contingent risks to which an office is subject: its certain expenses are the ordinary charges of management, including rent, salaries, interest of sums lying at the banker's, &c., advertisements, and the *commission*, as it is called, which most of the offices pay to those who bring them business.

Commission, in general, means either a per centage paid to a factor for the transaction of business, or a voluntary relinquishment in favour of the person who brings business of a part of the profit which the said person, being honourably free to choose between one competitor and another, has brought to the trader who, therefore, allows the commission. It answers to the profit which the retail dealer is allowed by the wholesale merchant from whom he buys. But, when an insurance office announces to the solicitor, attorney, or agent of a party desiring to insure, that they will allow him a liberal *commission*, the term has a different meaning. As between one office and another, the attorney is in a judicial capacity; and, as regards his client, *he is already the paid protector of the interests of another person.* He has, therefore, no liberty of choice between one office and another, but is already bound to choose that which he judges best for his client. All who have written on the subject of late years have attacked this *bribe*, for such it is; but they have directed all their censures against the offices, as if they were the only parties to blame. If, indeed, the bribe had been offered to the needy and ignorant only, this partial distribution of blame might have been allowed; but when the parties who receive the bribe are men of education, and moving

in those professions which bring the successful to affluence, I do not see the justice of allowing them to escape.
I have little doubt that an increasing sense of right and
wrong will banish this unworthy practice, either by
failure of givers or receivers.   A barrister cannot offer
an attorney commission on the briefs which he brings,
nor can a physician pay an apothecary for his recommendation ; a jury never receives a hint that the plaintiff
will give commission on the damages which they award ;
and the time will come when the offer of money to a
person whose unbiassed opinion is already the property
of another, will be deemed to be what it really is,
namely, *bribery and corruption*.   It is one among many
proofs how low is the standard of collective morality ;
and how easy it is for honourable individuals to do in
concert that from which they would separately shrink.

It appears, then, from all which precedes, that the
ordinary risks of an insurance office are alterations of,
and mistakes in determining, the rate of mortality, and
reduction of the rate of interest: which are guarded
against by assuming a rate of mortality beyond all
question greater than exists, and a rate of interest below
that which the funds will yield. At the peace of 1815,
every insurance office used the Northampton table at
3 per cent.   This was at a time when the real rate of
interest was higher than at present, and the offices must
have made considerable profit.   It was well known that
they did so ; and, accordingly, new offices were formed,
and have continued to be formed up to the present
time, some upon lower premiums than others, and most
of them returning all or part of the profits to the insured.   At the same time, an opinion has become very
prevalent, that it is possible for such offices to maintain
their ground at *much* lower rates of premium than
those in use ; a notion which I proceed to examine.

Mr. Finlaison, whose experience in such matters is
well known to the public, and for whose opinion I entertain a high respect, stands foremost among those
who contend for low rates of premium, having pub-

lished a table, which he certifies to be " abundantly safe
and practicable," and " so high as to insure, beyond all
doubt, a surplus of profit;" which table charges premiums at the ages in which most insurances are made,
falling short of those actually in use about 15 per cent.
These premiums are supposed not chargeable with the
management of the office, and at a rate of interest of
3½ per cent. I take Mr. Finlaison's proposition as a
modified one, for there are some which go beyond it.

On the other hand, the late Mr. Morgan could never
be persuaded that it was safe to abandon the Northampton table; and considered that the superior vitality
of the members of the Equitable was altogether a consequence of their being select lives. He seems to have
thought that, whatever run of success an office might
have, it should always be on the look out for reverses;
and that even the enormous accumulations of his office
were no more than the seven good harvests, a provision
for other seven of a different character.

In holding an opinion which comes between that of
these two authorities, I form it on a ground on which
neither would have rested the truth or falsehood of his
own. I consider the fluctuations of mortality as very
little to be feared, compared with those of the rate of
interest. It has long been matter of observation, that
the phenomena of the natural state of man vary but
little compared with those of his social condition. The
price of provisions swings to and fro like a pendulum;
the variations of mortality which follow its changes,
though sensible, bear no proportion to the magnitude of
their cause. The rate of interest has been halved
within the memory of man, and a heavy war might
double it again. That same war, with all its casualties,
direct and indirect, included, would not alter the mortality of the country by any serious amount. I consider it, then, as next to certain, that the insurance
offices have more to look for, whether as matter of hope
or fear, from the fluctuations of the rate of interest,
than from those of mortality. If the interest of money

could be made as stable as the duration of human life, I could then see no objection to an immediate and considerable reduction of the premiums charged, to an amount at least equal to that proposed by Mr. Finlaison. But here lies the difficulty; that these tables, at $3\frac{1}{2}$ per cent., already involve a rate of interest which the office cannot much exceed, if at all; so that the security which the precautions, nominally made against mortality, really afforded against fluctuations of interest, is partially or wholly destroyed, while no safeguard is introduced to supply its place.

An office raises its premiums either because its previous notions of existing mortality were wrong, or because it finds that it had calculated upon too high a rate of interest. A mistake on either of these points might be compensated by a contrary mistake as to the other. Now, though the offices which existed during the war have demonstrated that the mortality and rate of interest together yielded a large profit, it by no means follows that one of those causes of profit may be fully corrected, while the other has been correcting itself. To make both perfectly accurate, would bring the office to the very line which divides security from insecurity; a position which it would not be safe to endeavour to maintain. We are already in a very different position as to the rate of interest, which has been gradually falling since the war. The opinion as to the extent to which tables of mortality may be safely corrected, is formed upon arguments which dwell on the favourable rate of mortality, without sufficiently considering the counterpoise (for, as far as it goes, it is a counterpoise) existing in the alteration of the value of money.

Assuming the necessity of calculating upon a rate of interest something less than that which can actually be attained, I should think that no office would be justified in supposing more than 3 per cent., *with tables which are sufficiently high to come any ways near to the actual experience of mortality.* With regard to one point, and that of fundamental importance, namely, the possibility of a still further fall in the rate of interest, it may even be doubted whether, *with such tables*, a still lower rate of interest should not be allowed. But I am not here advocating one result or another, but only the necessity of taking into consideration all the possible sources of danger. To those who would use tables of greater vitality, I concede that, so far as mortality alone is concerned, the alteration is admissible; and for this reason, that experience shows human life to be of a higher value than formerly; but the concession is accompanied by the requisition of a lower rate of interest, and for the selfsame reason, that experience shows the value of money to be less than it was.

The preceding conclusion is reinforced by the consideration, that the worst is to be made of every circumstance in our previous calculations. When mortality is diminishing, the whole diminution is not to be allowed; but when it is increasing, a larger increase is to be contemplated. A person who would walk dry-shod on the sea shore, must not advance so fast as the ebb, and must retreat faster than the flow. Upon this consideration, the necessity of providing for a further fall in the interest of money is increased; or, which amounts to the same thing, the amount by which the favourable alteration in the rate of mortality may be allowed to affect the premiums is less than it would be if it were certain that the value of money would remain unaltered.

A very common security or guarantee to the public is the announcement of a large subscribed capital, either paid up in whole or part, or liable to be called for. This is equivalent to the personal security of a number of shareholders, collectively making themselves answerable for the engagements of the office up to a certain amount. Such a provision in itself is an obvious good; but, it being remembered that this security must be paid for, it becomes a question how much it is worth, and whether it may not be bought at too high a price. It is easily understood that the consideration which tempts men to lend names or money to an insurance office, is the offer of payment for the risk, or of higher than market interest for the money.   If the capital be paid up, the office makes common interest upon it, which is returned, with an augmentation, to the proprietors : if the capital be only paid in part, or merely nominal, still the office has to pay something more than it receives.

Now, I take it for granted that an office charging premiums* such as are commonly demanded, managed with prudence and economy, and successful in obtaining business, will not ultimately need any capital at all : firstly, because the premiums are such as must, in the long run, realise a profit after paying the expenses of management ; so that the only use of the capital would be as a provision against extraordinary temporary fluctuation: secondly, because a sufficient supply of business renders the probability of ruinous fluctuation extremely small, and altogether beneath consideration.† Now, since it is well known that the premiums are sufficient, it follows that the only need which a commencing insurance has of capital is for safeguard against the early expenses of management, and against failure of business: as follows.

The expenses of carrying on an insurance office, though they vary somewhat with the amount of business, yet do not by any means increase as fast.   In the first year of its existence, it would not be surprising if all the premiums paid were swallowed up by house-rent, salaries, &c. ; while, in process of time, increase of business might reduce such expenditure to 2 per cent. upon the yearly premiums.   Some capital, therefore, is necessary at the commencement ; for, if there be none,

---

* If the premiums were really too low, capital would be an injury, and not a benefit ; for, since this capital is really paid for, in whole or in part, out of premiums, it would not preserve the office from insolvency, but would rather accelerate its progress towards bankruptcy.

† The most probable cause of ruin to the insurance offices, or rather the least improbable, is a national bankruptcy.   Any contingency, then, which is much less likely than a national bankruptcy, need not be considered.

those who first insure their lives are entirely dependent upon the future success of the office. But this capital need not be large : in the present state of things, an engaged capital of one hundred thousand pounds is certainly above the mark, even for an office which is entirely without connection, and starts without one single life insured. If, as very often happens, a tolerably large number of customers has been obtained before the prospectus of the office is announced, then a capital, the interest of which will cover the expenses of management, is sufficient. But here it must be observed that the proprietors of this capital run some risk of losing a portion of their principal, and a still greater one of losing the interest for a limited time. This risk is the greater the smaller the original subscription, and it must be paid for accordingly. At the same time, it must be remembered that the mere existence of the capital diminishes the risk, by making it the interest of every proprietor to procure business for the office. The connection thus created is the secret of the successful start which has frequently been made; and it may be considered as very unlikely that an office will fail, from want of business, which is so well supported in the first instance as is implied when a capital of the preceding amount is announced.

There is, however, one case in which a larger capital is desirable, and even requisite; that is, where an office is established which is to insure some new and yet untried risk. Whatever pains may be taken in such a case to procure facts and deduce proper tables, there is always a risk that the experience of the office may be at variance with the facts of the tables. When, for instance, the general conclusions drawn from the mortality of towns were first applied to the insurance of life, it was a risk of unknown amount as to whether the lives of those who would come to insure would be of the same class as those from which the tables were made. They might turn out better, or worse. This risk has been tried, and found to be in favour of the offices; but in another speculation, of another kind, the same species of risk might give a contrary result.

Among the sources from which the insurance offices have drawn profit, we must reckon lapsed policies. It has frequently happened that an individual insuring his life has continued to pay the premiums for a few years, and then, either through incapacity to continue the payment, or because the object of his insurance was otherwise attained, has allowed his policy to lapse to the office by non-payment. The office, of course, is benefited, but not, as might be supposed, by the total amount of his premiums. What they have received does not all become profit by the lapse of the policy, but only that portion by which the premium for the whole life exceeds the premium for a temporary insurance. Every premium which is paid by an insurer contains the consideration given for the chance of his dying in each and every subsequent year. If, then, he remain a member of the office, and stand the risk of death during a certain number of years, all such part of his premiums as was consideration for the risks of those years became due to the office, and was taken by the office, as compensation for those risks, and cannot therefore be said to fall to them as profit upon the lapse of the policy. Two individuals, A and B, go to the office on the same day, and insure their lives for the same sum, A upon his whole life, and B for seven years. A pays, say 10l. of premium, and B 7l. At the end of seven years, A allows his policy to lapse, just at the time when B's policy expires by its own construction. What does the office gain by the lapse? Evidently the temporary annuity of 3l., by which the two premiums differ. The 7l. paid by A out of 10l. is not more than sufficient to pay his share of the claims which arose during the years which he continued in the office: the remaining 3l. was a reserve for future years, which becomes profit to the office on his declining to stand the risks of those years.

Perhaps no part of the subject is less understood than

this.   Persons having insured for their whole lives, and being afterwards desirous to discontinue, are surprised to find that they cannot get for their policies even as much as the amount of their premiums, to say nothing of interest.   Each of them reasons thus : — Since I did not die, the office lost nothing by me, and, as it has turned out, ran no risk : why, then, should they not restore me the premiums which I have paid ? To which it should be answered: Because the risk, which turned out favourably in your case, did not produce the same result in another case ; and it is the very essence of an insurance office, that those who live pay for those who die. If you can induce the executors of those who have died during your tenure of your policy to refund what they have received from the office, with compound interest, then the office will repay you your premiums, also, with compound interest.   The above-mentioned reasoning of the insured party is much on a par with that of the judge in Godsal's case.

A respectable weekly newspaper has lately allowed the following doctrine to be promulgated in its columns ; namely, that it is an undeniable fact, demonstrable by the books of any insurance office, that very much the larger portion of their profits has always arisen from lapsed policies ! Till I saw that article, I could hardly have believed that even a newspaper would have admitted so palpable a mistake.   On the supposition (no matter how false) that all the back premiums of a lapsed policy are, as they say in book-keeping, to be carried to profit and loss, how could such an assertion be made, in the face of the well-known fact, that premiums are deduced from a table of much higher mortality than that actually experienced ?   Those persons who, one with another, were expected to live twenty years, have lived twenty-four years.   A small proportion of them have allowed their policies to lapse, enough to give, perhaps, a perceptible profit to the office, but not enough materially to increase its funds ; for it must be remembered that, though the number of policies allowed to lapse bears a proportion to the whole which might give some colour to the preceding assertion, yet the value of these policies is generally small. It is seldom that a policy is abandoned which involves a large sum, or on which many premiums have been paid. If, instead of comparing the number abandoned with the whole number of policies, we were to calculate the value of those policies, and compare them with the value of all the liabilities of the office, the former would be found a very small portion of the latter. It is well that it has been so, for this source of profit is diminishing as the subject becomes better understood. It is known that a policy of a very few years' standing is worth *something*, and had better be sold at any price than abandoned.

All that precedes has reference to the relation in which the office stands to the public, and to the collective body of the insured. All dangers, and all remedies, have been considered merely with reference to the general security of the establishment, and without inquiring into the effect produced on the relative interests of the insured. Since it is the first principle that no interest of one or the other class of insurers must be consulted to the detriment of the whole, the order of discussion which I have followed is necessary to the subject. It now remains to treat of the internal management of an office, and to this subject I proceed in the next chapter.

CHAPTER XII.

ON THE ADJUSTMENT OF THE INTERESTS OF THE DIFFERENT MEMBERS IN AN INSURANCE OFFICE.

THERE is not a circumstance against which it is necessary to guard in the general management of an office, but what is accompanied by this inconvenience, that the measures adopted, whether of precaution or remedy, may be made to press unequally upon the different classes of insurers. If we take, for instance, a fixed rate of interest, sufficiently below that which can really be obtained, we find that many of those insured must pay their premiums at a time when interest is comparatively higher, and *vice versâ.* With regard to the tables of mortality, most probably (it has always so happened) a table which is generally too high will be unequally too high; so that some classes of insurers will contribute more largely to the safety fund than others. And even in the distribution of the profits, however good the will may be to apportion them duly, there are yet practical difficulties in selecting an equitable method out of those which do not require calculations of insupportable minuteness.

It will only here be necessary to dwell upon two points, the distribution of the premiums, and the method of appropriating the profits.

In the last chapter, in speaking of the use of too high a table of mortality, as a safeguard, I was merely considering the collective security of the office. There are two different ways of answering the same end : either by using a table of mortality confessedly too high, or constructing premiums from a true table of mortality, and increasing these by such a percentage as will produce the same receipts to the office. For general security, these two plans are equally good ; but they may produce very different consequences upon the relative state of the members. For instance, the Northampton table, which is the basis of most of those now in use, is certainly. as already noticed, too favourable to the older lives. Mr. Morgan gives the following table *, exhibiting the number who did die, and those who should have died, if the Northampton table had been correct, all in the twelve years preceding 1828.

* View of the Rise and Progress of the Equitable Society, London, 1828, age 42.

Age.	Number.	Of whom did die.	Of whom should have died.
20 — 30	4,720	29	68
30 — 40	15,951	106	243
40 — 50	27,072	201	506
50 — 60	23,307	339	545
60 — 70	14,705	426	502
70 — 80	5,056	289	290
80 — 95	701	99	94

From this comparison, Mr. Morgan concluded that the superior vitality of the young and middle ages was the effect of selection, which wore out, so to speak, after the age at which no new members were admitted; thereby proving, in his opinion, at once the effect of selection, and the excellence of the Northampton table. Now, it obviously cannot prove both of these things: granting the latter, it would certainly go a great way to prove the former; and granting the former, it does not impugn the latter: which is all that can be said. But, if it should happen that the mortality of the Northampton table is near the truth at the older ages, and very much above it at the younger, the sort of result shown in the preceding comparison would follow of course; and this circumstance, demonstrated as it is by other and independent tables, is, no doubt, the true explanation.

If such be the case, where is the fairness of using a table which demands premiums very much larger than the real risks from the young, while it admits older lives on more easy terms? Ought the older lives to enjoy any privilege in this respect? Quite the reverse; for, (page 253.) belonging to a class which is less known, and entering also in smaller numbers, with results therefore more subject to fluctuation, the percentage, added to the premiums deduced from a true table, ought rather to be larger in the case of old lives than in that of young ones. The best customers, both in number and quality, ought not to come worst off.

The proposed table of Mr. Finlaison (page 259) affords a striking illustration of this point. It is accompanied by a table representing the average premiums of all the offices. At the age of thirty, Mr. Finlaison proposes to demand 17 per cent. less than the average of what is now asked by the offices ; at the age of 60, this same able and strenuous advocate of reduction would only reduce the average premium of the offices by $3\frac{1}{2}$ per cent. I now put down the present value of 100*l.*, payable at the end of the year in which a life drops, from the Northampton and Carlisle tables, at 3 per cent., and for different ages, together with the percentage which must be taken from the former to reduce it to the latter.

Age.	Northampton.	Carlisle.	Percentage of difference.
20	£ 42·8	£ 33·9	20·8
30	47·8	40·0	16·1
40	53·8	47·1	12·5
45	57·2	50·8	11·2
50	60·9	55·4	9·0
55	64·6	60·9	5·7
60	68·6	66·5	3·1
65	72·9	71·1	2·5

In offices, then, which continue to use the Northampton table throughout, the *safety rate* is levied upon those who enter at the age of 20, to the amount of 21 per cent. out of the total sum they pay; while on those aged 65 it only amounts to $2\frac{1}{2}$ per cent. The Carlisle table represents the experience of the Equitable Society very nearly.

Again, the Amicable Society now charges premiums deduced from its own experience, and in which the fundamental inequality of the Northampton table is corrected. It will be worth while to compare the average of all the offices given by Mr. Finlaison, with the present premiums charged by the Amicable. The supposition is for 100*l*. insured.

Age.	Average.	Amicable.	Mr. F.'s proposed Premiums.
20	£2·02	£2·03	£1·76
30	2·50	2·53	2·07
40	3·26	3·25	2·78
50	4·47	4·83	4·06
55	5·38	5·90	5·00
60	6·58	7·33	6·25

From such comparisons as the preceding, I have long been of opinion that, safe as the offices are, each considered as a whole, the proportions of the premiums demanded at different ages are, in the first instance, inequitable. To a certain extent, the young are made to work for the old; that is to say, the person who insures early in life, the more prudent of the two, is made to pay a part of the premium of the one who does not begin till he is old.

The evil is not so great as it might at first sight appear, for two reasons : firstly, because those who enter at the older ages are few in number compared with those who begin between 30 and 50 years of age; secondly, because many offices make compensation to the younger members in the division of the profits. Still, however, the inequality is of a sufficient magnitude to demand alteration, which will be brought about in an obvious way; namely, by the younger insurers giving the preference to those offices in which, premiums and returns considered together, the inequality is the least.

There is another point, though not of so much consequence, in which an inequality falls more heavily upon the young than upon the old; namely, the method of paying the expenses of management. The yearly contribution of every member to this fund ought to be the same. Suppose, then, that from every premium a given sum is subtracted, to answer this end, the inequality of the remainders is increased; it being obvious that any disproportion which exists between two numbers is made larger by taking away the same from both.

The way to correct the inequality, without altering the actual receipts of the office, is as follows. The proportions in which the different ages exist in the office at any one time can be pretty nearly found. Let the office table of premiums be taken, and from it let an average premium be formed, by taking into account as well the several premiums, as the numbers who pay them. Suppose, for instance, that A persons pay the premium a, B pay b, &c. &c.; then the average premium is found by dividing the sum of the products of A and a, B and b, &c., by the sum of A, B, &c. Let the actual average premium be called P; and let the average premium, formed in the same manner from a true table of mortality (in which a, b, &c. are different, but A, B, &c. the same as before), be Q. Let P exceed Q by k per cent. of Q; then the premiums given by the true table, increased by k per cent., are those which should be substituted for the existing premiums, in order that all inequalities may be corrected, without diminishing the receipts of the office. It matters nothing, in the preceding rule, whether the premiums of what has been called the true table are correct or not, so long as their proportions are correct; and one office might, by this rule, adopt the proportions of another, without altering its own receipts.

If such a process as the preceding were performed, deducting from the receipts required by the office the whole expense of management, and afterwards adding the last-mentioned item in equal shares to all the *policies*, the distribution of the premiums would be theoretically perfect. It remains to consider the more difficult part of the question,—the method of dividing the profits.

Hitherto, I have had no occasion to speak of a most important difference of system which distinguishes one office from another; the distinction of *mutual* and *proprietary*. The former have no capital, except what arises from their own accumulations, and each member is a guarantee to the rest for the fulfilment of all engagements. If the office possess a charter, this guarantee operates no further than to pledge the prémiums already paid by any member for the discharge of all claims which arise before his own, since a corporation is considered in law as an individual. If, on the other hand, there be no charter, the whole fortune of every member is pledged for the discharge of all claims. The risk, however, at the commencement is not great in character, and small in amount; and the quantity of risk diminishes so much faster than the amount increases, that it may safely be said there is nothing in the commercial world which approaches, even remotely, to the security of a well established and prudently managed insurance office.

A proprietary insurance office has a capital, the proprietors of which may or may not be insured in the office, and for which such a bonus is paid, in addition to the market rate of interest, as is mentioned in p. 263. It would perhaps be difficult, at the present time, to establish a new proprietary office with a very large capital. The public now begins to see that much capital is not necessary, and that nearly all the bonus which is paid for its use is so much taken away from the savings of the insured, without any adequate benefit received in return. One by one, the proprietary offices must (as some have done) admit the insured to a share in the profits: the necessity for which will be taught by the decline of business, if not previously learnt.

The question as to how profits should be divided, is of the same nature in both species of offices; the difference being, that the offices which are partly proprietary have less to distribute among the insured than those which are mutual. The first inquiry must be, What is the profit of an insurance office; and how is the amount to be ascertained? Firstly, as to the profit which an insurance office may be expected to realise, judging by the premiums they receive, and the mortality they have hitherto experienced. Certain limits may be obtained, which may sometimes serve as a useful check.

Perhaps the average age of admission to an insurance office is about 40, as many entering younger as older. The average premium charged by the offices at that age is 3·26*l*. per cent. Now the most extreme supposition which can be imagined in favour of the insured is, that the Carlisle table should be taken as the law of mortality, and 4 per cent. as the interest of money. Upon these suppositions, the accumulations of the office would amount, upon a premium of 3·26*l*., at the death of parties aged 40, one with another, to 137*l*. But this pushes every favourable supposition to its extreme, and moreover allows nothing for expenses of management. I am inclined to think, however, that the usual premiums will, as long as the rate of mortality continues at its present amount, yield about 125*l*. for 100*l*. nominally insured, and perhaps something more.

It must not be left out of sight, that the offices consider every person as having the age which he will attain at his *next* birth-day. If, for instance, a person who attains 40 years of age on the 12th of March were to insure his life on the 13th, he would be said to be 41 years of age, and would have to pay accordingly. The effect of this very proper * regulation is, that, one party with another, all are half a year younger than their *office age*. Again, all the tables are computed on the supposition that interest is made yearly, whereas in fact it is made quarterly. Circumstances of this sort, trivial as they appear, do nevertheless produce a sensible effect in a large number of years. To the above we must add the profits arising from the purchase of policies, which is always done by the offices on terms very favourable to themselves; fines for non-payment of premiums; the profits of lapsed policies; and so on.

Leaving all speculation as to the probable profits, I now proceed to show how to ascertain, from the

---

* Proper as long as there is no subdivision of a year. I think the offices might very rationally divide the year into quarters.

actual statistics of an office, what its real condition is. And here I must observe, that though in the construction of premiums, a table of more than the real mortality must be used, yet no such thing is absolutely necessary in the valuation of its liabilities and assets. Here truth, and not security, is the object; and if by any means a true table can be obtained, its results should be calculated; though I do not say that in the declaration of profit, such results should be admitted to their full extent. The most simple theoretical way of conducting the process, is to ascertain the value of every policy, as in page 218.; that is, to ascertain how much should be given to the holder of each policy to renounce his claim, the office also abandoning the future premiums. When this is done, it is obvious that the office is not solvent, unless the assets arising from the accumulations of former years be sufficient to pay the values of all the policies, and thus to buy them all up. Supposing the office able to do this, with a capital remaining larger than would be necessary to create a permanent fund for the expenses of management, the surplus of that capital is profit. Otherwise, calculate the present value of all premiums due to the office, and also the present value of all claims to which it is liable. To the former add the sum total of the assets of the office, and to the latter add the present value of a perpetuity equal to the expenses of management. Thus, let

P = present value of all premiums.

C = present value of all claims.

A = total assets of the office.

M = present value of all expenses of management.

If then P and A together exceed C and M together, the office is solvent, and the excess is profit.

On each of these items a few remarks may be made.

(P.) All the parties who are of the same office age, may have their several policies considered as one collective policy, in respect of which the sum of the premiums is paid as one premium, and the sum of the

possible claims is one claim.   But as these premiums
are payable at all periods of the year, they may be considered as, one with another, due at six months after
the valuation, at which time the present office age of
the parties may be considered to be their real age.

(C.) All bonuses which have actually been added to
policies (if any) must be included in the claims; and
the value of each claim must be carefully found, with
reference to the time after death at which it is paid.
(See Appendix the Second.)

(A.) The principal of the assets must be deduced
entirely by means of the income it yields, and must be
ascertained from the income by means of the rate of
interest assumed.   On this subject, which contains a difficulty of a peculiar character, see the Sixth Appendix.

(M.) Against the expenses of management may be
set, as far as they go, the incidental profits, when they
can be tolerably well ascertained.

The profit being thus found, and that share of it
which belongs to the insured (if the office be not
mutual), it remains to inquire, What principle of division
should be adopted?   And, firstly, it may be doubted
whether the whole of the profit is immediately divisible,
consistently with prudence.   To use an astronomical
phrase, the increase of the surplus is partly secular, and
partly periodic; that is to say, instead of a steady and
uniform increase, there is a fluctuating rate of augmentation, compounded of that permanent rate which
the largeness of the premiums necessarily gives, and
the alternate accelerations and retardations occasioned
by the departures of the incidents of the several years
from the average.   The only way of obtaining the permanent part of the surplus is by estimating it on the
average of a considerable number of past years, regard
being had to the relative, not the absolute, surplus.
Let us suppose, for instance, that the present value of
all claims is ascertained to be one million, and the present
value of all premiums 700,000*l.*, the office possessing
besides (clear of charges of management) 500,000*l.*:

there is then a surplus of 200,000*l.* ; which having been accumulated out of premiums, and profits having been regularly paid up to the present time, it may be presumed that the premiums themselves are capable of maintaining this rate of surplus. The office must then be presumed able to pay 120*l.* for every 100*l.* insured.

But it is important to note, that the present rate of profit must not always be assumed as that which can be permanently maintained. Suppose, for instance, an office which begins for the first time to divide profits : its accumulations are therefore, in part, the reserves of profit which should have been added to former claims, had any division of surplus previously existed. The same remark may be necessary when any change is made in the way of dividing profits, since the surplus existing at the moment of the change is the result of a former state of things. Thus, an office which has proceeded injudiciously, in making too large divisions, may possibly, when it adopts a more prudent system, be justified in forming a system which would require a larger surplus than the one which it actually possesses at the time of discovering the error ; for the then existing surplus has been unduly weakened, and is not to be considered as representing the permanent effect of the improved mode of proceeding.

I have stated, that the percentage which can be added to each 100*l.* insured should be determined by the average of a number of years. If this number be too great, the incidental fluctuations of mortality may be compensated ; but at the same time the real and secular changes of mortality may be prevented from producing their proper effect. As long as the value of life is increasing, too long an average is a defect on the safe side : but if it were diminishing, it might happen that the mean of a number of preceding years would present a higher result than would be consistent with security. As yet the offices have had nothing to encounter except the diminution of mortality, and its consequences ; but

in constructing rules for their own guidance, they should
be careful not to fall into such errors on the safe side
as become errors on the wrong side when circumstances change.   I hold an opinion which I think, from
his writings, was also that of the late Mr. Morgan;
namely, that an insurance office must consider the last
half century as having been a period of circumstances
singularly favourable for the formation and growth of
such institutions, more so than it would be wise to expect
for the future.   Perhaps from five to ten years is the
length of time for which the preceding average should
be computed.

The valuations should, if possible, be made *yearly*.
No check which can be devised is so likely to be useful
as yearly valuation ; and it is absolutely necessary to any
system which gives the real amount of their premiums
to the insured.   In a mutual insurance office, starting
without much capital, it would be madness to rest upon
any tables and to neglect valuations; unless, as before
remarked, the returns made to the insured are meant to
be very much below their payments.   And in conjunction
with yearly valuations should come yearly divisions of
profits, or something equivalent.   There is, I believe, a
prejudice against frequent divisions in the minds of
many who have derived their ideas on the subject from
the former practice of offices.   But surely, provided that
the proper amount of profit be divided yearly, and no
more, it matters nothing whether the apportionment be
made seven times in seven years, or once only, as far as
security is concerned.   For it is to be remembered, that
yearly division of profits does not imply an annual expenditure, but only an annual distribution of future expenditure.   In septennial divisions, one of two things always
takes place : either the profits are made contingent upon
a party surviving one or more periods of division, which
creates great inequalities between the lot of different
persons (the very thing an insurance office was intended
to avoid); or it declares beforehand, what the profits
shall be during periods of seven years.   In the latter

case the annual division is unquestionably the more safe; since it is easier to predict the capabilities of one year than of seven.

In writing upon any point connected with insurance, the practice of the Equitable Society naturally suggests itself. Nevertheless, I always consider that society as a distinct and anomalous establishment, existing at this moment under circumstances of an unique character. It is the result of an experiment which it was most important to try ; but which having been tried, need not be repeated. Its history is briefly this : — The Amicable Society, which, in the year 1760, was the only one existing, was originally founded rather on principles of mutual benevolence, than of mutual insurance, as now understood. A certain number of persons (the only restriction being that their ages should be between twelve and forty-five), each paying the same sum yearly, the whole fund of each year (or the greater part) was divided among the representatives of those who died within the year.* The Equitable Society was founded upon the principle of apportioning the payments to the risk of life. The tables were constructed by Dodson, who, as Mr. Morgan remarks, " for greater security assumed the probabilities of life in London, during a period of twenty years ; which, including the year 1740, when the mortality was almost equal to that of a plague, rendered such premiums much higher than they ought to have been, even according to the ordinary probabilities of life in London itself." The truth of this remark will sufficiently appear, from comparing the average of the present office premiums with the original Equitable premiums, as given in the following table. And even these premiums were increased on the most frivolous pretexts. Thus *female* life and *young* life were considered as more than usually hazardous, and paid for accordingly.

---

* The Amicable Society now retains only one of its original characters ; namely, that all members, whatever may be their age at death, or the term of their continuance in the society, participate equally in the profits.

Age.	Equitable Premium, 1771.	Equitable Premium, 1779.	Average present Premium.
	£ s. d.	£ s. d.	£ s. d.
14	2 17 0	2 5 5	. . . .
20	3 9 4	2 12 10	2 0 0
25	3 14 0	3 0 6	2 4 0
30	3 18 7	3 8 11	2 10 0
40	4 17 9	4 7 11	3 5 0
49	6 2 5	5 10 2	4 6 0

Mr. Morgan says, "that for the first twenty years, the society possessed such an excess of income, that being suffered to accumulate without interruption, it contributed, in a great measure, to form the basis of its future opulence." This circumstance, with the great number of policies which were abandoned* in the early stages of its career, and the increase of interest during the war, are quite sufficient to explain the wealth which the Equitable Society has accumulated: to these must be added the parsimony with which, at first, additions were made to the policies. The whole was an experiment, on a graduated scale of premiums, made with a caution, which, though it turned out to be superfluous, could not be known to be such, except by the result. It was at the same time a venture, and by many considered as a hazardous one; for instance, the law officers of the Crown refused a charter, on account of the lowness of the premiums. The hazard having been run, and having turned out profitably, the proceeds belong to those who ran it, and to those who, by their own free consent, became their lineal successors. Nor is it the least remarkable circumstance connected with this society, that the immense funds at its disposal have been always opened, though under restrictions, to the public. Though this has been done in a way which renders the participation of the new insurer in the

* Perhaps Mr. Morgan's statement on this point may have led to the statement alluded to in page 266.

previous accumulations a remote contingency, still it *is* done, and by a body who might without any bar, legal or moral, immediately close their doors, and divide the whole among themselves.

I have made the preceding remarks, in order that it may be clear how little the history or practice of the Equitable Society should have any direct authoritative bearing on the spirit in which the management of a more modern office should be carried on. The general lesson taught by it is, — be cautious ; but, among other things, be cautious of carrying caution so far as to leave a part of your own property for the benefit of those who are in no way related to you. If there be a Charybdis in an insurance office, there is also a Scylla : the mutual insurer, who is too much afraid of dispensing the profits to those who die *before* him, will have to leave his own share for those who die *after* him. Reversing the fable of Spenser, we should write upon the door of every mutual office but one, *be wary* ; but upon that one should be written, *be not too wary*, and over it, "Equitable Society."

An insurance office has no existence separate from that of its insurers ; and no public duty to fulfil, except to collect, improve, and *equalize* their premiums (p. 238.) : therefore, their most important object, next to the fulfilment of their guaranteed engagements, is the distribution of their profits in such manner that every one may obtain his due share. The question now becomes, What is the due share of each party ? This is, in some measure, a question of previous contract, though there are those who consider that there must be a right and a wrong way. For instance, Mr. M'Kean, the compiler of the tables alluded to in page 191., and of a useful work * which accompanies them, says, "Our conclusion, and a most important one, lies conspicuous on the very surface. It is impossible that ALL the

---

* " Exposition of the practical Life Tables, &c. London : Butterworth, Richardson, &c. 1837." This work is, I believe, sold separately.

offices above mentioned can be correct or just in their laws for dividing the surplus. If the plan of the *Equitable* is right, then most unquestionably the plan of the *Atlas* is wrong, and great injustice is done to the younger members, and so *vice versâ*. But, is this a state of things in which so important a system as that of life insurance, based, as that system is, on mathematical science, ought or can continue to exist? Certainly not."

On this I observe, that though life insurance be an application of (not based upon) mathematical science, yet that the entrance of exact numerical reasoning is subsequent to the admission of certain principles, and the experimental acquisition of certain facts. It is not by mathematics we learn that life is uncertain in individual cases, but nearly certain in the mass — that it is the duty of every one to provide for his family — and that this can be done without contingency, if those who survive the average term agree to surrender a part of their substance to those who do not. Calculation will point out the amount which, upon any given principle of division, belongs to one or another of the insured; but before we can come to this point, it must be settled with what intention the surplus was paid; which may be different in different offices. The following considerations might be addressed to any person who intends to insure his life: — You are aware that the premium demanded of you is, avowedly, more than has hitherto been found sufficient for the purpose, the reason being, that it is impossible to settle the exact amount, on account of our not knowing whether the future and the past will coincide in giving the same law of mortality, and the same interest of money. The surplus arising from this overcharge, for the future existence of which it is hundreds to one, is now at your own disposal, and you must choose between one office and another, according to your intentions with regard to its ultimate destination. Firstly, if you doubt the general security of the plan of insurance, and are desirous of an absolute guarantee, independently of accumulations from premiums, there are offices which will, in consideration of the surplus aforesaid, pledge their proprietary capitals for the satisfaction of your ultimate demand upon them. Secondly, if, being of the opinion aforesaid, you think the whole surplus too much to pay for the guarantee, there are proprietary offices which retain a part of the profit in consideration of the risk of their capital, and return the remainder. Thirdly, if you wish the surplus premium, as fast as it is proved to be such, to be applied in obviating the necessity of any further overcharges, there are offices which divide the profits during the life of the insured, by means of a reduction of premium. Fourthly, if you wish the surplus to accumulate, and, feeling confidence in your own life, are willing to risk losing it (the *surplus*, remember) entirely if you die young, on condition of having it proportionally increased if you live to be old, there are offices which divide all or most of the profits among old members. Fifthly, if you would prefer a certainty of profit, die when you may, there are offices which at once admit new members who die early to a full participation in all advantages. The choice between these several modes must be made by yourself, according to your own inclinations, views of fairness, or particular circumstances.

There are three modes of division which deserve particular notice; namely, periodical additions to the policies, periodical diminutions of premium, and addition to the policy at death to an amount depending upon the assets of the office, without reference to the time during which the insured has paid premiums. I may, perhaps, be thought to treat this subject with prolixity; notwithstanding, knowing that this part of the subject has created more discussion of late years than any other, I think an attempt to compare the principles of different plans not out of place.

The considerations which follow will apply to all offices which divide any profits whatever: the inquiry being, not how much surplus should be divided, but in what proportions a given sum should be divided among the insured.

Let us return to the original constitution of an insurance office (page 238.), derived from the statement of its main object; namely, that it is a savings' bank with a power of equalizing those results in which the different durations of life would cause differences. Suppose that such an office sets out with premiums imagined to be no more than sufficient, but which are afterwards found to be more than sufficient, leaving an admitted amount of surplus in hand. The first thought would be of *restitution*; namely, rendering back to each individual the amount which he had *bonâ fide* contributed towards the surplus. To do this properly, it must first be settled whether the insurance office is one or many. Does each age insure itself, or do the separate ages insure both themselves and each other? If the premiums were properly proportioned, there would be no occasion to ask this question : but if the incomers of one age pay unduly as compared with those of another, then it is but fair that they should receive in proportion. In the distribution of premiums, which I have described in p. 270., it is equitable that a remedy should be provided, by virtue of which those who enter the office young should receive more than the rest. And it is, for this reason, desirable that the proportions of the division should be regulated by a true table of mortality.

Let P be the real premium, and $P + p$ the office premium ; and let the death of an individual take place after he has been n years insured, and just before the $(n + 1)$th premium is paid. If the office had been a compound interest savings' bank, the deceased would, at his death, have been entitled to the following amount.

$P + p$ improved at compound interest for n years

$P + p$ n-1

. . . .

. . . .

$P + p$ . . . . 1 year.

But under the conditions of insurance, the part P, with

its accumulations, is the consideration for the sum insured ; the remaining part p, with its accumulations, is due under the name of profit or restitution, in a strictly mutual office.

The application of the preceding method would require that a calculation should be made once in every year of the quantity p and its accumulations, for every individual insured. This having been done, and the surplus $A + P - C$ having been calculated from a true table of mortality, it is then known in what proportion any two individuals insured are claimants upon this fund. Suppose that p and its accumulations amount, in the case of the persons X and Y, to 100l. and 150l. Suppose that $A + P - C$ is 100,000l., and that the sum of all the excesses of premium with their accumulations, of which the 100l. and 150l. just mentioned are items, is 120,000l. It matters nothing that the last sum is greater than 100,000l., since we are not speaking of a fund on which there are definite claims, but of one the nature of which it is to be of uncertain amount. The use of the items 100l. and 150l., and of the sum total of 120,000l., is to enable us to divide the real fund of 100,000l. among those who raised it, in the proportions in which they contributed towards it. Thus if X and Y were to die in the year of the valuation, it would be fair that they should receive such proportions of the 100,000l. as 100l. and 150l. are of 120,000l.; that is, five-sixths of 100l. and 150l. This method proceeds upon the principle that all the excess of premium is taken in trust as a guarantee for the main fund, and is to be returned if not wanted, or such proportion of it as is not wanted. It confines the insurance, or provision against the uncertainty of life, entirely to a stipulated sum, and regards all that part of the premium which is not really wanted to provide this sum, for one man with another, as paid into a common savings' bank, in which no equalization is supposed.

The labour of making the calculations would, I imagine, prevent any office from adopting the preceding plan, so as to carry it into execution yearly. With a good system, however, the difficulty of managing the details of such a scheme would not be so great as at first sight might be supposed. Upon its principle hang the two first plans of division mentioned; namely, periodical additions to the policies, and periodical diminutions of premuim. In both of these, the advantage of the insured is increased by the length of his life; that is to say, the excesses of his premiums are placed to his credit in the first, and considered as having been prospective payments of his future premiums in the second. But nevertheless there runs through the offices which adopt these plans more or less of a practice which prevents the surplus from being divided among the insured in equitable proportions. Suppose that there is a septennial *bonus,* as it is called, which was declared in the year 1830. Immediately after the award, two persons, A and B, aged 30 and 60, enter the office each upon a policy of 100*l.,* and were both alive when the bonus of 1837 was declared. This bonus is generally a percentage, not upon the amount of premiums paid, but upon the sum insured, and both would have the same addition made to the 100*l.* for which they have insured. But have both contributed to the accumulations of the office in the proportion which would render this mode of division equitable? To consider this point, remember that a promise to pay, say 5*l.,* at the death of a person aged 67, is of much more value than the same at the death of a person aged 37. The older life therefore receives much more than the younger life. But he has paid much more. That is true; but at the same time he has occasioned a greater risk to the office, and it is the excess of his premium above the risk (and not the whole premium) which the office acknowledges in declaring the bonus. From page 270. it sufficiently appears that the premiums of the older ages are already too small in comparison with those of the younger: this mode of dividing the surplus, therefore, only tends to increase the existing injustice. The only remedy is, to make use of the process laid down in the preceding page ; and having ascertained the amount of what each person has paid over and above what was necessary, to consider each person as entitled to the sum which his overplus would purchase at his death,. if the bonus be made by addition to his policy ; or to a diminution of premium answering to the annuity on his life, which the overplus would buy, if the bonus be made by diminution of premium.

The knowledge, therefore, of the *real* premium is necessary for an equitable distribution of the surplus, upon the supposition that the said distribution is made on the principle of dividing the surplus fund among the contributors in proportion to their contributions. Every plan which, ceteris paribus, makes equal additions to the policies of different ages, is inequitable. I repeat again, that in the preceding cases, the principle of division ought to be considered as arising from the combination of an insurance office and a savings' bank ; the portion of premium which covers the risk of life being paid to the former, and the remainder to the latter.

The third method of division supposes the establishment to be entirely an insurance office, and not at all a savings' bank. Its object is to make the returns to the different members both equal and equitable. Considering that the real risk of life is not perfectly ascertained, and that if it were it would not be safe to reduce the premiums to the lowest theoretical safety-point, such an office, instead of demanding a premium avowedly too high for the sum insured, and engaging to return all or part of the surplus, considers the sum insured as indefinite, except only in so far as a minimum is named, below which it is not to fall. Thus such an office, receiving, say 3*l.* of premium, from a person aged 34, for what is called, in compliance with custom, a policy of 100*l.*, does in fact make the following bargain:—The office engages to return, at the death of the party, let that take place when it may, such a sum as will represent the average accumulation of an annuity of 3*l.* continued during the life of a person aged 34, be that sum more or less ; with this additional limitation, that the office undertakes that the said accumulation shall not be less than 100*l*. This last guarantee, though necessary for the satisfaction of the public, is in truth so certain, from the amount of the premium demanded, that a person acquainted with the subject looks upon the possibility of the funds of the society suffering from it as an extremely remote chance.

In order, however, to make the proceedings of such an office equitable, the proportions of the premiums paid by parties of different ages must be fairly regulated. On the supposition that the inequality pointed out in page 270. is allowed to exist, the preceding methods of division may be (I do not say are) adjusted so that every interest shall be consulted. But in the present plan, it is impracticable to remedy any such defect of proportion, at least without dividing the establishment into as many different offices as there are ages, which would not be easy, and perhaps not very safe. The simple rule for determining the relative premiums is to make them proportional to the real premiums, with the exception of a given addition to each (not premium, but) policy, for expenses of management. In a large office, however, the expenses of management may be made a part of the percentage addition to the premiums.

The method of division in such an office is extremely simple, and has been already described in page 276. Subtracting the present value of all the claims, that is, of all the minimum claims, reckoned as 100*l*. for each tabular premium paid, from the sum of the present values of all premiums, and of the assets of the office, the proportion which this remainder is of the present value of all the claims expresses the fraction of 100*l*. which may be added to each 100*l*. insured.

Let A, the assets * of the office, be 500,000*l*.; P, the present value of all premiums, 600,000*l*.; and C, the prseent value of all claims, 850.000*l*. : then $A + P - C$,

---

* Diminished for the expenses of management, as in page 275.

the surplus, is 250,000*l.*, which being 25 parts out of 85 of the whole claims, or $29\frac{1}{17}$ per cent., will afford $129\frac{7}{17}l$. for every 100*l.*, which is guaranteed. Those who die in the year of this valuation, may therefore receive that sum.

The principle on which the preceding division is made, is, that if the same state of things continue, every one will in turn receive the same dividend. But, can such a prediction be made? Undoubtedly not, for the fluctuations, both of those who come into the office, and those who go out, will tend to produce variations. It is very unlikely that any office should maintain itself for a long series of years nearly in the same position ; and, since the idea of allowing any permanent diminution of the surplus must not be admitted, there is no alternative except an arrangement for a gradual increase, which it is the object of this mode of division to make as slow as is consistent with the certainty of having it. But in this case, it may seem as if the old system were revived, and a fund instituted by the present insurers, for the sole benefit of those who come after them. There is, however, an important difference between never paying more than the guaranteed minimum, so that all the surplus goes towards that fund, and drawing upon the surplus nearly to the full amount which safety would allow, leaving only such a trifle to augment the fund as is requisite to avoid too large an out-going. The old principle, then, which formerly prevented any bonus whatsoever, is here merely applied to such an extent as to keep the bonus within proper limits.

If the tables of mortality by which the profits are divided, be actual representatives of existing mortality, and if the number of members remain nearly the same, the indications of these tables, implicitly followed, would soon reduce the surplus of the office to that which is barely necessary for the extreme payment which the premiums will admit. To take a case : suppose that the premiums will in the long run pay 125*l.*

for every 100*l*. guaranteed; the present value of all
the claims is 1,000,000*l*., that of all the premiums
700,000*l*., and the value of the assets of the office
600,000*l*. The surplus is therefore 300,000*l*., and,
going upon real tables, the office begins to pay 130*l*. for
every 100*l*. guaranteed; and this it would be able to
do in favour of all who are insured at the time of the
preceding valuation. But part of this dividend does
not, and, by hypothesis, cannot, arise from the premiums: it is therefore paid entirely out of surplus,
and will gradually disappear. The dividend will be
reduced to 125*l*., about which it will fluctuate, being
sometimes a little less and sometimes a little more. An
increase of business in such an office would make the
surplus disappear more rapidly, since each new comer
brings in an equivalent to 125*l*. and those of the new
comers who die receive 130*l*. A diminution of business would produce a contrary effect; and a total ces-
sation of new comers would allow the dividend to remain at 130*l*. As far as any danger from fluctuations
of mortality is concerned, I do not see any objection to
such a division as the preceding: but when it is remembered that the possible diminution of the rate of
interest must also be provided for, I think it would be
prudent to reserve a small proportion of the surplus
for accumulation.

There are two ways in which this reserve may be
made; firstly, by employing a table of less than the
real mortality in the valuation of the claims and premiums; secondly, by calculating the surplus from a
real table, and dividing as upon the supposition that a
given fraction of this surplus, say one eighth or one
tenth, should be expunged in the calculation. The
latter plan is the best of the two, in every respect but
one, as follows. The mutual insurance office must be a
republic, and many of its members have very little information upon the questions which are, from time to
time, submitted to them. They are easily dazzled by
the appearance of surplus, and are quick to believe that

a larger division might be made in their favour. Add to this that the older members carry with them in the discussion of questions, that influence which age naturally and properly gives in the management of important affairs; and as to which the conduct of an insurance office only forms an exception, because questions arise in which the interests of the old and young clash * with each other, which is nowhere else the case. Under such circumstances the disposition to break in upon the surplus is the fault to which the body has a tendency, and it is not a bad thing to place some small difficulties in the way of doing this. Now if a fraction of the surplus be withdrawn from the calculation of the dividend, it is very easy to change one fraction into another. A vote of the general meeting, and a few strokes of the actuary's pen, and the thing is done. But when the requisite fraction of the surplus is deducted by the supposition of a lower rate of vitality (or of interest) than actually prevails, no change can be made without the entrance of a large number of important considerations, the discussion of which occupies some time, and places a useful check in the way of the restless.

But is it then proposed that every office shall be provided with a fund, which, though slowly, is yet indefinitely, to increase? Not necessarily; for the reserved portion of one year is not put aside, and considered as inalienable, but enters into the surplus of the next year. There may be, then, a limit to the increase of the surplus, as follows. Suppose the office to be in a stationary state, having arrived at the point where the influx of the new members compensates the efflux occasioned by death or surrender. The receipts of the office consist entirely in premiums and produce of capital, the expenditure in management and payment of claims. As long as the surplus increases, the sum of the first pair

---

* The members of a mutual insurance office are not properly represented in their list of directors, unless the individuals composing it are of very different ages.

of items will exceed that of the second; and, whatever may be laid by in each year, it produces a larger sur-plus, and larger payments on account of claims, in the next year. If, then, the surplus could increase without limit, so would the dividends ; but if the surplus have a limit, the dividends also have a limit: and it is plain that the limit arrives, when the yearly outgoings from claims and management are equal to the receipts from premiums and interest of capital. A mathematical in-vestigation of the conditions necessary in order that the fund may increase, but not without limit, gives the following result :

Suppose an insurance office, constructed upon the preceding principles, to have arrived at its stationary state, with respect to influx and efflux of members, and make the following suppositions :

A The assets of the office, for precision, say Janu-ary 1, 1838.

P The *real* present value of all premiums from members then in existence.

C The *real* present value of all claims (not includ-ing additions) to which the office is then liable.

m The expenses of management till January 1, 1839.

p The amount which will accrue from premiums and interest of premiums by January 1, 1839.

c The amount of claims (not including additions from the surplus fund), which will be paid before January 1, 1839.

r The interest of one pound for one year.

t The fraction which is taken of the tabular surplus fund in the computation of the dividend.

We suppose (as must be the case in an old office), C greater than P, and (as must be the case in a solvent office) A and P together greater than C.

1. In order that there may be a surplus fund in-creasing, but not without limit, find the fraction which a year's interest on C is of *c*. Then *t*, or the fraction of the surplus fund (or of $A + P - C$), which enters into the formation of the dividend, must exceed that

fraction which a year's interest on C is of *c,* otherwise the fund would increase without limit.

2. Neither can there be such a fund unless the sum of *m* and *c* should fall short of the sum of *p,* and of a year's interest on the excess of C over P. But, when this is the case, the limiting *surplus* capital is found by dividing the excess of the second total just mentioned over the first, by a divisor obtained as follows : — multiply together *t* and *c,* divide the product by C, and subtract *r* from the quotient. To this surplus capital, add the excess of C over P, and the limiting capital is obtained.

3. If it should happen that the limiting surplus capital is less than the actually existing surplus, it is a sign that the action of the preceding plan would diminish the surplus towards that limit instead of increasing it. In such a case, the surplus is already too large for the value of *t* to increase it; and if *t* be not diminished, that is, if less of the tabular surplus be not taken into the computation of the dividend, the fund will diminish.

It is not to be supposed that any office will ever reach a stationary state ; but the approach may be near enough to make the preceding process of some use in the determination of the dividends due to the insured. If, following the plan which the preceding problem supposes, we were to inquire what value should be given to the fraction *t,* the answer to the question must depend on the reduction of interest which is supposed within the bounds of probability. Suppose the present rate of interest to be $3\frac{1}{2}$ per cent. and that the extreme limit is supposed to be $2\frac{1}{2}$ per cent, in such a case the value of P and C must be calculated at $2\frac{1}{2}$ per cent., and such a limiting surplus must be fixed upon as will, at that rate of interest, enable the office to pay at least its guaranteed claims But it is impossible to lay down an entire system of rules for the regulation of a species of undertaking which depends on the fluctuations of the state of society. Whatever maxims may be collected, and however sound they may be, skill and judgment will always be requisite to apply them to the cases which arise. In this respect the offices resemble the individual problems which arise in life contingencies. Many as are the cases which have been described in books upon the subject, almost every application of them requires attention to some cir‑ cumstance peculiar to the instance in question.

CHAPTER XIII.

MISCELLANEOUS SUBJECTS CONNECTED WITH IN‑ SURANCE, ETC.

THE limits of this treatise will only afford a few words on several points of interest, which I will therefore condense into one chapter, taking the subjects as they arise.

The management of annuity offices is somewhat more easy than that of insurance establishments; and the maxims of security in the former are, of course, the direct reverse of those in the latter, so far as any considerations of mortality are concerned. Tables must be assumed of higher than the real vitality, and a rate of interest somewhat below, or at least not above, that which can actually be obtained.

Those who wish to buy annuities on the firmest possible basis, may deal with the government. The commissioners for the reduction of the national debt are empowered to grant annuities in lieu of stock, on terms calculated from the *government tables* (page 168). The rates are high; and though a private office may really be as solvent as the nation, yet confidence springs from opinion, and the security of the national debt must always be thought the very best. The patriotic annuitant, too, may reflect that the profit derived from him goes to the reduction of the national debt.

The distinction of male and female life becomes of importance in the granting of annuities. The insurance offices have not as yet, except, I believe, in one or two instances, begun to recognise the distinction, which is of the less consequence, since, with respect to the office, it is keeping on the safe side, and, with respect to the public, very few female lives are insured. But the exact reverse takes place with regard to annuities ; it would be insecure to grant them to females on the same terms as to males ; and a very large proportion of the whole number of annuitants is of the former sex.

Annuities might be granted by an office which should undertake a return of profits, in the form of a payment to the executors at the death of the party ; and an association of mutual annuitants would not be of difficult formation. The principal objection would be, the smallness of the number of persons who buy annuities, compared with those who insure their lives. If, however, such an office were to grant reversionary annuities, their field would be very much widened. Several of the insurance offices grant annuities, but none, I believe, in which the annuitants are sharers in the profits.

The details of a *Friendly Society* comprise every possible species of life contingency. They grant weekly payments during sickness, annuities in old age, and sums payable at death, in consideration of weekly premiums. These institutions, combined with Savings' Banks, and aided by the removal of the abuses of the Poor Law, will, in time, raise the labouring classes of this country to a degree of independence which they have never known. But, as might have been expected, the management of these important institutions has, in many instances, been wanting in prudence ; and I am afraid it is hopeless to expect that the unity of system, which must prevail before a thorough knowledge of the advantages they offer can get abroad, can be attained while their several administrations are unconnected, and at liberty to pursue all possible variety of plans, subject only to the certificate of an actuary that each proposition is not unsafe. But something more than safety is required : an equitable distribution of benefits, and a certainty of the most careful management, are as necessary to the universal formation of these societies as an opinion of their safety. The government, which has within these few years been compelled, by the most decided necessity, to apply a very severe and searching remedy to an abuse of long standing, owes the labouring classes a strong expression of sympathy with the numerous cases of hardship which such a measure must create, and with the excellent conduct and temper under its operation which has pervaded the classes most immediately affected by it. It is to be regretted that the change itself was not accompanied by acts of parliament for the *encouragement* and *aid* of societies such as those of which I am now speaking, in addition to those which already existed for their *regulation*. The most determined opponent of the protective principle would hardly dispute the policy of giving effective help to the efforts of self-support, at the moment when the aid of the parish, which had been the resource against poverty, became only the last security against starvation. If the nation had been obliged to abandon a distant colony, in circumstances of danger and distress, there is no doubt that the settlers would have been furnished with arms, arsenals, ships, money, and all that could enable them to do whatever might be done for their own defence and support. Has similar help in similar circumstances been given at home ? Is the labouring man, thus suddenly thrown into a position where the power and the habit of depending on himself are necessary to a degree of which his training never implied the existence, one bit nearer to the acquisition of the power or the formation of the habit, by any aid of the legislature? Have even the opponents of the measure, with their professions of benevolence, ever pressed, or even suggested, the duty of showing the labouring man, not only that by combination his class can provide for itself, but that the community which found it necessary to make a change involving him in years of uncertainty and possible hardship, was desirous that he should have that knowledge, and willing to aid him in attaining its full benefits?

It is not too late to take the necessary steps; and any one who imagines a legislature able to feel, or to think, will see the means of addressing himself to the first faculty by such considerations as the preceding, and to the second by urging the policy of giving every class a share in the artificial system of property on which the country now depends. At present, the *property* of a labouring man is all tangible, and immediately at hand; it would not be a great wonder if he were found to have no clear opinion of the rights of a landlord, a fund-holder, a mortgagee, or an annuitant. But if he himself were in possession of any of those claims which, by means of law, can be created, enforced, or transferred by virtue of the possession of a bit of paper — still more, if the support of his old age and of his sick bed were connected with this purely legal tenure of his past savings, he would then be interested in the preservation of the existing system by the share of it which belongs to himself.

The friendly societies, numerous as they are, are by no means universally distributed; and if they were, the smallness of their several amounts of investment must occasion the expenses of management to bear a larger proportion to the whole than would be the case if all were united. Besides which, it happens every now and then that the affairs of such a society fall into disorder from want of skill or care. The government has lent considerable assistance by allowing their investments a larger rate of interest than could elsewhere be obtained; but this aid, independently of its being but little known by the class whom it most concerns, does not guarantee the proper use of the funds so invested. If one large office were to be established in London, having the general management of the money raised, and the regulation of its distribution, it would not be difficult to find persons of station * and character throughout the country who would consent to act as agents, receiving the contributions and certifying the claims. The expense of management might be borne for a few years by the public purse, and this burden might be gradually thrown on the establishment itself. No very great difficulties could arise in the formation of such an institution, and certainly none the expense of conquering which would not be trifling in comparison of the greatness of the object gained. The act which should establish this universal Friendly Society would, in two generations, become the real poor law.

The subjects of fire and of marine insurance are founded on principles of great simplicity, though it is not easy to procure exact data for the computation of risks. As there exist no offices which are managed on the republican method of a mutual Life Insurance Company, no publication of the results of experience has been made. If every loss by fire or sea were a total loss, it would only be necessary to ask what proportion of all the houses or ships now existing is burnt or wrecked in a year or on a voyage, and the premium for insuring a house for one year, or a ship for one voyage, would immediately follow. Thus, if of all the ships which sail to the West Indies, one in a hundred is lost, the lowest premium at which an insurance could take place is one per cent., and all demanded above that proportion would be profit. It would not, perhaps, be very easy to ascertain this proportion with exactness, and the difficulty is increased if ships or houses be divided into different classes as to security, since the risks of each class must be ascertained separately. But

---

* Many of the Friendly Societies now established depend almost entirely upon the superintendence of the clergy or local gentry.

the greatest obstacle to a satisfactory adjustment of risks, lies in the necessity of taking into account the chances of only partial loss, which would make the tables (if they could be procured) nearly as complicated as life tables.

On the subject of marine insurance, nothing is known to the public, as to the experience of the underwriters; and, as it is not directly interested in the subject, it would be difficult to create any disposition to inquiry. The mercantile world, how-ever, and the underwriters themselves, have a direct interest in the dissemination of such information, for reasons which it is no pleasant task to state, both on account of their invidious character, and their obvious want of connexion with the general objects of this treatise. But the latter circumstance may, perhaps, not be disadvantageous, since the statement of the exist-ence of an imputation, coming from a quarter in which there is no interest whatever, either in the continuance or discontinuance of any present condition of things, need not excite any disposition, except that of calmly weighing whether it is necessary or not to produce a refutation.

Some years ago, I heard the following opinion stated in a mixed company, in reference to a then proposed attempt to render ships incapable of actually sinking, however much they and their cargo might be damaged; namely, that the mercantile world would not be inclined to patronise an invention which would make the seaman safer than the ship. Some time afterwards, I saw an article in a periodical journal, distinctly written for the purpose of making its readers believe that, in conse-quence of insurance, unsafe ships are allowed to be used, to an extent which has caused much more loss of life and property than could have been experienced if no such institution had existed. Other allusions, more or less direct, in various publications, have convinced me that one of two things must be true, either such an impression has a party who acknowledge it, or authentic information upon the subject is so difficult to be obtained, that the one, two, or ten, who believe it, or profess to believe it, feel that no answer can be made to the assertion.

That there are men in the *carrying* world (if mercantile world be too wide a phrase for the subject) who would, from a pitiful economy, expose the seaman to risks which a little outlay might prevent, is very possible; there are men of such a spirit in every world: that there are others who would consider such conduct as little short of murder, a like analogy would equally justify us in asserting. Which class has predominated can only be absolutely known to the public by results, without which there is but general opinion upon character to aid any individual in forming his conclusion. It is in human nature that the insured should not be so careful as one who stands risk; and it is, unfortunately, the general experience of men acting in bodies, that they are not found to be swayed by the principles which would be acknowledged and acted upon by them severally. Putting these things together, it is not wonderful that, in any case where suspicion might attach to a body of men, there should be quarters in which it does attach. It would not be wonderful, either, if the suspicion were found to be perfectly groundless; but correct feeling would point out the desirableness of forestalling such suspicion, if possible, by the publication of all necessary information. In the present instance, it would be well that the proportion of loss, among insured vessels, should be known; it would not be necessary to state the values of the several vessels, since the simple account of the number insured, and the number on which a claim has been paid, in various years, would be sufficient. The onus of proving that the loss on uninsured vessels, or on vessels which sailed before insurance was known, is or was greater than that on insured vessels, would lie upon those who make the charge. All persons, in the case of any body of men, must hold every thing short of absolute proof against them to count for nothing, when they show themselves ready to communicate those materials out of which a misdemeanor, if there be one, might be substantiated.

The offices for the insurance of fire have not given any account of the proportion of insured houses upon which claims have arisen. Their usual annual charge is, I believe, about one part in a thousand of the sum insured, upon premises of ordinary risk, such as a dwelling-house in London. There are higher rates for more hazardous insurances, constructed, I should imagine, very much from mere estimation of the risk. But the government steps in between the insurer and the insured, and imposes a duty on each policy which nearly trebles the annual payment upon it. This has been called a tax upon prudence, and in like manner the stamp duty might be called a tax upon justice. I am afraid that if nothing commendable suffered under an impost, reformation would thrive more than revenue; and a deficiency of means to pay the interest of the debt would be a heavier tax on prudence, justice, and every thing else, than any minister has yet contemplated. But it may not therefore follow that the particular tax in question is politic, still less that its amount is justifiable. The reason of the tax is plainly this: the moral security offered by the fire office is worth so much more than competition will allow them to ask, that the impost is one which does not fall so heavily as it would do if levied in many other quarters. Nobody can question the truth of this; but, nevertheless, the amount of the tax imposed by the legislature must be owned to be excessive, and likely to act as a prohibition in the case of poor persons occupying small premises.

But there is a mode of overthrowing this tax, or, at least, of bringing the government to terms, to which I can see no impediment, practical or moral. It is the application of the principle of mutual insurance by a number of individuals acting in a private capacity, and not opening a public office. Suppose a thousand individuals, registering their names, to appoint three men of undoubted character to receive contributions of one guinea a year each. If the subscribers be occupiers of dwelling-houses in London, there is no doubt that this sum would be amply sufficient to insure a thousand guineas to each. If three years were to elapse without a fire taking place, the subscription might be suspended, until circumstances should diminish the fund; which, improving in the mean time at interest, would become every year more capable of meeting demands upon it. There would be no need of any legal security, if the trustees were well chosen; and a short agreement would explain the understanding on which the parties contribute. As soon as a few such clubs were formed, the inutility of imposing a tax on one particular way of effecting an object would become apparent.

It would be lucky for the preceding plan, if it were the decided opinion of lawyers that the courts of equity would not entertain any application for inquiry into the state or management of such funds; since, in that case, the law of honour would be sufficient. It has always been found, that whenever the law of the land refuses to protect a proceeding which is fair and equal in itself, a stronger law claims jurisdiction. The parties benefited in the end would be the fire offices, since such a method of resisting this excessive tax would inevitably procure its abolition.

There is another tax which, though not so disproportionate in its amount, is much worse in its principle than that on policies of fire insurance; namely, the tax on policies of life insurance. It must be remembered, that the income of which the savings are invested in this manner, has already undergone a considerable amount of taxation. If any investment of such savings be taxed, all should be treated alike.

The abolition of lotteries happily leaves nothing to be said upon the subject of gambling, encouraged and promoted by the government; and the recent decision of the French legislature, by which the public gaming-houses have been suppressed, must be a source of congratulation, both from the excellence of the measure itself, and the prospect of imitation which it opens, on the part of other continental powers.   But, at the same time, it cannot be denied that, however desirable it may be that no community should give to gambling that appearance of sanction which is implied in regulation, the refusal of the latter is accompanied by evils, of which it is never possible to say positively that they fall short of those which would be produced by sufferance accompanied by restriction.   In this country, there are the means of gambling open to every class of the community, and there can be no doubt that those who avail themselves of them are subject to imposition in a degree which could not be the case if the play were accompanied by publicity.   The classes of rank and wealth have the power of forming themselves into clubs, in which illegal games are played without the possibility of detection, and in such institutions there can be no doubt, with rare and occasional instances of exception, the play is conducted at least with fairness.   But no such thing can be supposed with regard to the numerous receptacles in London and other large towns, and which are believed to exist in different forms, suited to all classes of society.   The difficulty of obtaining legal proof renders conviction next to impossible ; and the occurrences which sometimes take place at the sessions, prove that, even when enough of evidence is obtained to hold parties to bail, the accused can generally find the means of preventing the evidence from being forthcoming to sustain the indictment.   Under such circumstances, gambling in its worst form thrives in defiance of law.   Nevertheless, the good consequences of discouragement are visible throughout the country.   There is no people in the world among whom so little of direct gambling is found.

The infatuation which leads persons to suppose that they can ultimately win from a hank, which has chosen a game in which the chances are against the player, is one which can only be cured, if at all, by a quiet study of the theory of probabilities. Perhaps some of our readers may suppose, that the persons who thus court ruin, do it under the notion that the results given by that theory are dubious, or derived from unpractical speculation, or perhaps absolutely false. So far is this from being the case, that though they undoubtedly fall into error by forming their notions from observation unaided by theory, yet their error frequently consists in representing games of chance as being more unfavourable to themselves than they really are. Though the true premises should lead them to the conclusion that success is next to impossible, they cannot learn the truth even from a mistake which should teach it *à fortiori.* The author of the article " GAMING," in the *Penny Cyclopædia,* states, apparently from his own knowledge, that it is customary to consider the chances of the bank at the game of *rouge-et-noir,* as $7\frac{1}{2}$ per cent. above those of the player. Now, it can be immediately shown, from the first appendix, that when a player puts down a stake, his chances of doubling his stake, of losing it, and of simply recovering it, are as 8903, 9122, and 1975. Now 9122 does not exceed 8903 by $7\frac{1}{2}$ per cent. of 8903, but only by about $2\frac{1}{2}$ per cent. If, however, the preceding assertion meant that the game was considered as a simple one, in which the chances were as $46\frac{1}{4}$ to $53\frac{3}{4}$, the error was very large indeed. So far as this one instance goes, it should seem that the warning against this game, as derived from observation of its results, was yet stronger than that which would have been given by the theory of the game. The same author adds, that he heard it frequently asserted by constant frequenters of the Parisian gaming-houses, that it was absolutely *impossible* for any one to win in the long run.

Still, however, to the hopeless attempt of squaring the circle, or of finding perpetual motion, we have to add that of discovering a method of certainly winning at play: the attempt at which has been the ruin of many a speculator. The gaming banks have discovered the secret, which is simply to embark considerable capital, and to play with chances unequally in their favour. To produce in the young mind a conviction that events will happen, in the long run, in a fixed, and not in what is called a fortuitous manner, should be an object of education, in order to produce that soundness of views on the results of gambling which is a sure protection against the temptation. By trying experiments upon what are called chance events, such as might easily be done with a pack of cards, or a few dice, it might easily be made to appear that no large number of events will present any marked deviations from the general average which the knowledge of this theory points out before-hand. Persons aware of the truth of the law just stated, may often be able to apply it advantageously. I received the following anecdote from a distinguished naval officer, who was once employed to bring home a cargo of dollars. At the end of the voyage it was discovered that one of the boxes which contained them had been forced ; and on making further search, a large bag of dollars was discovered in the possession of some one on board. The coins in the different boxes were a mixture of all manner of dates and sovereigns ; and it occurred to the commander, that if the contents of the boxes were sorted, a comparison of the proportions of the different sorts in the bag with those in the box which had been opened, would be strong presumptive evidence one way or the other. This comparison was accordingly made, and the agreement between the distribution of the several coins in the bag and those in the box, was such as to leave no doubt as to the former having formed a part of the latter.

THE

QUARTERLY REVIEW.

ART. I.—*An Essay on Probabilities, and on their Application to Life Contingencies and Insurance Offices.* By Augustus de Morgan, of Trinity College, Cambridge. London, 12mo. 1838.

MR. DE MORGAN—known favourably in the scientific world as Professor of Mathematics in University College, London, and Secretary of the Royal Astronomical Society—is, we believe, connected as Actuary, or otherwise, with one of those numerous Insurance-offices, of which he treats generally in the volume before us. It is chiefly employed, however, in elucidating the doctrine of what mortal men call *Chances*—a subject of great intricacy, which, towards the latter end of the seventeenth century, first engaged the attention of Huygens, Pascal, Bernouilli, and some others; and which was shortly afterwards taken up by De Moivre—several of whose brilliant results, as Mr. de Morgan observes, were left to us without the knowledge of the steps which led to them, and the *tables of mortality* constructed by whom were for a long time almost exclusively adopted. Our Professor treats at some length of the nature of Direct and Inverse Probabilities, of various Tables and their use, adaptation of Probabilities to Life Contingencies, Annuities, value of Reversions, &c., giving the solution of numerous problems, rules, and examples to elucidate their application. He also undertakes to expound the chances of dice-throwing and card-playing; but we have no desire to meddle with this part of his subject, even though the tendency of the study should be ' to convert games of chance into something more resembling games of skill,' being persuaded that skill among gamblers is a dangerous weapon. Of the Professor's thirteen chapters, three only are appropriated to Life Insurance, and the practice and management of Insurance-offices: from these we shall occasionally quote, and to them alone confine the few observations we have to offer on this clever but unequal volume.

Mr. de Morgan is friendly, as every humane person must be, to these institutions, through the means of which a certain provision can be made, on moderate terms, for the fatherless and widows; but he goes beyond this, and appears to think that the *theory* of Insurance and Annuities might be greatly extended, even ‘to an agreement of a community to consider the goods of its individual members as common.’ Such projects have been put forth from time to time, but hitherto they have been generally considered as the visionary product of fantastic heads. He shall, however, speak for himself :—

‘The theory of insurance, with its kindred science of annuities, deserves the attention of the academical bodies. Stripped of its technical terms and its commercial associations, it may be presented in a point of view which will give it strong moral claims to notice. Though based upon self-interest, yet it is the most enlightened and benevolent form which the projects of self-interest ever took. It is, in fact, in a limited sense, and a practicable method, the agreement of a community to consider the goods of its individual members as common. It is an agreement that those whose fortune it shall be to have more than average success shall resign the overplus in favour of those who have less. And though, as yet, it has only been applied to the reparation of the evils arising from storm, fire, premature death, disease, and old age, yet there is no placing a limit to the extensions which its application might receive, if the public were fully aware of its principles, and of the safety with which they may be put in practice.’—*Preface,* p. xv.

Not a few sensible people are of opinion that, as regards ‘the reparation of evils,’ such as cases of fire and premature death, both the theory and the practice of insurance have already been carried quite far enough. We confess we are inclined to be of this way of thinking, and can only hope that the many knots of projectors who have been so ready, of late years, to exhibit in this ‘most enlightened and benevolent form which the projects of self-interest ever took,’ may be able to hold their ground. Professor de Morgan, however, appears to entertain a more favourable opinion than we are disposed to adopt. He says,—

‘The expenses of carrying on an assurance office, though they vary somewhat with the amount of business, yet do not by any means increase as fast. In the first year of its existence it would not be surprising if all the premiums paid were swallowed up by house-rent, salaries, &c.; while, in process of time, increase of business might reduce such expenditure to 2 per cent. upon the yearly premiums. Some capital, therefore, is necessary at the commencement; for, if there be none, those who first insure their lives are entirely dependent upon the future success of the office. But this capital need not be large: in the present state of things, an engaged capital of one hundred thousand pounds is certainly above the mark, even for an office which is entirely without connexion, and starts without one single life insured. If, as very often happens, a tolerably large number of customers has been obtained before the prospectus of the office is announced, then a capital, the interest of which will cover the expenses of management, is sufficient.

But here it must be observed that the proprietors of this capital run some risk of losing a portion of their principal, and a still greater one of losing the interest for a limited time. This risk is the greater the smaller the original subscription, and it must be paid for accordingly. At the same time it must be remembered that the mere existence of the capital diminishes the risk, by making it the interest of every proprietor to procure business for the office. The connexion thus created is the secret of the successful start which has frequently been made; and it may be considered as very unlikely that an office will fail, from want of business, which is so well supported in the first instance as is implied when a capital of the preceding amount is announced.'—p. 264.

An *engaged* capital of one hundred thousand pounds sounds well; but if such ever existed, and 5 per cent. be allowed to those who subscribe it, it contributes only to its own destruction, and to swell the debt of the incipient undertaking;—but we shall enter a little more into detail concerning the nature and progress of these institutions. The subject is not new to us. Twelve years ago (Quarterly Rev. No. 69), we took a comprehensive view of the several Life Assurance Offices then existing: pointing out the great benefits they had conferred on families of almost every class, especially of those who had only a life-interest in their incomes—but, at the same time, not concealing their defects, nor passing over certain abuses to which they are liable. The insurance companies which we then referred to amounted to thirty-two, but we believe not less than forty were in being at the time. They have since, however, increased to a most extraordinary extent; and that, we believe, with very doubtful advantage, either to themselves or the community. ‘In 1806,’—thus advertises in 1839 the secretary of the Provident Life Office,—‘there were only *eight* life offices in London, including the Provident. Since then their number has increased to nearly *one hundred*: of these, about *thirty* have broken up, and *seventy-two* is their number in the London Directory for the present year.’

We have no wish to inquire into the secret histories of these *thirty up-breaks*, few of which could have occurred without serious loss and inconvenience to others besides the shareholders. Before many of them started there were offices enough, well established, and quite adequate to supply the wants of the public; and in the race against these old favourites some may have found it impossible to get on, even though the managers might be honest and able men, who neither applied funds improperly, nor entered into indiscreet engagements. At all events no warning has been taken by their downfall. Even since this year began we suspect a new office has figured for every month that has elapsed. The start, in fact, is easy. A busy, bustling attorney, with some half-dozen or a dozen others, who call themselves directors, with a secretary or actuary, and a medical gentleman, draw up a prospectus in which higher benefits, and lower terms, are held out than in any previously existing office, and every possible accommodation offered to all such as may be induced to deal with this tempting novelty. Very little money is required to set the machine a-going. A nominal capital of 500,000*l*. or 1,000,000*l*. (seldom less than the former) heads the prospectus : but the only present demand, on a subscription share, is some 2*l*., 3*l*., or 5*l*. ; and, to induce friends and others to *take shares*, an immediate interest of 4*l*. or 5*l*. per cent. is promised on the subscribed capital, though the said capital itself, invested in government securities, can be producing little more than 3 per cent. Here, then, amidst so many flattering superficialities, is at once a direct and continuous reduction of the subscribed capital. Then the directors, the secretary, and actuary, the doctor, and a clerk or two, must be paid salaries ; a house must be hired and fitted up ; and every one must know that no trifling quantity of this kind of business, of slow growth in new, and gradual even in old offices, will be found sufficient for meeting all these contingencies and permanent expenses. Moreover, the old offices are, or at least profess to be, careful to take only such applicants as are in a sound state of health ; but many of the new ones do not hesitate to invite, openly, persons of a far different description. ' I should be very sorry,' says the late actuary of the *Equitable*, ' to see this society descend to the quackery of pretending to determine how many years should be added to the age of a person, according as he is afflicted with asthma, dropsy, palsy, &c., in order to fix the premium at which his life is to be insured.' It is at least obvious that to conduct an office on the principle which this gentleman pronounces 'quackery,' must require very great additional delicacy of calculation, and occasion, therefore, a large increase in the expence of management.

It has been not an uncommon practice (adopted by some that do not require it) to blazon at the head of their advertisements long lists of noble patrons, honorary presidents, and trustees— (lords, dukes, princes of the blood—even the Queen has not escaped)—patrons who can afford them no patronage—trustees who have no trust—presidents who never preside—in short an array of grand names that are mere decoy-ducks. One of the newest offices, we perceive, has no less than four English and four Scotch peers for its *supporters !* The author just quoted, in repudiating practices which were adopted by the Equitable at its first establishment, and afterwards abandoned—such as raising their 25th policy at once to No. 275—says,

'Another expedient, equally dishonourable, was adopted for the like purpose of adding to the importance of the Society, by holding forth, with their permission, the names of Lord Willoughby de Parham and others as Directors, who had not the least interest or concern in its affairs ; and at the end of two years, when, it is probable, deceit was deemed no longer necessary, thanks were absolutely voted to Lord Willoughby *for the use of his name in sustaining the reputation of the Society. . . . .* No aid derived from a corrupt source can be regarded as honourable, nor is it easy to say which are the most reprehensible—the gentlemen that lend their names, or the Society that makes use of them, for the purpose of misleading the public.'—*Rise and Progress of the Equitable Society.*

If the noble personages now alluded to have, out of pure, but mistaken, good nature, been prevailed on to lend the use of their names, we agree with this writer in condemning the practice as a source of corruption : if they have *taken shares* in the several concerns, they are no doubt aware that they are responsible, not merely for the amount actually subscribed, but for their full share of the nominal advertised capital ; and it is by no means legally certain that, without holding shares, the lending of their names does not incur the same degree of responsibility. If there be any among them who have not sanctioned the use of their names, we would recommend them to follow the recent example of the Duke of Wellington.

Some eight or nine months ago there appeared in the newspapers the report of the case brought before the Insolvent Debtors' Court of a clerk to a company called 'The London Equitable,' who stated that he had come from the country in consequence of an advertisement in the papers.   On repairing to the office, he said, he was told that on depositing 100*l.* he should forthwith have the appointment of Secretary, and speedily be promoted to the rank of Director.   He soon discovered, however, that all the names in the list of Directors, with the exception of two, were fictitious,— not merely men of straw, but a collection of assumed names, whose owners had no existence.   He stated that the capital of this Company was advertised to be 500,000*l.*, in 50,000 shares of 10*l.* each, and that a deposit of 2*l.* a share was required to be paid down.   The Duke of Wellington was the declared *patron,* the Bank of England were the *cashiers,* and a long array of imposing names graced the prospectus.   The Duke, however, as usual, 'hit the nail on the head'—he applied at once to a police magistrate, requesting that an inquiry might be made into the nature of the affair.   The result was, that this bubble Company immediately exploded—the poor Secretary lost his

100*l.* and got into debt—and the two worthies who projected
the fraud were discovered to have disappeared with whatever
other moneys might have been advanced by their dupes. This
we are afraid is by no means a solitary case, for John Bull, with
all his mother-wit, has at all times been the ready dupe of adventurers, projectors, and speculators. It is matter of history
that, about the period of the South Sea concern, more than 200
visionary projects for accumulating wealth were formed, all of
which shared the fate of the grand bubble, burst, and 'dissolved
into thin air.'*

Many of the new Insurance Companies, in order to attract
customers, have reduced the rates of their premiums below what
the probabilities of human life, deduced from long and varied
experience and observation, will warrant. There is one office in
King-William Street, ' The Standard of England,' which advertises
' *lower* rates of premium than those of any other office : *hence*' (says
the advertisement) ' an immediate and certain bonus is given to
the assured, instead of the remote and contingent advantage offered
by *some* Companies, of a participation in their profits.' We
demur to this '*hence*'—and maintain that ' lower rates' are incompatible with ' an immediate and certain bonus.' This office, in
fact, has been little more than two years in existence, so that its
' lower rates ' could at best be considered only in the light of an
experiment ;—but its rates do *not* appear to be ' *lower* than those
of any other office.' The *Independent and West Middlesex Assurance Company*, of the same standing with the former, advertise
terms still lower ! Thus :—

	Age 30			40			50		
Standard	1	19	7	2	13	3	3	18	8
West Middlesex . .	1	15	0	2	10	0	3	5	0

We should say that, without extraordinary good management,
an extensive and healthy body of the assured, and the exercise of
most rigid economy, these rates of premium, in both cases, are too
low to be safe. But the latter office offers so extraordinary a
display of private liberality for ' immediate public benefits,' that
we are tempted to place on our page its oft-repeated and almost
daily notice in the newspapers, precisely in its own shape, words,
and figures.

* Of all the schemes of that era *four* only have survived, and these still exist in
full vigour, because founded on good sense and honest principles—the Royal
Exchange Assurance Company, the London Assurance Company, the York Build-
ings Company, and the English Copper Company.

' IMMEDIATE BENEFITS OFFERED TO THE PUBLIC.

L IFE ANNUITY RATES, calculated on Equitable
Principles ! ! !

POR RXAMPLE.

For every 100*l.* deposited, this Association will grant the Annuity placed opposite
the Age of the party depositing.—From 50*l.* and upwards, in proportion.

Age. 30 to 40	to 45	to 50	to 55	to 60	to 65	to 70	to 75	to 80
£. s. d.	£. s. d.	£. s. d.	£. s. d.	£. s. d.	£. s. d.	£. s. d.	£. s. d.	£. s. d
8 0 0	8 10 0	9 0 0	9 10 0	10 10 0	12 10 0	15 10 0	20 0 0	25 0 0
Pr.Ct.	Pr.Ct.	Pr.Ct.	Pr.Ct.	Pr. Ct.	Pr. Ct.	Pr. Ct.	Pr.Ct.	Pr.Ct.

LIFE AND FIRE INSURANCE RATES

Reduced 30 per Cent. per Annum.

LIFE ASSURANCE RATES.

Age 20 to 25	to 30	to 35	35	38	to 45	to 50
£. s. d.	£. s. d.	£. s. d.	£. s. d.	£. s. d.	£. s. d.	£. s. d.
Premium.. 1 11 0	1 15 0	2 0 0	2 6 0	2 10 0	2 15 0	3 5 0

This Company make no Charges for intermediate Ages under 50 Years.

FIRE INSURANCE RATES.

Common Insurance.

		s.	d.	
Private Houses and Shops (not hazardous)	. . .	1	0	per Cent.
Hazardous		2	0	
Double Hazardous		3	6	
Farming Stock		1	6	

INDEPENDENT AND WEST MIDDLESEX ASSURANCE COMPANY,

Opposite the Bazaar, Baker-street, Portman-square, London ; St. David's-street,
Edinburgh ; Ingram-street, Glasgow ; and Sackville-street, Dublin.

Established and empowered under the several Acts of Parliament of 14th Geo.
3rd, c. 48 ;—22nd Geo. 3rd,—53rd Geo. 3rd, c. 141, and 3rd Geo. 4, c. 92 ;
1st Vic. c. 10.

Capital, ONE MILLION.

(By order of the Board.)

Resident Secretary, Mr. WILLIAM HOLE.

Bankers—{ The Bank of England.
Bank of Ireland.
Western Bank of Scotland.'

Bravo! we know nothing equal to this. Take just one example, from the terms of this advertisement, to give an idea of
the liberality of the ' Independent and West Middlesex.' A
person from thirty to forty years of age, say thirty-four, deposits 100*l.*, for which he is to receive an annuity of 8*l.* per
annum. He insures his life for 100*l.* at a premium of 2*l.* per
cent. per annum, and receives therefore a clear annuity of 6*l.*
per cent. in money. Allow the office to make 4*l.* interest on
the 100*l.* deposited, (which is more than any of the government
securities will give,) and consequently the company, by paying
8*l.* and receiving 6*l.*, makes an annual sacrifice of 2*l.* per cent.

during the life of the annuitant, without the possibility, as appears to us, of redeeming the loss, for on his death the 100*l.* deposited must be repaid to the representatives, being the sum assured. What mystery there may be in this transaction it is impossible for us to unriddle. But we may observe that the liberal annuity tables of government, for the age of thirty-four, when the price of consols is 93, give an annuity for 100*l. stock* of 5*l.* 3*s.* 7*d.*, or, which is the same thing, for 100*l.* sterling, 5*l.* 11*s.* 4*d.*, making thus, by this office, a further ' sacrifice to public benefit' of 2*l.* 8*s.* 3*d.* per cent. Can this deceive any one with comprehension beyond that of an idiot ? Can any one be simple enough to imagine that James Drummond and James Alexander, of Charing Cross and Carlton House Gardens, (names which figure in the list of its Directors,) are to be found in Baker Street, opposite the Bazaar ?

This Independent Company, established opposite the Bazaar in Baker Street, affords almost a solitary instance of an office of this kind being removed to a great distance from any other ; for it is a curious feature, in the localities of these institutions, to find the new offices always endeavouring to cluster round the old ones. Thus, in New Bridge Street and Chatham Place, we find no less than fifteen brisk rivals elbowing the ancient fixtures of the Rock and the Equitable. In the new street in the City, bearing the name of King William, new Insurance Companies have sprung up like mushrooms, some of them perhaps not much better rooted than this species of fungus. It has been said that this noble street, with its splendid-*fronted* houses, consists chiefly of gin-palaces and insurance offices, twelve or thirteen of the latter squeezing round the two old-established companies, the London Life and Edinburgh. Again, in Waterloo Place and Regent Street, we find six or seven close to the Asylum and Palladium.

There is a reason for this: the new ones, as we have observed, being comparatively unscrupulous in their reception of subjects, and outbidding each other in the diminution of premiums, follow up their scheme by being ready on the spot to entertain the applications of those *rejected* by the senior establishments. A person applies at some old office for an insurance on his life ; the doctor finds him plethoric, asthmatic, consumptive, or dropsical ; he tells him his life is not considered to be insurable : the disappointed stranger (or his agent) asks what he is to do, it being of the greatest importance he should effect an assurance. The answer probably is, ' Knock at the next door, where they are not quite so nice as we are.' Another finds the premium of the old office too high, and is unwilling to give it : he is recommended to the next door but one. The only chances, in fact, that most of the new offices have for obtaining business, lie in outbidding one another in the reduction of the premiums, and in receiving persons with bodily infirmities, or such as may be going to unhealthy climates; but they depend mostly on the reduction of the premiums. Now we contend that it is a fallacy to suppose that the reduction of a few shillings per cent. in the premium can be of any advantage to the insured, more especially where there is a participation of profits, while it operates as a serious drawback on the profits of the office, and consequently of the insured also. The higher the premium, and the stricter the caution in taking none but good lives, the larger will be the profits to be divided. It was by these means that the Equitable was enabled to amass its eleven or twelve millions; and to divide such an enormous share of profits among the insured. The Northampton Tables were generally its guide, and those insuring were not only required to produce testimonials of sound health, but in most cases to appear personally before a board of directors; and the consequence was, as the late Actuary tells us, that from the Equitable experience it was found that, where *three* persons were expected to die, *two* only actually died.

Mr. de Morgan observes that, with a merchant or a banker, the liability to a demand and the demand itself come so nearly upon one another, that real insolvency and bankruptcy are seldom far asunder.

'When credit cannot be sustained by monthly, and even daily, proofs of substance, it takes its departure altogether: but it is not necessarily so with an insurance office, of whose existence it is the essence to be always receiving consideration for bills which, one with another, have a long time to run. Such an establishment may be in reality *insolvent* many years before the symptoms of *bankruptcy* come on. As no large concern of the kind has hitherto failed, it is difficult to say how they would finally come on: but this much is certain, that an insurance office which could really pay only ten shillings in the pound might, by introducing a better system, or by mere force of circumstances, not only recover its ground, but ultimately become exceedingly profitable. But I throw this part of the argument (though it shows a strong principle of vitality inherent in the constitution of such offices) out of the question: for, surely, no sane and honest person would trifle with important matters so far as to assert that the possibility of temporary insolvency, to be redeemed by the chapter of accidents or prudence, when it was wanted, should enter into the deliberate calculations on which men should be invited to stake the subsistence of their children.'—p. 252.

We entirely agree with Mr. de Morgan that no sane or honest person would trifle with such matters as this—but we must dissent from his opinion as to the easy recovery of an office that could only pay ten shillings in the pound.

Taking into consideration the vast importance of the subject to thousands and tens of thousands of families, no man could, perhaps, serve society more essentially than by affording the public at large some distinct *data* for making a prudential choice among so many rival Insurance Offices: but the attempt would be extremely invidious; and we are sensible, moreover, that *we* could not, if we would, do the thing completely and satisfactorily. Perhaps the safest general rule is, to look well at the list of directors. If these are men of known integrity, of aptitude for business, moving in some public sphere, and of substantial property, one may feel himself on pretty safe ground: such men are not likely to lend their names to any visionary undertaking, nor to require any ostentatious array of noble lords, honourables, or right honourables, to bolster up the institution which they direct. We may be permitted, however, to classify the several offices into their septennial periods of existence, as affording some aid towards the guidance of persons intending to assure their lives. The letter *x* precedes the Mutual Assurance Companies, *y* the Proprietary Assurance Companies, and *z* the mixed Mutual and Proprietary.

z	Argus, established in .	1834
z	Britannia	1837
y	British Colonial . .	1838
y	Family Endowment .	1835
y	Freemasons and General	1838
x	Hand-in-Hand . . .	1836
y	Independent . . .	1836
y	Legal and General . .	1836
x	Metropolitan . . .	1835
y	Minerva	1836
x	Mutual Life . . .	1834
z	National Endowment .	1838
y	National Loan Fund, &c.	1837
y	Protector	1836
z	Standard of England .	1836
y	United Kingdom . .	1834
y	Universal	1834
y	Victoria	1838
z	Westminster and General	1837
y	York and London . .	1834

First period.
From one year to seven.
Experimental.
Of the twenty offices included in this class, it will be seen there are three under two years old, four under one, and six not three years in existence.

Second Period.
From seven years to fourteen.
Probationary.
It may be remarked, that while twenty new offices were created in the last five years, these four offices only sprung up in the nine years preceding.

y	Crown	1825
y	National	1830
z	Promoter	1826
y	University	1825

Third Period. From fourteen years to twenty-one. Generally in *a salutary state.*	*z* Alliance	1824
	z Asylum	1824
	y British Commercial .	1820
	y Clerical, Medical, &c. .	1824
	y Economic	1823
	z Edinburgh	1823
	y European	1819
	y Guardian	1821
	y Imperial	1820
	y Law Life	1823
	y Palladium	1824
	y Scottish Union . . .	1824
Fourth Period. From twenty-one years and up- wards. *General stability.*	*z* Albion	1805
	x Amicable	1706
	y Atlas	1808
	y Caledonian	1805
	y Eagle	1807
	x Equitable	1762
	z Globe	1803
	y Hope	1807
	x London Life Association	1806
	y Licensed Victuallers .	1721
	z London	1721
	y North British . . .	1809
	z Pelican	1797
	y Provident	1806
	z Rock	1806
	z Royal Exchange . .	1720
	x Scottish Widows' Fund	1815
	y Union	1714
	y West of England . .	1807
	y Westminster Society .	1792

These lists are deficient by some fifteen or sixteen, (the new ones of this year not included,) but the information they afford may be found useful in the way of caution. At the same time, we desire to be understood as not doubting that, in the first list, consisting of twenty offices, in which the oldest has been only five years in existence, there may be some so well conducted,—under respectable managers of known integrity and character,—as to invite a constant stream of business, notwithstanding their minority; while there may also be some few in the older classes, not of that high public estimation as to induce those who have looked narrowly into the nature and conduct of Assurance Companies to intrust them with their own interests, or recommend them to their friends.

If the question were to be decided by numbers—(the second class *y*, containing thirty-five companies out of the fifty-six named; the third class containing fourteen companies; and the first class only seven)—the choice would undoubtedly fall on the Proprietary Companies. The distinction of Mutual and Proprietary seems intended to combine the other two, but, we suspect, under no fixed limits or regulations. The Rock is a Proprietary Office, and differs only, as we believe, in one respect from the others, and that is, that none but the assured can hold shares. What the London and Westminster Mutual Life Assurance Society may mean by the following statement, we pretend not to comprehend:—it says that the principle upon which it is founded is mutual, and that ' A mutual assurance *draws a distinct and broad line* between it and *all proprietary companies ;*' but in the very next line we are told, ' This society not only embodies *all the new features* of modern proprietary companies, but also preserves the characteristics of Mutual Assurance Societies.' This is rather puzzling, and we leave it to others to unravel ; but Mr. de Morgan's brief account of the first two (x and y) is clear enough.

' The former have no capital, except what arises from their own accumulations, and each member is a guarantee to the rest for the fulfilment of all engagements. If the office possess a charter, this guarantee operates no further than to pledge the premiums already paid by any member for the discharge of all claims which arise before his own, since a corporation is considered in law as an individual. If, on the other hand, there be no charter, the whole fortune of every member is pledged for the discharge of all claims. The risk, however, at the commencement is not great in character, and small in amount; and the quantity of risk diminishes so much faster than the amount increases, that it may safely be said there is nothing in the commercial world which approaches, even remotely, to the security of a well-established and prudently-managed insurance office.

' A proprietary insurance office has a capital, the proprietors of which may or may not be insured in the office, and for which a bonus is paid in addition to the market rate of interest. It would perhaps be difficult, at the present time, to establish a new proprietary office with a very large capital. The public now begins to see that much capital is not necessary, and that nearly all the bonus which is paid for its use is so much taken away from the savings of the insured, without any adequate benefit received in return. One by one, the proprietary offices must (as some have done) admit the insured to a share in the profits,—the necessity for which will be taught by the decline of business, if not previously learnt.'—pp. 272, 273.

The leaning of Mr. de Morgan, though he does not say so in express terms, is evidently in favour of Proprietary Companies, as requiring less caution than the Mutual—and this, notwithstanding the successful practice of the Equitable Society. ' I always,' he says, ' consider that society as a distinct and anomalous establishment, existing at this moment under circumstances of an unique character. It is the result of an experiment which it was most important to try; but which, having been tried, need not be repeated. Its present state is, in fact, the result of a *monopoly* which never can be repeated. When it was established, in 1762, the *Amicable*, which had existed from the beginning of the century, was the only society formed for the purpose of making assurances on lives; and in speaking of *that*, a writer already quoted observes, ' Nothing could exceed the injustice and improvidence of a plan which made no distinction between the old and the young in its premiums, and, by the annual division of its surplus, kept the society in a state of perpetual infancy.'

Our present author, among other remarks on the fashionable puffs, says :—

'Of one thing I am certain, that the magnificent style in which the prospectuses frequently indulge might often remind their readers of the unparalleled benefits which are promised by another description of traders, who vie with each other in describing the rare qualities of their several *blackings*. If there be in this country a person whose ambition it is *to walk in the brightest boots to the cheapest insurance office*, he has my pity : for, grant that he is ever able to settle where to send his servant, and it remains as difficult a question to what quarter he shall turn his own steps. The matter would be of no great consequence if persons desiring to insure could be told at once to throw aside every prospectus which contains a puff : unfortunately this cannot be done, as there are offices which may be in many circumstances the most eligible, and which adopt this method of advertising their claims. If these pompous announcements be intended to profess that every subscriber shall receive more than he pays, their falsehood is as obvious as their meaning : if not, their meaning is altogether concealed.

' Public ignorance of the principles of insurance is the thing to which these advertisements appeal : when it shall come to be clearly understood that *in every office some must pay more than they receive, in order that others may receive more than they pay*, such attempts to persuade the public of a certainty of universal profit will entirely cease.'— Preface, pp. xv., xvi.

When a person is making up his mind as to the choice of an office, it is very natural that his election should be likely to fall on that which offers the most reasonable terms—that is to say, where the amount of premium to be paid for a hundred pounds is less than in others : but this difference in the premium is not the only thing to be regarded. The difference of a few shillings per cent., more especially in a proprietary and participating establishment, is, we repeat, of little importance, provided they keep within the limits of those tables which have been constructed on the law of mortality, as deduced from the most approved statistical information, collected and registered from details of numerous large and distinet masses of the population of this and other countries. As Mr. de Morgan observes—

'There may be danger in the assumption of any table formed from experience; and this ought to operate powerfully as a caution against lightly admitting a change of premiums, on the authority of any small number of facts. But more particularly should this be attended to in the formation of new varieties of contingency offices, the chances of which have not yet stood the test of experience.'—p. 242.

The Professor treats in some detail of the valuation and distribution of the profits arising from insurances; and under this part of the subject, the matter being differently arranged in different offices, the following considerations, he says, might be addressed to any person who intends to assure his life :—

'You are aware that the premium demanded of you is, avowedly, more than has hitherto been found sufficient for the purpose, the reason being, that it is impossible to settle the exact amount, on account of our not knowing whether the future and the past will coincide in giving the same law of mortality, and the same interest of money. The surplus arising from this overcharge, for the future existence of which it is hundreds to one, is now at your own disposal, and you must choose between one office and another, according to your intentions with regard to its ultimate destination. Firstly, if you doubt the general security of the plan of insurance, and are desirous of an absolute guarantee, independently of accumulations from premiums, there are offices which will, in consideration of the surplus aforesaid, pledge their proprietary capitals for the satisfaction of your ultimate demand upon them. Secondly, if, being of the opinion aforesaid, you think the whole surplus too much to pay for the guarantee, there are proprietary offices which retain a part of the profit in consideration of the risk of their capital, and return the remainder. Thirdly, if you wish the surplus premium, as fast as it is proved to be such, to be applied in obviating the necessity of any further overcharges, there are offices which divide the profits during the life of the insured, by means of a reduction of premium. Foorthly, if you wish the surplus to accumulate, and, feeling confidence in your own life, are willing to risk losing it (the *surplus*, remember) entirely if you die young, on condition of having it proportionally increased if you live to be old, there are offices which divide all or most of the profits among old members. Fifthly, if you would prefer a certainty of profit, die when you may, there are offices which at once admit new members who die early to a full participation in all advantages. The choice between these several modes must be made by yourself, according to your own inclinations, views of fairness, or particular circumstances.'—pp. 282, 283.

The great importance of choosing an office which allows a participation of profits, is exemplified by a Report put forth by the 'Rock,' in which it is stated that 'In the case of a royal personage, lately deceased, whose life was largely assured for the benefit of his family, the Directors found, by a document in their possession, that, out of eleven offices granting him policies, all at the same time, and at a rate of premium varying from 4*l*. 4*s*. 2*d*. to 5*l*. 0*s*. 2*d*. per cent. (that of the Rock being 4*l*. 8*s*. 2*d*.), only *five* made any return of premium or additional bonus; and that, of these five, the Rock paid more bonus than either of the other four, in the proportion of 55*l*. 6*s*. to 88*l*. 17*s*. 9*d*., to 55*l*. 12*s*. to 32*l*. 2*s*., and to 19*l*. 4*s*. 8*d*., on and over every one hundred pounds assured in each respectively.'

Most of the offices, except those on the strict mutual principle, have three modes of distributing profits to the assured, who is generally allowed to make his choice among them. The first is that of fixed periodical additions to policies or sums assured : the second, periodical diminution of premiums—deferred payment of premiums, or payment of them for a fixed number of years—for all of which an equitable rate is professed to be calculated : the third is the addition to policies at deaths, according to the state of profits at the time, without reference to any particular periods of distribution. In the first of these, which is the most common, there is a great difference in different offices. Some make no distinction, in the sums to be appropriated, between the young and old assured; and some allow no portion to those who commence their assurance beyond a certain age. Some, perhaps the greater part of the proprietary offices, divide septennially; others quinquennially, and a few, but very few, annually,—to commence after the payment of a certain number of premiums. This last may perhaps be considered as the most equitable mode, enabling the survivors, in most cases, to receive a share of the profits proportioned to the sums they have paid in premiums; but it is the least of all favourable to the increase of the assets of the office,—a very considerable portion of their capitals arising from profits derived from the length of time between the periodical divisions. The Equitable, the only one that has adopted the decennial rule, has enriched itself chiefly by its long periodical division.

To illustrate this, let us suppose the assured to die just before he has completed the period of ten years : his representatives receive no part of the profits which have accrued in that time; nay, we are told, as to some offices, that if the 31st December, for instance, should be the termination of the *period*, and if the assured should die before *midnight* of that day, though he had paid all the premiums required within the period, his executor would be considered as entitled only to the bare sum assured, and not to any share of the profits. If this be so, such a practice, we hesitate not to say, is unjust, and we have no doubt that, upon trial, it would be pronounced illegal. If the last premium of the period be paid up—it matters not in what month, week, or day the assured dies—the executor ought to receive the fair share of the profits. A respectable office would not attempt to take an advantage of this kind. It is enough that all the profits are withheld from those who die before the payment of the stipulated number of premiums. The longer the interval of the periods of division, the greater will be the probable number that may be expected to die without participation, and,' consequently; the larger the profits of the office and of those who survive.* Another source of profit to the offices arises from lapsed policies, the premiums paid upon them being so much pure gain. Formerly they were much more numerous than at present. The competition among offices, each trying to beat the other down, has taught those who assure, that a policy even of a very few years' standing is worth something, and most of the offices do not decline giving something for it (though considerably less than the amount of the premiums paid). If more should be demanded on the score of the office having incurred no loss by the risk, and having enjoyed the accumulated interest, Mr. de Morgan furnishes the answer which the office might give : · The risk which turned out favourably in your case did not produce the same result in another—and it is the very essence of an insurance office, that those who live pay for those who die ;' but he should have added—and those who die before the completion of a period pay to those who outlive it.

There is, however, we really believe, a great degree of liberality shown by the established offices to the assured or their representatives, whenever a case deserving benevolent consideration occurs; and it must be owned they have good reason to be cautious in this department of their procedure. We understand that instances of gross deception are not uncommon, such as the substitution of a healthy subject for examination by the medical officer in the place of one that would be rejected, concealment of disease, forged certificates of age to lower the rate of premium, &c. When a creditor proposes an insurance on the life of his debtor, it is particularly necessary to be satisfied of the identity of the latter, as this step is rarely had recourse to be-

---

* The general use, by insurance offices, of the word 'profits' is an abuse of the term, they being wholly contingent and remote. It cannot for a moment be questioned that; instead of 'profit,' the insurance office must sustain a loss by every insurer who dies before the amount paid by him in premiums, with the accumulated interest, shall be equivalent to the amount of his policy—say from 15 to 35 annual premiums, according to the age of the insured—yet, in most of these offices, the representatives share in the *profits*, should the insured die immediately after seven payments. The equitable rule would be, to assign the *bonus* to such only as had survived the expectation of life, according to the generally received law of mortality ; or who had paid in premiums, with interest upon them, a sum equal to that for which the life was insured.

fore an apprehension is entertained of approaching death. Such and many other deceptions are practised against insurance offices; and, although the strongest evidence may have been produced in a court of justice to prove the fraud, the office, whether as plaintiff or defendant, has almost always failed, by the leaning of the jury to the weak, and against the strong: the one party is poor, the other is rich—the one is an individual, the other a company—and the verdict is too often given in direct contradiction to the summing up of the judge. It is quite fair that when there is a doubt the individual should have the benefit; but jurors should remember that they are SWORN to apply all their faculties in arriving at the just decision.

By the act of 14 Geo. III. chap. 38, levelled at *gambling*, the insurance offices were meant to be protected against one very important risk of fraud. It enacts that no insurance on life shall be valid unless the party insuring has a plain legitimate interest in the party whose name is inserted in the policy. By the laws of France and most of the continental states, all insurances of this class are absolutely forbidden, not for the prevention of gambling, (which is rather encouraged,) but in order to guard society against the risk of the persons assuring contriving the death of the assured. Now we are sorry to say that this is supposed to have happened in a few instances in our own country, and the tendency to it ought to be more strictly prohibited by law. In short, a decisive blow should be struck at the practice of assigning policies to, or purchasing them in the market by, those who are strangers to the parties whose names the policies bear, and who can have no other interest in them than the desire that such policies should speedily become claims —whose interest lies in the death, not in the life of the *assured*.

A very odd case was tried recently before Lord Abinger. Two young women, the daughters of a deceased officer, with no other property whatsoever but pensions of 10*l.* a-year from the Ordnance, lived a few miles out of town with a person who had married, we believe, their sister-in-law, also in very reduced circumstances. However, they all came to London as the winter was setting in, took lodgings, and the elder girl, having just attained her twenty-first year, was sent sometimes alone, sometimes with her married sister, to no less than eight or ten offices, to effect an insurance at each on her own life. Being extremely handsome, and in the full bloom and vigour of health, she was admired and courteously received at the several establishments; and, strange as it may appear, though she could assign no other reason for wishing to assure her life, than that she was told it was right to do so, she actually succeeded, with five of the offices, in effecting policies in her own name, some for two, others for three years, for no less a sum in all than 16,000*l.*! This was about the end of November, 1830. One evening in December the whole party went together to the theatre—they took some oysters and other refreshments on their return—this young and beautiful person went to bed—from which she never arose, but to be placed in her coffin. A *post-mortem* examination took place; a great effusion was found on the brain, caused by extraordinary violence of vomiting, the consequence, it was stated, of some powders given by her sister-in-law. The husband, as *trustee*, lost no time in applying for the amount of two of the policies that had been assigned to him, but the offices very properly refused payment: they ought to have refused the insurance. He takes the alarm and goes with his family to France, and some years afterwards brings his action through an agent, not venturing, it would seem, to appear himself; and *for once* the insurance office got a verdict in its favour!

The Act of 14 Geo. III. is in fact a dead letter. It merely enacts the voidance of the policy. Will the holder, if rejected, prosecute the claim?—would he be entitled to a verdict?—what damages could he obtain? The two parties, the assured and the office, are frequently *participes criminis*, and both interested in keeping up the policy; and what is a third party (who holds the policy) to gain by rendering it void? The only gainer would be the office, from the premiums that may have been paid: *the Act does not say that they shall be refunded, nor does it award any penalty on the offenders.*

In our former article we noticed the indignation with which Mr. Babbage commented on the practice of almost all the Companies in paying a commission to agents, solicitors, or brokers who bring assurances to their respective offices. He relates, among others, the case of a clergyman who desired his attorney to make choice of an office to assure his life for 2000*l.* The attorney applied to the office for which he was agent, and which happened to be one of the few which made no return of any part of the profits. The consequence was, that at the clergyman's death the family received only the original sum, 2000*l.*, whereas, had the attorney gone to the Equitable, he would have received for the widow and orphan children 3200*l.* If this agent concealed from his employer that such a result would be among the probabilities, he no doubt acted dishonestly; but we cannot agree in the sweeping inference of Mr. Babbage. The following is the view which Mr. de Morgan takes of this matter:—

' As between one office and another, the attorney is in a judicial capacity; and, as regards his client, *he is already the paid protector of the interests of another person.* He has, therefore, no liberty of choice between one office and another, but is already bound to choose that which he judges best for his client. All who have written on the subject of late years have attacked this *bribe*, for such it is; but they have directed all their censures against the offices, as if they were the only parties to blame. If, indeed, the bribe had been offered to the needy and ignorant only, this partial distribution of blame might have been allowed; but when the parties who receive the bribe are men of education, and moving in those professions which bring the successful to affluence, I do not see the justice of allowing them to escape. I have little doubt that an increasing sense of right and wrong will banish this unworthy practice, either by failure of givers or receivers. A barrister cannot offer an attorney commission on the briefs which he brings, nor can a physician pay an apothecary for his recommendation; a jury never receives a hint that the plaintiff will give commission on the damages which they award; and the time will come when the offer of money to a person whose unbiassed opinion is already the property of another will be deemed to be what it really is, namely, *bribery and corruption.* It is one among many proofs how low is the standard of collective morality; and how easy it is for honourable individuals to do in concert that from which they would separately shrink.'—pp. 258, 259.

We suspect Mr. de Morgan to be much better versed in the doctrine of chances and probabilities than in the intercourse between barristers and attorneys, doctors and apothecaries; but we would ask him, what is a poor man, living in the heart of Wales, and wishing to effect an insurance, to do, but apply to his man of business, or the agent of some office, who must take his examination, send it up to the office, employ a medical man, &c. &c.; and can it be expected he shall do all this without remuneration? We believe that the whole of the country business with the offices in London is, and must be, transacted through agency; and, though each agent may have his peculiar office, yet it is undoubtedly his duty to explain to his private employer, as far as he knows, the different terms on which different offices grant assurances. For residents in London, we believe, agency is not given, as the party can himself apply.

On the whole we cannot consider these institutions in any other light than as great public benefits, of which almost every class of society may avail themselves with advantage to their rising families. Like all other human institutions, they are liable to be misconducted and abused; the good, however, we are satisfied, greatly predominates. Take, for instance, a case of very common occurrence: suppose a clergyman, happy in his domestic circle, educating his children liberally, and with his 400*l.* or 500*l.* a-year distributing consolation to his parishioners. Possessing

o nly a life interest in his income, no sooner is the thread snapped
than beggary stares his family in the face—the widow and children
are at once turned out upon the wide world, or doomed perhaps
to receive a grudging pittance from some relation. Now, all
this might have been avoided by an appropriation of some 50*l.* or
60*l.* a-year out of the life income, through the instrumentality of
an assurance office.

It is the same in almost every walk of life. Lawyers, phy-
sicians, surgeons, and apothecaries, marrying. young, and solely
dependent on their practice ; officers of the army and navy, who
can lay by a pittance of their pay ; clerks in public offices, in
banks, and counting-houses ; tradesmen and artificers,—in short
almost every description of persons may profit in this manner,
and a great mass of misery be avoided by the sacrifice of a very
small portion of income. Even the highest personages of the
realm, not excluding royalty itself, may profit by these offices,
when embarrassed in pecuniary matters ; by them the pressure
f debt may be relieved, and the creditor satisfied, and incum-
brances on entailed estates removed, on reasonable and honourable conditions, infinitely preferable to what can be had from
turning to the common run of money-lenders.

We do not think it worth while to go into any argument with
certain persons who object to all life-assurance as a species of
gambling—nor with those who, looking to the incorrect phrase,
lose sight of what is really meant, and prose about impious interference with the *fiat* of Providence. There is, however, a more
business-like class who object to the plan. These contend that,
if the annual sums paid by the assured, as premiums, were put out
at compound interest, the produce would exceed what the assured
or his representatives will receive from the office. This is looking
at the subject in a very narrow and mistaken point of view : it
supposes life certain to a given extent. Mr. de Morgan says the
best thing an individual could do with a small sum (say 100*l.*), so
as to have perfect security for its return, would be to invest it in
the funds at $3\frac{1}{2}$ per cent. ' He might also invest the interest,
and thus obtain compound interest :' but he observes, ' it is not
easy for an individual to do this : unless he provide an agent to
draw the dividends immediately on their becoming due, various
circumstances will happen to prevent the immediate investment
of the interest. It is not at all an unfair calculation to suppose
that, upon each half-yearly dividend, a month will be lost, so that
nominal compound interest for forty-two years will only be really
for thirty-five years.' But he has elsewhere assigned a much
better reason for giving a preference to assurance offices. He
says :—

' Probably, if the following question were put to all those whose lives are now insured, What is the *advantage* which you derive from investing your surplus income in an insurance office? more than half would reply, The *certainty* of my executors receiving a sum at my death, were that to take place to-morrow. This is but half an answer; for not only does the office undertake the equalization of life, as above described, but also the *return of the sums invested, with compound interest.*'—p. 239.

The object is to provide a *certainty* against the casualties of life which render it *uncertain;* and to secure a sum of money greater than would be secured by any other means, let death come when it may. It is not a question whether 1000*l.* placed in the funds to accumulate (which every one has not the means of doing), or the insurance of a life for 1000*l.*, is preferable—the question is simply this, whether it is more advantageous to cause a small annual sum to be paid *for insuring* 1000*l.*, or to place the amount of that small sum annually, at compound interest, in the funds. Let us take an example from two or three different offices, and see what the several results will be.

A young man of thirty years of age insures his life for 1000*l.*, say with the Rock—the premium 2*l.* 12*s.* per cent., or thereabouts; the probability of his life may be taken at thirty years. Now 2*l.* 12*s.* put out at 3 per cent. compound interest, for thirty years, would produce (omitting fractions)   .   .   . £1236
The sum insured is £1000

His loss by insuring would thus be £236
But the Rock divides profits septennially—at least 8 per cent. each period, of which may be reckoned four in thirty years—the bonus then would be .   . £320

The gain by insuring, instead of funding at compound interest £8S

Try the same case in the Palladium—
The loss as before would be   .   .   ,   . £236
By a statement of profits now before us, a life of thirty would receive every seven years about 86*l.* 10*s.*, and for four periods the bonus would be   .   .   . £346

Gain by an assurance in the Palladium   .   .   . £109

Taking the age of fifty, the result would be pretty nearly the same; but if we suppose the assured to have died within the first period of seven years—say at the end of six years—all other points

the same, the accumulated compound interest on 2*l*. 12*s*. for
1000*l*., would amount to £168
But the survivor would receive by insuring the life . £1000

The gain in this case to the assured, and consequent loss
to the office is £832

In the Equitable, as at present constituted, the young insured
would not fare so well: let us take the case as before of the
probability of a life reaching thirty years. The plan of excluding all the assured from any participation of profits, until they
come within the 5000 oldest subscribers, is not a trifling feature:—one must live, on an average of chances, at least fifteen
years before he reaches admission into that enviable number; and in the next fifteen, should he survive, he might, perhaps,
get the profits of one decennial period; which, after deducting
the premium and simple interest upon them, will give him at the
end of thirty years, at the most, about 150*l*. But, if the young
obtain only so small a pittance, an insurance made at an advanced
age is ruinous. Take an example of one supposed to be made in
the year 1820 for 1000*l*., the age fifty-five, premium 53*l*. In
fifteen years, that is in 1835, he might hope to get within the
envied pale; but the division of profits being in 1839, he will
then have assigned to him (payable at his death) 3 per cent. for
the remaining four or five years, say 150*l*. At this time, that is
in nineteen years, he will have paid in premiums with interest at
3 per cent. £1331
Will be entitled (when the policy becomes a claim) to £150

Balance of money advanced, with interest . . . £1181

He is now in his seventy-fifth year, and enters on a fresh
decennial period, which if he should survive, and it is about ten
to one against him, he will have paid a further sum of . £607
His share of profits will now be about . . . £300

There remains a loss of £307
Add former loss £1181

£1488
Deduct original sum insured £1000

The actual loss to the assured, and gain to the office . £488

How different would the result have been under the old regulations! In this case the representatives of the assured would

have received 1610*l.*, in addition to the original 1000*l.*, instead of sustaining the above loss : for we have the late actuary's own statement, put forth somewhat triumphantly, that the Equitable, up to the year 1820, had added to a policy of twenty years' standing 77 per cent. ; to one of thirty years' 161 per cent. ; to one of forty years' 280 per cent. ; and to one of fifty years' 401 per cent. ! and yet, knowing well what the result of the change must inevitably be, he actually triumphed in the loss which the insured must incur, and in the certainty of the great benefit which the office would receive, from the device of his own ingenuity. Commenting on the history and practice of the Equitable Society, our Professor pithily says :—

' The general lesson taught by it is,—be cautious ; but, among other things, be cautious of carrying caution so far as to leave a part of your own property for the benefit of those who are in no way related to you. If there be a Charybdis in an insurance office, there is also a Scylla : the mutual insurer, who is too much afraid of dispensing the profits to those who die *before* him, will have to leave his own share for those who die *after* him. Reversing the fable of Spenser, we should write upon the door of every mutual office but one, *Be wary;* but upon that one should be written, *Be not too wary,* and over it, " Equitable Society." ' p. 281.

Our sole object in recurring to this subject has been to inculcate the necessity of exercising great caution in a very delicate matter of practice. We cannot shut our eyes and ears to the numberless cases in which quiet individuals and families, especially those residing at a distance from town, are injured from placing rash reliance on the pompous invitations of speculating quacks—nor do we think, on the other hand, that the established reputation of an insurance company ought to protect its peculiar manœuvres from scrutiny. Study well, we repeat, the names of the real working directors—distrust placardings of dukes and lords, who can know nothing about the matter, and probably never heard of it—and look sharp, when you see unparalleled advantages offered, as to the number of years during which the generous association propounding such benefits has been able to exhibit its attractions. *Per contra*, do not allow yourself to be inveigled into an absurdly disadvantageous arrangement, merely because the establishment that offers it is of old standing, undoubted firmness, and thinks it may take any liberties with the gaping mass.

Beaumont,
Observations, Cautionary and Recommendatory

John A. Beaumont, *Observations, Cautionary and Recommendatory, on Life Assurance* (London: Green & Co, 1841)

This is another of many discussions about the growth and practices of life assurance at a time when the business was being rapidly extended. Beaumont's background had been with the County Fire Office, from where, around 1830, he had campaigned for the establishment of a joint fire-engine brigade. By 1841 his attention had turned to life assurance. He was one of several authors who moved the discussion of the life assurance business away from the organisation and practical difficulties of the business, as seen from within, to a perhaps more considered and impartial concern about the problems and abuses that were perceived to be growing in an ever more complex life assurance market. However, he still writes from a perspective within the industry and with the industry's interests firmly in view. He develops his concerns and suggests remedies in another pamphlet in 1852 (see below, vol. 6, pp. 25–36).

LIFE-ASSURANCE.

OF the *principle* of assuring or securing money, to the use and for the benefit of those who come after us, there can be but one opinion : it is not less the dictate of reason and of natural religion, than it is the benevolent and provident inculcation of our common christianity. Hence the pupil of Gamaliel lays it down as an irrefutable axiom, that, " if any provide not for his own, and especially for those of his own house, he denies the faith itself, and is even worse than an unbeliever." And, if this be conceded, the most eligible *mode* of carrying the principle into effect is well worthy of our very attentive consideration, and the only point on which a difference of opinion ought to, or can, exist. This *modus agendi* it is the object of the writer of the present brief sketch to exhibit, not only to the conviction of the hitherto-uninsured, but, it is hoped, to their preference and adoption of that class of insurance which is stable, safe, and sound; and not of that which, either originating in ignorance or in knavery, is conducted with mismanagement or improvidence, and ends in disappointment and distress, if not in beggary, to those who have looked to and relied on it, as their last, perhaps their only, hope.

That life-assurance and annuity-offices, when conducted on sound principles, are a great boon to society, is sufficiently obvious; but, the injuries which must be eventually inflicted on the community, by those whose specious and alluring promises and prospects of gain are based on erroneous calculations, or commenced for the purpose of raising a fund, only to be embezzled or dissipated by directors, managers, actuaries, secretaries, and other *employeés*, may not be quite so public, if even at all known; because the cupidity of those, who thus experimentalise on the credulity of the public, is practised with too much apparent candour to excite suspicion ; and the proneness of mankind to novelty, however extravagant and absurd, too frequently obscures the understanding of the eager, who are not initiated into the secret.

Nothing is more easy than for a few artful and needy adven-

turers—bankrupts in reputation and fortune—to start an establishment of an imposing character in architectural appearance, with
stuccoed front, in some dingy street of the metropolis, where the
haunts of commerce, and the accumulations of ill-scavengered
streets, shall present a sufficiently strong contrast, and give
advantage in favour of modern erections over unpretending and
time-worn edifices   Neither is it a difficult task, in these speculative times, to fit up the interior with mahogany-desks and costly
furniture, and to place behind them a few clerks, with fashionably-
cut coats on their backs, pen in ear, steel-pen in hand, and
liveried porter at the door, to give an air of importance, respectability, and pressure of business.   Nor is it found to be more
difficult to get a few sham customers to peep in, as is done at
mock auctions, as decoy-ducks to the rest of the community.
The British public—intelligent, sharp-sighted, scrutinizing, as it
is styled—is mightily deceived by appearances like these; and
when, in addition to these appliances, the neatly-folded prospectus makes its appearance, headed by a list of directors, including
of course a chairman, with the usual appurtenances of physician,
surgeon, actuary, secretary, banker, standing counsel, solicitor,
and the whole paraphernalia of deception, it is scarcely possible
to resist the temptation.   The provident father, who contrives to
spare a few pounds annually from his scanty income, that he may
provide a fund for his dependent family after his decease; the
fond husband, who is desirous that the partner of his life shall not
be left penniless, in the event of the premature termination of his
existence, is captivated with plausible appearances, and with
names simulating respectability; and his humane and benevolent
intentions, in regard to the objects of his affection or solicitude,
render him blind to trickery, liable to imposition, and incredulous
of good advice, if even he ask it.

It is, we repeat, the disinterested object of the writer of the
present article, to warn the public against such new-fangled
institutions; and, at the same time, to direct their attention to those
of proved respectability and well-tested strength of capital.   All
other aim he utterly disclaims, being wholly unconnected with all and
every speculation or enterprise, whatever be its name or nature.

Few people are, perhaps, altogether ignorant of the principles of life assurance. Most persons are aware that there are two classes of assurance-offices—one really, if even not so denominated, proprietary, proffering a *share* of the profits; and the other mutual, professing to devote the *whole* of the profits to the insured. Each of these may have its peculiar advantages over the other. The great point in both is, permanency and real capital : to obtain which continuance or stability, both available capital and prudent management are obviously indispensable. The advantages of the proprietary life-offices are, their age and their investment of capital: with them, the whole scheme is one of honourable and fair mercantile speculation. The contract of those who insure with them is invariable ; whilst the interest of the proprietors themselves is to make the institutions as stable, uniform, and permanent, as any human establishment can possibly be. The advantages, which the mutual insurance-offices possess, and profess to afford, consist, principally, in the interest which those who insure are supposed to derive from the profits of the establishments. Of these, some profess to divide the profits triennially, quinquennially, or septennially ; offering an accruement of bonus, after the expiration of a definite period of so many years' annual payment; and benefiting the insurer, at his option, either by augmenting his original policy, or by reducing his subsequent annual payment of premium, until another definite series of years shall have rendered the means of a second and a third similar and optional disposal of the profits of the concern, by what may be called the ascending or descending scale.

It cannot be doubted that the security, for obtaining good management of the business of such monetary societies, is much greater in the older or proprietary insurance-offices, than in the modern mutual societies. The guarantee of the capital of the proprietors of these is afforded to those who insure ; and it is not reasonable to suppose, that such proprietors will wilfully waste their own capital in reckless and improvident speculation. There are no over-strained statements made, or tempting inducement held out, by them; but, on the contrary, almost all the respectable proprietary life assurance-offices adopt the same, or nearly the same, tables of calculation, and these are in favour of an ever-accumulating capital to the company. It is not so with most of the mutual life assurance-offices, which are not only founded on erroneous principles, in regard to calculation, but seem to think only of the premature division of early profits, to the detriment of future accumulation;—a principle this, which strikes at the root of permanent security.

The following general conclusions, then, may warrantably be drawn from the few foregoing remarks :—

1. That every scheme for making persons, who insure their lives, joint and equal participators in the success of the institution or society with which they insure, is a departure from the original object and intention of life-assurance ; which is, or should be, a permanent and invariable contract, and not a trading partnership, all the members of which form a joint stock fund.

2. That tontines, lotteries, and all similar associations for *mutual* benefit and protection, are, doubtless, laudable institutions, when conducted on honourable, safe, and judicious, principles ; but, they are still so much dependent on results and management, that they never can afford that protection which is obtained by an assurance, where a permanent security, such as that alluded to, exists, to insure the fulfilment of the contract.

It should be observed, that almost all the life-assurance-offices, which have been recently established, are on the *mutual* principle ; and the temptation held out by an early participation of benefits, hereafter to be made, is attended with proportionate danger, as to eventual security, which, in offices of adequate capital, does not exist. Ultimate success is, therefore, in peril, in proportion to the present advantages held out to induce insurances. *Qui trop embrasse, mal étreint.*

The remarks which have been made, on the "grasp all lose all" system, it is hoped, will not deter persons from effecting life-insurances on correct principles. We consider it to be not only the obvious policy, but the incumbent duty, of all persons of moderate income, to lay by a part of it, by which a fund may be obtained, after they have closed their career of earthly exist-ence, for the support of their families. It is selfishness, if not profligacy, of the worst kind, for persons to waste the whole of their income in present enjoyment, regardless of future consequences to those, whose society contributes to their present happiness, and whose future prosperity and comfort should be the object of their anxious care. It does, we confess, appear to us most surprising, that,—although the system of life-assurances has been known to the British public ever since the reign of Queen Anne, when the " Amicable Society " was first established in this metropolis,—only about 80,000 persons, out of a population of about 20 millions, or 1 in 62 of heads of families, have, as yet, availed themselves of its advantages! Life-insurances appear to us not only the most provident and safe, but among the most honourable, means of protecting, from want and penury, the too-often-helpless beings, who may survive; but they afford, also, the best opportunity of enabling parents to make a provision for their children, suitable to the station which they should maintain in society; and which they themselves have either permitted, or, in most instances, induced, them to assume and occupy.

But, while we are, we scruple not to avow, anxious to impress on the minds of the fathers of families, generally, the propriety, advantage, and duty, of availing themselves of the benefits of life-assurance, we earnestly entreat them to exercise due caution and discrimination as it regards the offices in which to ensure. Let them, as they value the comfort and happiness of their families, prefer stability to cheapness, permanency of advantage to present gains; and, as a necessary consequence, let them prefer the respectability of well-established proprietary life assurance-offices, to the glowing expectations held out by the many mutual-benefit-institutions, which, without any greater recommendation to adoption, than those held out, are fraught with defeat to the hopes, and consequent destruction to the well-being, of those dependent on them.

It may be suggested that the person to whom an assignment is made of a life-policy, in cases of loan, bond, deposit, or other security, will do well, by personal inspection of the records of the office, to see not only that his assignment is duly registered and acknowledged there, but also that no other assignment has been, or, without his notice or concurrence, shall be, made of the document in question ; and that all office-notices of coming payments shall be sent to him, either in addition to, or in lieu of, the notice heretofore sent to the insurer himself: this will appear needless to those who have not had too much reason to regret their want of caution in this particular. It is not every lawyer that can tell us *whose* bond is valid, when another creditor or claimant exhibits a similar security,—the expensive aid of a court of law, equity, or chancery, being sometimes found necessary, before the several claims can be adjusted.

The writer would leave his duty incomplete if he neglected to refer his readers to the able *exposé* of such impositions, by that upright, uncompromising, and independent, magistrate, Alderman Sir Peter Laurie, recently made at the Mansion-House, on the bursting of that bubble, "The Independent and West Middlesex Assurance-company," in which he stated, that not only had the company itself been broken up, but that the whole of the executive, directors and manager, had decamped *on the very day they were under obligation to pay Five Thousand Pounds on Annuities!* embezzling, abstracting, and appropriating to themselves, in their abduction, not only very little short of One Hundred Thousand Pounds of *Annuities*, the cash-deposits of those credulous victims who, allured by their attractive advertisements, had deposited their savings or earnings, as the seed-corn of a future harvest; but also half that sum paid to the company for life-policies, and for assurance against fires; amounting, together, to the enormous sum of One Hundred and Fifty Thousand Pounds! Sir Peter observed, in his exposure, that "there were several flash establishments in the metropolis, at that moment, obtaining large sums of money fraudulently. The ingenuity exhibited in the management of the concern, relative to which he appeared at the Mansion-House that day, was very remarkable ; but crimes of *ingenuity were on the increase.* The Independent and West Middlesex Assurance-company pretended to have been established in the year 1696, with a capital of One Million sterling ; and here it ended, with all its professed advantages, after having really existed no more than four years, during which period it was engaged in plundering the public, and in enriching a few miscreants, who were, at that mo ment, enjoying the fruits of their iniquity."

Scarcely was the ink, in which we had written the last sentence, dry, when our table was loaded, and our ears and eyes assailed, with so many, and such convincing proofs of the nefarious villainy of the above sham establishment, that we were all but overwhelmed by the flood of distressing intelligence brought to us. Nothing, since the bursting of the great South Sea bubble, in 1721, or the panic of 1825-6, has ever approached this in atrocious impudence, scheming imposition, and ruinous effects. Widows, wards, and orphans—servants, labourers, and legatees, who either had monies left to them or, by their frugality and economy had acquired a slender pittance, or a moderate competence—or, by their providence, temperance, and self-denial, had earned and saved wherewith to support them in sickness, adversity, or old age—all these enticed and attracted by this maelstrom, have lost,

" At one fell swoop,"

their little all—earnings, savings, profits, gifts, legacies; and, therein, their whole living! Where is the county, town, or village, in the provinces, Great Britain and Ireland, in which are not now to be heard the unavailing lamentation, cutting self-reproaches, and irremediable regrets, of the unhappy dupes? Let the following, selected out of a mass of instances, tell their tale of sorrow, to the ears and hearts of a generous and indignant nation :—

That zealous magistrate, Sir Peter Laurie, whose ear is ever open to the injured, and whose heart is ever ready to sympathise with the distressed—publicly addressing Mr. Alderman Pirie—states (on the authority of a letter from the editor of a *Glasgow Paper)* that, among the many robberies, committed by the penniless and characterless *quatré,* who originated this imposture, which, for extent and heartlessness far exceeded anything within his memory that it was deplorable to see the number of victims, poor and aged, who had embarked, in this sea-unworthy vessel, all they had in the world, appealing, in vain, to those who, themselves victimized, were unable to render them assistance.

Alderman Pirie (who has been equally successful in denuding and annihilating the Australian Bank) in reply to, and in confirmation of his worthy brother alderman's heart-rending statement, said, that he also had been recently apprised of the extensive *ruin* which had arisen from the over-weaning confidence which the too credulous and miserably duped annuitants and depositors had unavoidably reposed in this infamous mock company : adding, that its bankrupt and menial conductors (two are characterless and out-of place gentleman's servants, and the other two uncertificated bankrupts), had, during their course of plunder, resided in splendid houses, and kept magnificent establishments.

Sir Peter replied, that the chief actors in this tragedy had absconded, and fled to the continent with their illgotten gains ; and that the highly respectable houses of Farquhar & Co., in Broad Street, and of Biggs & Co., living at the west end of the town, were then engaged, the former for the Irish and Scotch, and the latter for the London victims—who ought to make one purse, and a common cause, in the prosecution, to try to bring to condign punishment the four setters-up of this mockery of security, *whose only assurance was their own impudence,* and their only safety, their temporary escape.   The leading features in this monstrous vice and villainy remain to be unmasked. Not only did its projectors occupy a noble house, in one of the most wealthy, fashionable, highly-rented, and aristocratic streets in the west end of the metropolis (27, Baker Street); but they assumed the garb of candour, tempered with caution,* and of respectability, guarded by formality, in all their external dealings with the unenquiring public.   All was done, apparently, under legal advice—the advisers, doubtless, co-plotters ; and, as such, partakers in the plunder.   This gave a character of stability to the concern, and either prevented suspicion, or threw dust in the eyes of its customers or dealers.   To crown the whole, in order to

---

* They talked much, and wrote more, of enrolling deeds in the Court of Chancery : they invited and courted inquiry !   In their specious prospectus, they referred to Acts of Parliament extending over a period of forty years !— all pure inventions, not to be found in the statute-book !   Here, we cannot help observing, we read, cite, and requote ; and no one takes the trouble to examine, compare, or verify; and this in the nineteenth century !   We exclaim, on every fresh recurrence of imposition, " *Quis putaret?* " and, the hour after, are ourselves the dupes of the next fair-spoken scheme !

appear disinterested benefactors of their species, they even started a loan company, for the accommodation and benefit of those who could not avail themselves of the vaunted and tempting benefits which their office held out to eager and infatuated expectants; and, with *noli me tangere*, as their motto, and jealous of their honor, they even prosecuted the proprietor of a Scotch paper, for only hinting at their want of respectability; but, happily, took nothing by this motion.

The Lord Mayor (before whom the indefatigable Sir Peter, again exposed this *charlatanerie)* said, he found, that, under existing circumstances, the office of magistrate, as regarded the accused parties, who promised so much, and did so little,

> " Who keep the word of promise, to the ear,
> And break it to the hope,"

could not be made available beyond the mere, but unlimited, exposure of these fraudulent transactions; yet he trusted that the press would willingly avail itself of his statement in order to make known this widely spread devastation, as a future caution to prevent the introduction of so much misery into families. One unfortunate dupe, driven to despair, in the *acmé* of his agony, had attempted self-destruction! They had taken from him all; and, probably, he exclaimed with the man of Mount Ephraim, "What have I more?" A female sufferer had, ever since, hourly drooped; and, at last, has died of a broken heart, with all the horrors of a workhouse before her. An aged laundress, involved in this wide-spread desolation, is in a state bordering on madness. An aged infirm man, has now no alternative but the poorhouse or madhouse. These four deplorable cases were laid before him, by Mr. Smith, the landlord of these heartless scoundrels, bankrupts in character and in finance, a quartumvirate composed of the discarded of society.

Sir Peter said, among those unfortunates, a clergyman, of Cheltenham, had sent him a letter, of which the following is an extract:—" Although I should be sorry to trespass on your valuable time, yet I feel assured you will extend your indulgent attention, a few minutes, whilst I briefly state the particulars of my aggravated case. I am a clergyman, with a contracted income; and have brought up a family respectably: amongst others, a son, aged 27, who, for many years, has been suffering from the sad malady of epilepsy, rendering him incapable of exerting himself towards his own livelihood. Desirous that, at my decease, he should not become a burthen to his brothers and sisters, I laid out very nearly £2,000 in the purchase of an annuity for him in the West Middlesex Assurance Company: having lived the greater part of my life in the country and not so conversant in worldly matters, as a mode of business, some allowance might well be made, if a want of caution should be imputed to me; but I must state, that I did not enter into this transaction without some consideration and enquiry, which were so far satisfied, by an assurance from the company, that the annuity-deed should be signed by three* of the directors, and that a memorial of the bond should be enrolled in the Court of Chancery, pursuant to an Act of Parliament, made for that purpose; which is also stated at the back of the parchment bond, one with a £12, the other a £6 stamp. This blow to me is the more severe, from its having been just preceded by a brother-in-law having died insolvent, to whom I had lent £1,500, towards bringing up a family of eleven children; so that my income is reduced nearly £200."

To satisfy himself of the truth of the many reported instances of fraud practised by this band of conspirators, and both to disabuse and caution the credulous and unsuspecting, Sir Peter requested Mr. Farquhar, of the house of Johnston & Co., Solicitors, New Broad Street (who are employed against these " men of straw, " but adepts in roguery), to communicate with him on the subject; a call which that gentleman promptly obeyed. Among other informations then and there disclosed, but, for obvious reasons not proper, now, to be fully made public, Mr. F. stated, that the original deed of settlement of the *soi-disant* company had been burnt! and the managers had endeavoured

---

* To a deed of this sort, to a Mrs. Barker, are appended the names of " John Wilson, Thomas Knowles, and William Edward Taylor, Acting Managers," attested as " in the presence of George Williams, Solicitor, No. 2, Hart Street, Bloomsbury;" and " William Hole, Secretary, 27, Brook Street, Portman Square,"—all *ignota farina*.

to get hold of the notary's copy, which had been sent to Scotland, (where they had the unblushing effrontery to bring an action for heavy damages in order to establish their suspected reputation!) but, happily, that document was safe in the hands of the proper officer of the court of session. If they had succeeded in their object, all further trace of the company would have been lost. In the very formation of this deed of settlement, signatures had been purchased, like the once-famous, not to say infamous, witnesses, in the purlieus of the Old Bailey, at five shillings per head! Sir Peter, rather facetiously, observed, that it was not a little remarkable, that the Scots, whose conceded character for long, if not for double, sight was proverbial, in all money matters were, as it regarded the thing 'yclept the West Middlesex *four-berie*, stone blind.

Mr. Smith, the landlord of the elegantly-furnished mansion, finds, too late, that, in getting such high-flown and swift-flighted tenants, more innocently than the men of Jerusalem, he had made his house "a den of thieves." To aid the cause of justice, he, at the request of Sir Peter, has, on the *French-leave* decamping* of his tenants, removed to Messrs. Johnston & Co., the few books and papers which had not, previously, been either subduced or destroyed by the "managing" gentry; all of whom have *levanted*, choosing the time, and leaving the aftercomer to pay the piper: " *Occupet extremum scabies.*"

Among the servants, not in their secrets, the porter states, that, about a fortnight before the bubble burst, and the thieves decamped with the spoil—leaving neither stick nor stool—two pipes of wine, sent to the house, were bottled off hastily, and divided among the managers and secretary, who sent the prey to their respective houses!

Their country agents appear to have received 50 per cent., for the first year, and for the six following years, 15 per cent., on all the grist they could bring or send to the mill, in the shape of transferred fire-assurances: on life-assurances, 20 per cent., at first; and 5 per cent on annuities, for the gross payments: pretty

* Will not Lord Palmerston aid in their capture, by an appeal to the foreign courts? Why is there not some internation rule in all cases of this nature? Time is not always found for the writ, " *Ne excat regno.*"

pickings these, a fact which of itself should have shown the rottenness of the concern.

Sir Peter Laurie is not, we are happy to be able to state, the only public-spirited individual who has lent the influence of his name and character to the detection and developement of this species of chicanery and robbery.   One, whom to name is to praise ; as distinguished for wisdom and eloquence, as he is for courage and conduct ; the *decus et tutamen* of his admiring and grateful country ; and whom this gang of swindlers, this *officina malorum* had advertised, with unheard-of audacity, as the patron of one of their bantlings—a loan and deposit company—until his Grace indignantly repudiated the affiliation, has shown himself in this, as in every other public matter, the unflinching advocate of the oppressed, the unbending opponent of fraud, and the stern lover of justice.   Need we name the Duke of Wellington ? the favourite of his sovereign, the *point d'affaires* of his friends, the pride of the army, the terror of our enemies, the *dernier ressort* of the injured, and the idol of the eye !   Long may he live to enlighten the counsels, guard the liberties, and influence the legislative deliberations, of his countrymen — the senate !   " Great in the council as the tented field."

> " *Serus in cœlum redeat ! diuque*
> *Lætus intersis populo Britanno ?*
> *Neve te, nostris vitiis iniquum.*
> *Ocior aura tollet.*"—HORACE

But the heart sickens at our recital ; we, therefore, conclude, with saying, that in our hope and suggestion we cordially join the shrewd and indefatigable baronet ; viz., that the Government or Parliament will take up and investigate, in committee, the whole subject of fire, life, and annuity insurance and assurance-companies.   We want no monopoly : we recommend not any undue controul : we advise not the slightest infringement of our monetary, or other honourable commercial associations.   What we wish we had almost said, *demand*, is, a minute and rigid inquiry into the stability and respectability of parties proposing to set on foot all future institutions of the kind ; ample security of and from each and all ; a registration of their establishment ; certificates of the solvency of the parties applying for enrolment; a security, in case of embezzlement or bankruptcy; a deposit, in the public funds, of two-thirds of their declared published capital; an annually-attested statement (all under penalties) of their transactions; a *bond fide* guarantee to all depositors, to the full extent of their claims ; and an applicability to the full amount of their dealings of responsibility and attachment to the estates of each separate president, trustee, director, governor, manager, and secretary, engaged or employed; whether their property be real *(not entailed)*, funded, or unemployed personal.

Without the least partiality to, or preference of, the great, in matters of this nature, but, with profound esteem and gratitude to our country's true defenders and benefactors, we felicitate ourselves, and congratulate them also, that the report, that the Marquis of Wellesley (who so long, and so ably, as Governor-General of India, enlarged our dominions, crippled our enemies, and enhanced and multiplied our revenues) had deposited, and *lost*, the £30,000 which the East India Company had awarded to him, in return for his unexampled services, is (agreeably with the statement of Mr. Farquhar and Sir Peter Laurie) wholly without foundation. Would that we could say the same of many others! These deluded people, alas! must, either go to the parish workhouse, or perhaps sweep the crossings, or become cads to coach-stands, or, being guilty of the crime of poverty, live and exist in the sympathies of their repenting relatives! their mouths filled with unsparing anti-benedictions, loud and deep, on the heads of their betrayers, and lamenting to the latest their being led by the nose to the "grave of hope," the parochial bastile!

" Abandon hope, all ye who enter here."

Should we after this disgusting *eclaircissement*, be asked to give an opinion of the course of all this long train of evils, we reply, it is to be found in the cupidity of the money-maker, in the desire, resolve, and haste, to be rich ; and in the subtle craft of man's arch enemy. " He,' says the prince of sages, " who maketh haste to be rich, shall not be innocent." " They, that *will* be rich," (it is the dictation of inspiration itself), " fall into temptation and a snare:" such have, heretofore, as now, " pierced themselves through with many sorrows." Lynx-eyed as men are, in some, in most, matters, in this they display obtuseness and credulity unparalled in the wide creation even of creatures acknowledged to be far inferior to our race, and possessing nothing but instinct for their guide. "Surely, in vain, is the net spread in the sight of any bird;" whereas man, the lord of the creation — man, the vice-regent of his maker—not seeing the hook, catches at the *gilded* bait and plunges into the open nets, which the Great Fisher and Fowler of souls holds out to him, and is, to his cost, caught, and devoured! nor will even this *exposé* hurt him! To-morrow he will act on other fresh victims of duplicity and cozenage, to prey on the same food day after day: *telle est la vie.*

As a " beacon light of truth " to the unwary (since we cannot remedy the past) we now offer to our countrymen these our hints, advice, and admonitions. Let our readers be satisfied that those offices which offer the smaller profits have the more solid foundations; and let them be equally assured that those hacknied clap-traps of greedy speculators, however musical to the public ear, such as " cheap insurance," " sole-participators," " quick returns, small origins, large profits," emanate from those who would deceive others or are themselves deceived; and who, whether to be ranked in this or in that category, are ill-fitted to lead the public in matters of so much importance. No *wise* man *can*, no *honest* man *will*, no *good* man *dares* to hope, or to wish, to expect, or to try, to gain by the loss, to rise by the fall, or build on the ruin of his fellow man—this is the natural property of the leech and the vampire.—" Live and let live," should be every man's motto.—" Do as you would be done unto," should be our golden rule. The light which has penetrated into the dark practices of the West Middlesex deception, may gleam before long through the dusty casements of other institutions, which like Cæsar's wife are not beyond suspicion.

GREEN & Co., 3, Curzon Street, May Fair, Printers and Publishers, by Special Appointment, to the Queen and H. R. H. Prince Albert, (Parliamentary Chronicle Office).

Blayney,
Life Assurance Societies Considered

Frederick Blayney, *Life Assurances Societies Considered as to their Comparative Merits, &c.* (London: William Stevens, 1848)

A quite detailed discussion of the relative merits of the various life offices, which again reflects the continuing debate about the practices and procedures of the growing number of offices. It provides an insight to the industry several decades on from the discussions of Baily (1810), Farren (1824), and Babbage (1826).[1]

Note

1 See vol. 4.

LIFE ASSURANCE SOCIETIES,

&c. &c.

THAT life assurance is a species of lottery, by which an assurance office speculates upon the duration of every life it may assure, no one acquainted with the subject can deny; the former relying on the assured living to the age which persons at his time of life are usually expected to attain, and whether he lives to that age, or dies at any intermediate period, the office must in either case pay the sum assured; thus it may happen, that a life assured for £1000, or any other particular sum, may die within the first year of the assurance, and although one year's premium only is all that finds its way into the coffers of the office, they must still pay the sum assured, an incongruity which is tolerated by all the assurance offices to the present day in preference to the adoption of the principle of average loss, as in cases of fire and marine insurance, the latter being regarded as an invasion of the legitimate objects of life assurance, and the loss thus occasioned by the short-lived being counterbalanced by the contributions of the assured, who have lived long enough to survive the ordinary expectation of life. Before however an office will be persuaded to assure a life, it must be borne in mind that the health and constitution of the party must be duly certified to them as good and sound, not only by their own medical officer, but by one of his medical friends, and perhaps two other persons at least who are understood to have sufficient knowledge of the same. The assurance being thus based, and the assured put under a binding engagement to pay his premium within the time prescribed, and for the term agreed upon, on pain of forfeiting his policy and all the benefit thereof: and as the contributions so made may considerably exceed the sum assured, every prudent person who contemplates effecting an assurance upon his life must necessarily desire to become a member of that society in particular which offers the fairest prospect of *ultimate security* and *a due return* for the contributions he may be required to make to the funds of the same; hence it is *not* of the least importance in furtherance of an object so desirable as that of making some provision for his family, or other objects of his bounty, when he himself is no longer able to supply their daily wants, that he should at least be enabled to form a general opinion of the comparative merits of the various offices now extant, and thereby avoid placing his confidence where it is most likely to be abused, not forgetting how much depends on the prudent management and integrity of the office he may select. With these considerations it is the object of the following brief sketch to afford, as perfectly as the materials will admit, an analysis of the various systems and practices of the existing offices. (*a*)

Life assurance offices hitherto established have usually been classed under the following heads, that is to say :—

MUTUAL, PROPRIETARY, MIXED PROPRIETARY.

The *first* is understood to be composed of a society of persons who, by annual contribu-

(*a*) Without derogating from the value of several very useful works on this subject already before the public, it may be observed that not one of them, with a solitary exception or so, can be said to be impartially written, they

tions or premiums, create a capital or fund for *their own mutual benefit*, and who consequently share among themselves any profits or surplus, should the fund so created be more than sufficient to meet the objects for which it was intended it should be made available.

The *second* is composed of a class of persons who, in the spirit of trading and under the pretext of a guaranteed capital, take up the business of life assurance as a *source of profit* to themselves, to the exclusion of the persons who contribute the fund from which such profits arise; and, as an inducement for the assured to forego the advantage thus parted with, namely, all the surplus capital which may arise beyond satisfying claims, they have the assurance that a certain guaranteed capital (which is raised by shares) shall be forthcoming to make good deficiencies, should the fund raised by the contributions of the assured be found at any time inadequate to satisfy the claims as they may arise; thus the assured

having emanated from persons connected with assurance offices. The design of the writer of the following sheets (which are intended as an Appendix to his *Treatise* on the same subject published in 1837) is to distinguish such of the existing offices as are particularly entitled to public patronage.

may be regarded as a mere customer, who buys a specific sum and pays the price by periodical instalments, which, if sufficient to pay the sum assured twice over, he gains not one shilling advantage thereby.

The *third* of the above classes is constituted precisely as the second; instead however of sweeping all the profits into their own pockets, the parties constituting the shareholders, with less apparent zeal for gain, permit the assured to share with them in the profits according to their own notion of reciprocity of interests; under which some offices allow the assured one-half, or one-third, whilst others increase the benefit in the proportion of two-thirds, three-fourths, four-fifths, or the like, the result of all which operations is that the shareholders usually derive a very large share of the profits out of the funds contributed by the assured as a return for a guaranteed capital, which, perhaps, as to nineteen-twentieths, is merely nominal. And although upwards of 120 offices for the assurance of lives have been opened, (not to say established as to some of them) yet strange as it may appear, scarcely a dozen of that number have adopted the system of mutual assurance, owing, perhaps, to two supposed causes, the one the difficulty of find-

ing *a priori* a community of persons (*b*) sufficient in number, who alike cherish the twofold principle of universal and individual
benevolence, and who in their primitive character will become the capitalists for carrying
out their own architectural design until the
period of consummation shall have made them
the recipients of the first fruits. The other of
the two causes may be mainly attributable to
the incessant and persevering alarm put forth
by proprietary offices as to the risk supposed
to be attendant on the members of a mutual
guarantee society, by *calls* upon them to make
good losses or deficiencies, which in a proprietary would be met by their guaranteed
capital, but as no instance can be adduced of
such a contingency having happened either
to the one or the other, in any respectable
and well-conducted establishment, it must be
viewed as a mere hypothesis unsupported by
even the semblance of truth, to keep from view
the dearly purchased security of a guaranteed
capital.   And here may it not be asked, if

(*b*) The Scottish Widows Fund Society began business
with the trifling capital of £370 only, voluntarily subscribed by a number of individuals as patrons to the
Institution.—The Economic Society was also founded
upon a subscribed capital to meet the expenses of its
early growth, which has been since redeemed.

the subscribed capital of a proprietary had been put in requisition to meet any contingency which they guaranteed to provide for, but which they never thought of as likely to happen ; and if, peradventure, such an event did happen, and they themselves were put in *juxta-position* with the assured by operation of legal proceedings, might they not have acted as other honourable men similarly circumstanced have recently deigned to do, (although in connection with a very different business) evade payment even under the shelter of legal parlance, or perhaps deny their liability disjunctive of the assured themselves as *participes criminis*, and thus leave them to the tedious and uncertain remedy of a suit in equity ? (c) Before, therefore, a person embarks in a transaction so all important as that of making a provision for the objects of his bounty by the medium of an assurance on his life in the hope of securing to them all the advantages to be derived from such a source, he must

(c) In many of the deeds of settlement under which life assurance offices are established, a power is conferred upon the directors, in virtue of which they may wholly exhaust the *assurance* fund before one shilling of the guaranteed capital can be touched. In others it is expressly conditioned that the liability of the shareholders themselves shall be restricted.

endeavour to fortify himself against the specious and illusive representations too commonly made by offices, (who in their zeal to do
business hold out prospects which they themselves can scarcely hope to see realized,) and
consider well how far his own interests are
essentially identified.   Indeed numerous are
the schemes set on foot by way of allurement,
and to suit every possible object of the assured.
The ramifications of which are as varied as the
points of a mariner's compass, in which also
calculating ingenuity has taken no inconsiderable share in order to devise the ways and
means for meeting the required premiums,
so as to adapt the same to nearly all classes of
the community, the payment of which, for instance, may be made either in one gross sum, or
by yearly sums,—or deferred for a given number of years—or in a certain number of equal
annual payments, when they cease, and the
assured has no further payments to make
during his life,—or under the head credit, or
half credit, he may postpone the payment of
his premiums to a certain period, or forbear
the payment of half thereof; the unpaid portion to constitute a loan, and with interest
thereon be paid at a fixed period, or go in reduction of the sum to be ultimately paid under

the policy. Or the premiums may be calculated so as to commence and continue during the early years of assurance upon a reduced scale of payments, and increase during the latter years, which is termed " Ascending scale;" or, by the adoption of the converse of this, it may commence on an increased scale, and diminish in a corresponding degree during the latter years of the assurance, which is termed " Descending scale "—so as to throw the greater or lesser weight on the particular period referred to, as may in either case suit the convenience of the party. Or he may assure at a certain rate of premium, but unless he survives a certain period the policy becomes forfeited—so that the extinction of the policy as well as the premium happens at the particular period agreed upon. These and other schemes of the like nature are in common use among offices of modern growth; nevertheless, for reasons hereafter adduced, the safest course to adopt is perhaps not to insure at all till we are *satisfied* we can meet the premiums with uniform regularity and certainty.

Some few offices have made a distinction between *male and female lives*, by having tables of premiums calculated upon a somewhat lower scale for the latter than the for-

mer, under the generally received opinion,
that females on the average live longer than
the males (*d*)—a doctrine which has been

(*d*) No distinction has at present been made between
the married and unmarried, in like manner as between
the male and female; but if the following data can be
relied on, such a distinction will ere long become a matter
of consideration with assurance offices.   Some curious
facts (if they may be so called), on the subject of marriage as connected with longevity, are stated by Dr.
Caspar, in a letter of his, published at Berlin.   It had
been long ago vaguely asserted, that bachelors are less
long-lived than married men.   Hufeland and Deparcieux
were of this opinion, and Voltaire observed that there
were more suicides among those who had not given hos-
tages to fortune than among those who had.   Odier,
however, was the first who set on foot the inquiry with
exactitude, and he found (Bibl. Britannique, 1814) that
in the case of females the mean duration of life for the
married woman of 25 was above 36 years, while for the
unmarried it was about 30½.   At 30 there was a difference of four years in favour of the married, at 33 two
years, and so on.   With regard to men, we gather from
Deparcieux's, and the Amsterdam Tables, that the mortality of those from 30 to 45 years of age is 27 per cent.
for the unmarried, while it is but 18 for the married;
and that for 41 bachelors who attain the age of 40, there
are 78 married men.   The difference becomes still more
striking as age advances.   At the age of 60 there are but
22 unmarried men alive for 48 married; at 70, 11
bachelors for 27 married men, and at 80, for the three
bachelors who may chance to be alive, there are nine
Benedicts.   The same proportion very nearly holds good
with respect to the female sex ; 72 married women, for

mainly founded on the observation of mortality on the Government Tables; but as it appears to refer to a particular class of persons, it is but a naked confirmation of the assumed fact.

The practice now very general among assurance offices of having sets of tables, called *participating* and *non-participating*, is not, perhaps, of the least importance; the latter, which is the lower rate, being adapted to persons who effect assurances for short periods on the lives of their debtors, and who desire to do so at the lowest possible rate, beyond which they are calculated to divert the attention of the uninitiated in the business of life assurance from the more important object of reaping a greater benefit by ulterior profits, to attain which the original and fun-

example, attain the age of 45, while only 52 unmarried reach the same term of life.   M. Caspar, in conclusion, considers the point as now incontestably settled, that in both sexes marriage is conducive to longevity. To this we may likewise add, that the effect of locality upon life may at no distant period become the subject of tabular distinction as regards premiums, it appearing from the last report of the Registrar-General for Lancashire that in the Ulverstone district one person in four attains the age of 70, in Lancashire 1 in 6, in Preston 1 in 15, in Manchester 1 in 17, and in Liverpool 1 in 20 only.

damental principle as to our investments in matters of life assurance must still remain as our fixed rule—namely, by making annual payments in the shape of premiums, to secure to our representatives the largest possible sum in gross, or relieve ourselves, by diminishing the burden of such yearly payments at a time when we may feel its pressure; and whether this can be done through the medium of an assurance office, or a savings' bank, prudent and cautious deliberation only can determine. In the latter, the contribution and profits are at all times correctly ascertained and accounted for, so that at any given day the contributor can view the progress he is making in the object he contemplates; and if he fails in carrying out the same, his little wealth is still under his own control and disposition. Not so with an assurance—he may make contributions of premiums for a series of years, but should he in any succeeding year omit to make good his yearly payment within the prescribed time (e) all is lost, and he may in vain

(e) The practice of restricting the time or days of grace for payment of the premium to 30 days, and in some offices even to a shorter period, to avoid an absolute forfeiture of the policy is, to say the least of it, inequitable and arbitrary. In the Equitable Society, a case occurred, in which the party insured his life for

appeal to the clemency and consideration of
the office for a restitution of his rights; in
vain he may plead ignorance, inadvertence,

£5000, and having changed his residence, the usual
notice from the office did not reach him, and having
through mere casual inadvertence omitted to pay his
premium, the forfeiture of his policy was the subse-
quence; the omission, however, being brought to his
mind, he, by an appeal to the directors, and a compliance with the ordinary requisitions as to health, and
payment of penalty, ultimately obtained a new policy,
the effect of which, however, was to exclude him from
all the benefits in profits which had anteriorly arisen, and
which the society pocketed as so much clear gain, irrespective of the ulterior advantages to be reaped by such
a capital being worked at compound interest, against
which he appealed, again and again, to the tender mer-
cies of the directors. Their laws, like those of the Medes
and Persians, were unalterable, however stringent and
arbitrary. These cases have been of frequent occurrence
in the Equitable and other offices, and have as frequently
inflicted the most cruel disappointment, in some instances
absolute ruin and destitution to widows and orphans, as
the substitute for once contemplated independence.
Ought such an arbitrary rule to exist in a society for
mutual assurance, in which the immunities and rights
of its members ought, at least in principle, to be balanced,
and where fraud is not imputable? The terms usually
imposed on the forfeiture of a policy for non-payment
of a premium—namely, *payment of a fine,* and *satisfac-*
tory proof of the health of a party—are as to the latter
frequently an insuperable difficulty, and calculated to
open a door to fraud against the assured; for if on submitting to the scrutiny of the society's medical officer,

or inability, whether temporary or arising from reverse of circumstances, as to the cause of his unfortunate departure from his engagement; the answer is, " Sir, *your policy is forfeited, and all you have contributed is irrevocably lost.*"

We have no adequate means afforded us beyond actual experience, when dearly bought, for testing either the liberality, integrity, or stability of a proprietary company; neither the names attached nor the capital guaranteed can be made either subservient or available without the aid of one or other of Her Majesty's courts at Westminster Hall; and if honourable dealing is not rigidly regarded, it is more than probable that a proprietary body may, in the hour of danger, show less zeal for the interests of the assured, than a mutual guarantee society, in which the interests of each individual are identified with his co-members; when, therefore, we see at the head of a prospectus—Capital, one million, two millions, or perhaps five millions, it must neces-

it should be found that by accident or any other cause the health of the assured may not come within a corresponding standard, as on the policy being effected, he is at once told that the office will not renew the policy other than at a premium, which may be either very exorbitant, or far beyond his ability to pay.

sarily be understood to be almost valueless as to any benefit it will confer on any other persons than the proprietors themselves, under colour of which, however, a superstructure of wealth is raised of no ordinary magnitude. The architectural materials of a proprietary office, as already observed, are shares of a transferable nature; for instance, 20 shares of 50*l.* each, on which perhaps 2½ per cent. has been paid, are originally worth just the amount of the money paid for them as so much paid-up capital, and as the insurance office increases in years, so the value of the shares becomes greater by the share of profits periodically added thereto (*f*), besides bearing a large per

(*f*) The following will show the vast profits attendant on the operations of proprietary companies, by contrasting the highest market value of the shares of a few of the principal offices, with the prices originally paid for those shares.

	Office.	When Established.	Amount of Shares.	Amount paid up per Share.			Price per Share.			Profits per Cent.
				£	*s.*	*d.*	£	*s.*	*d.*	
1	Atlas	1808	50	5	0	0	17	0	0	240
2	Sun	1810	100	10	0	0	47	0	0	370
3	Imperial	1820	100	10	0	0	16	0	0	66
4	Guardian	1821	100	36	10	0	50	15	0	40
5	Law	1823	100	10	0	0	49	0	0	390
6	Legal	1836	50	2	0	0	6	10	0	225
7	Universal	1836	100	6	15	0	18	0	0	166

centage of interest, all of which the unlucky assured pay for; whilst in a mutual assurance society the advantage thus conferred on the shareholders would form part of the general stock, for the benefit of the contributors themselves.

Hence, mutual societies are evidently the best adapted to fulfil all the legitimate objects of life assurance; they are essentially benefit societies upon an extended scale; whatever surplus or profit is produced is divided amongst themselves at stated periods; whatever is taken more than is necessary to meet the society's engagements is returned. The disadvantage arising to a mutual society without a subscribed capital in its early outset is that of throwing an undue weight of expenses upon its accumulating funds; but if provided with a small temporary capital, to protect it against adverse fluctuation, and the unavoidable expenses which attend the infancy of almost every speculation, the society would have recourse to that medium, and subsequently repay its obligations, when maturity and a few successful years had sufficiently fostered its funds. In these times, and according to the ordinary rates of premiums now charged, a mutual society which is conducted with ordinary prudence may confi-

dently look for success as certain, and a
career of uninterrupted prosperity, by its funds
at all times exceeding its present liabilities;
and whatever such excess may be, it is profit,
and ought to be returned to the members
whose funds have yielded the same. The
most fruitful source of profit, perhaps, to an
assurance society, has arisen out of an excess
in the mortality of the representative table
above that of its actual experience (*g*), to

(*g*) The result of this experience in the Equitable and
Scottish Widows' Fund offices, which have adopted the
Northampton Tables, and as a consequence very high
premiums, has been in the former 100 to 87, and in the
latter 100 to 57; thus, where the table expected 100
would die, the number of defuncts was only 57, being
43 less than the predictions of the table. The Northampton Table, it will be remembered, was formed from
the Burial Registers of Northampton, between the years
1741 and 1780, and was the only one used by assurance
offices for a considerable period. The Carlisle Table,
which is now adopted by several offices, was formed
from materials which had reference to a subsequent
period, namely, from 1779 to 1787, and is considered
the most correct representative of healthy life of the two.
The Equitable Table (as it is called) was formed from the
experience of the Equitable Society, from its commencement to 1829, by a comparison of which with the Northampton Tables, a progressive increase in longevity has
been established; other proofs of which may be collected
from the more recent experience of the Scottish Provident
office, in which 68 deaths only had occurred for every

which may be added the realization of a greater per centage than 3*l.*, upon which these tables are calculated; to prevent, however, an unnecessary accumulation of this excess of capital, a restraint is usually put, so that few offices suffer this surplus to accumulate beyond a certain number of years, or some lives would be most unfairly benefited at the expense of others; thus from decennial to annual divisions of the surplus, the nearer they approach to the latter, the sooner they reach even-handed justice.

In conclusion, there is another point intimately connected with justice and honourable dealing, which is, that the representatives of persons who die by suicide, duelling, or the hands of justice, are restricted by many companies to such a value of their policies only as the latter may submit to pay. The *Amicable* office goes further, and refunds to the representatives the amount of contributions or premiums not exceeding the sum assured. Other offices, with apparent liberality, declare that their policies, in the hands of a third party, are not forfeited in cases of suicide, &c.;

100 that might have been expected according to the Government tables, and less than a half of what would have occurred according to the Northampton Table.

it may, however, be regarded as singular, that life assurance societies in general, whilst they profess to rank with the most philanthropic of institutions, as best calculated to enable the provident and benevolent part of the community to guard against calamities which are too frequently the consequence of premature death, meet cases of self-destruction with the most heartless apathy; so that under the pretext of *imaginary fraud,* the benevolent intention of the unfortunate victim is frustrated, and perhaps a suitable provision wrested from the hands of a widow and orphans. If it is true, as stated by those who are most competent to form a correct judgment on the subject, that the number of suicides in England does not exceed a thousand annually, (among whom few are of the class of persons who usually effect assurance on their lives,) the cases occurring to an individual office must be comparatively rare, even within a period of twenty years; and in the absence of all proof of a wilful fraud, beyond the belief that the act is ascribable either to a diseased state of the mental faculties, or to passions which ordinary judgment cannot restrain, the infliction of so arbitrary a penalty as a forfeiture is wholly incompatible with honourable dealing, and the principles which assurance companies profess to uphold. The conditions of a policy (of which the assured are generally left in ignorance) usually declare it void in case of suicide, the legal effect of which is a forfeiture of all benefit thereunder. This has been confirmed by a case recently decided by the Judges in the Exchequer Chamber, on a bill of exception in an action brought by the representatives of one Schwabe against the Argus Company, in which it was held, that a party assured, holding his policy in his own hands, who might commit suicide, forfeits his policy, and the office is not bound to pay the amount. In this case, however, the office, before the commencement of the action, went the length of offering a return of all the premiums paid. A return of the money contributed, with interest, would perhaps in all cases best accord with justice.

Having now referred to the most material points to be considered by persons as to the selection of an office, whether mutual or proprietary, it remains to detail, with sufficient minuteness, the comparative merits of each in the order in which they have been successively established.

AMICABLE.

This society (which for its antiquity takes precedence of every other institution of the like nature), in its original constitution being wholly unaided by any graduated scale of premiums, adopted the philanthropic principle of making each subscriber pay the same quantum of premium, whether young or old, so that the ultimate benefit was reaped in a larger amount by the older than the younger of the lives, the total of contributions by the latter being greater than by the former; but succeeding years introduced many wholesome regulations into the management of the business of the society, until it reached its present maturity. The last charter granted to this society prescribes a certain test as a rule for the future government and application of its funds, that is to say,

  1st. That in every year a valuation was to be made of all the premiums payable on existing policies, and of all the assets and liabilities of the society, and the sum ascertained which the society could afford to pay on every share as it became a claim.

2ndly. That the aggregate of the profits of every preceding seven years was to be divided by the number of shares (*h*) which had become claims during the same period, so as to ascertain the actual dividend to be paid on every share which became a claim in that year; and the calculation to be made according to a table of mortality deduced from the experience of the society, and each share being guaranteed to produce £200, independently of profits. This, with other calculations prescribed by the above charter, give to the society a system for distribution of its funds, by strictly arithmetical deduction.

UNION.

The first proprietary establishment for the assurance of lives was the Union, and commenced business at a time when it was so imperfectly understood, as to be regarded alike hazardous to the assurer and the assured, consequently the expectation of the latter was realized with greater certainty,

(*h*) Sums assured in this office are in shares, each of which are now guaranteed at £200.

only by a subscribed capital being raised in aid of the contribution fund, by which they guaranteed the full payment of the sums assured. And to persons who preferred the security of a subscribed capital, this office has taken the lead of several of its contemporaries, by awarding to the assured *a liberal share* of profits by septennial divisions, which under their present regimen are calculated not on the premium, but the sums assured, besides giving the assured the option of insuring with or without profits, in the latter of which the rates of premiums, being lower than in the former, are made to suit the convenience of persons who effect policies for short periods, for a temporary purpose only, in which the assured receives merely the amount of his policy, a practice now adopted by nearly all the proprietary offices.

LONDON ASSURANCE.

Within the brief period of seven years, the Union found a competitor in this office, which became incorporated by royal charter, (*i*) but

(*i*) Few assurance companies have availed themselves of the additional powers conferred on the Crown to grant charters of incorporation by the statute 6 Geo. IV. c. 91, although the same may be obtained with increased faci-

which did not until the year 1831 yield to
the principle of allowing the assured, whose
policies were of five years' duration, a participation in the profits (which after re-
serving a portion thereof, not exceeding one-
tenth, to be carried forward to the next quinquennial division), equal to *two-thirds*, to be
added as a bonus to the sum assured, with
the benefit also of exemption from any share

lities and diminished expenses, but have adopted the
more general practice of obtaining Acts of Parliament,
to enable them merely to sue and be sued. Some of the
newly established companies have, however, availed themselves of the general powers conferred by recent Acts
of Parliament as regard friendly societies and joint-stock
companies, viz. 10 Geo. IV. c. 56, 2 Will. IV. c. 37, 4 &
5 Will. IV. c. 40, and 7 & 8 Vict. c. 110. And among
the Acts passed in the last sessions was the 10th and 11th
Vict. c. 78, intituled, "An Act for the Registration, Incorporation, and Regulation of Joint Stock Companies,"
whereby it is provided that in addition to the particulars
which the promoters of every company are by the Act
(7 & 8 Vict. c. 110) required to return to the office for
registration of joint-stock companies, such promoters
shall also return to the office the following additional
particulars: 1st. The amount of proposed capital of the
company; and 2ndly. The amount and number of shares
into which the same is to be divided; and in the event
of dissolution or ultimate incorporation by Act of Parliament or royal charter, so as to be withdrawn from the
operation of the present Acts, that due notice thereof
shall be given to the registrar of joint-stock companies.

in the expenses of management, which fall exclusively on the corporation.

EQUITABLE.

As upwards of forty years succeeded the London before any other assurance office was established, it might be inferred that the business of life assurance progressed slowly, but whether owing to prejudice or the exorbitant premiums then charged, however justified by the extraordinary mortality which not unfrequently occurred in the principal cities and towns in the kingdom about the period referred to, by the prevalence of contagious and epidemic disorders, experience only can supply the place of positive data; suffice it to say, that large profits were the result of the business as carried on by the two contending proprietary offices, and as profits so gained were, in a corresponding ratio, held to be so much loss to the persons who had contributed towards the fund which had yielded those profits, that simple but indisputable fact naturally enough gave rise to the formation of the Equitable Society, on the principle of mutual contributionship (*k*),

(*k*) The constitution of the Equitable Society, as originally framed, has been essentially perverted by certain

or as it is more generally understood, "*mutual assurance*," and "*mutual guarantee*," but under rules and regulations more scientific than those on which the Amicable Society had been conducted, inasmuch as the funds were accumulated under a graduated scale (founded on the most accurate data that could be then collected), and for *the exclusive benefit* of those who contributed them, and who, although really and properly the arbiters of the issue attendant on the due administration and application of those funds, yet it would appear that the dread of a CALL to satisfy apprehended deficiencies was then regarded by many with as much fear as it is now held

exclusive rights and privileges, originated by certain bye-laws, which in effect have occasioned a most unequal, not to say unjust, distribution of its funds, by bestowing on the policy-holders of one generation that portion which properly belongs to another; for instance, persons who effected assurances in that office in 1837 would, by the operation of one of those bye-laws, succeed to partake of the profits sooner than those who effected assurances twenty years earlier, which at once explains the cause of the vast difference in the marketable value of their policies, and affords an additional proof of the mischiefs resulting from the long interval between the periods of apportioning the profits, which are decennial, a practice repudiated by nearly all other establishments of the kind as opposed to just and honest principles.

by all to be ridiculous; hence the true application of the principle of mutual assurance could only be by the contributors or members mutually guaranteeing for each other's fulfilment of the society's engagements, aided by their common fund, and its adaptation for the benefit of all, without even the presence of personal liability, although not then so generally understood (*l*). Chimerical, however, as were the prejudices against the Equitable Society, it cannot be denied that its career was eminently successful, although another 40 years passed by ere they found a competitor (*m*). In this society, the members are entitled to the *surplus income* under certain restrictions, one of which is, that the number which is entitled to a share thereof is constantly limited to 5000 of the members who have been longest in the society; and, as they die off, the vacancy thus occasioned

(*l*) So strong were the prejudices against the principle espoused by the Equitable Society, whether from the apprehended danger of an increase of establishments of the kind (similar institutions being then almost wholly unknown in France and other foreign countries), or lacking a pecuniary inducement or the bonâ fides of a proprietary, the Government refused to grant a charter on the society applying for one.

(*m*) The London Life Association, established in 1806.

is filled up by the next policy-holder in order of date, and, according to the number now assured, a person may be a member twenty years ere he can be one of the chosen number.

WESTMINSTER.

This society, in following the example set by the London Assurance as to the application of profits, came to the resolution some ten years since of conferring upon the assured the benefit of a participation therein, by making *certain and specific additions*, by way of bonus to their policies, which is understood to be equal to one per cent. per annum on the sum assured.

PELICAN.

This office has likewise found it necessary to succumb to the prevailing system of making a return of some portion of the surplus premiums to the assured, in aid of which a higher scale of premium than the one formerly adopted was deemed essential; and at the end of every seven years, after such a deduction for charges and management as may be thought reasonable, the directors propose to return to the holders of policies not less than *a moiety* of such surplus, which may be appropriated either by an immediate payment, in reduction of the future annual premiums, or as an addition to the policy.

GLOBE.

Whilst unyielding to the principle of dividing profits, the Globe Assurance Company hold out no inducement to those who desire to benefit by a participation therein, nor are their rates of premium materially below those of many other contemporaneous offices which divide profits with the assured.

ALBION.

This office also slumbered over the old state of things, until aroused by the attractive allurements held out by other offices of more modern origin, when *four-fifths* of the profits were proffered to the assured on policies effected ulterior to May, 1844, to be returned triennially by either of the three modes adopted by the Pelican. Policy holders, anterior to that period, are left to abide by their original compact.

ROYAL EXCHANGE.

This company being incorporated by royal charter in like manner as the London Assurance, have determined on following the precedent of the latter by conceding a portion of their profits on policies effected ulterior to the commencement of the year 1842, which it is understood is equal to *two-thirds* thereof, to be ascertained septennially, but not to apply to policies unless of three years' standing, with the option of having the same applied in reduction of the annual premiums or augmentation of the sum assured.

LONDON LIFE ASSOCIATION.

The London Life Association is distinguishable from the London Assurance Company (although sometimes mistaken for the latter), as adapting its principles to those of the Equitable Society, without however subjecting the assured to the arbitrary restrictions imposed by the latter. Thus, in the London Life Association, the assured are made participators in the *entire* surplus profits, which at short periods are applied in the gradual diminution of the annual premiums, until the same wholly cease to be payable, should the assured live long enough, (which many have, without exceeding the ordinary duration of life). By more recent regulations seven annual premiums must be contributed to entitle the party to share in the profits. In this office persons may also assure at reduced rates of premiums without profits.

ROCK.

Few companies have pursued a more steady and undeviating course of business than the Rock, which for upwards of forty years has yielded to the assured no inconsiderable share of their surplus capital, as will be seen by their last published statement referable thereto (*n*); and although their accustomed plan of limiting the share of profits to *two-thirds* yield less than might be acquired in a mutual assurance

(*n*) It is understood that the capital of this company, now invested in government securities, is little short of £3,000,000 in amount, respecting which a meeting has been lately convened, to take into consideration the expediency "Of extending the power given to the directors by one of their bye-laws, to the extent of authorizing loans and advances on the policies of the company, and investment in and loans on the security of debentures of railway companies, when it shall appear advisable to the directors."

society, yet it must not be forgotten that this office has distributed large amounts of profits at a time when other similar establishments have wholly excluded policy holders from any such benefit, and which must afford a strong inducement to those who desire the positive in preference to mere expectancy or promise. In this office the profits are applied by either of the usual modes, *i. e.* reduction of premiums or augmentation of policy.

PROVIDENT.

This company (*o*), at stated periods, ascertain what proportion of profits they intend for the assured, but whether it is equal to one-third, two-thirds, or the like of the surplus capital, must depend on the state of the materials at the time the calculations are made, the whole amount of premiums paid by the

(*o*) In reference to this office it may not be out of place here to remark, that few men have displayed greater skill and ability in the management of an insurance office, or in detecting and exposing the impolicy of the too rapid increase of rival establishments, than the late Mr. Barber Beaumont ; and, to crown a life of great usefulness, he has bequeathed a most magnificent sum for the formation of an institution for the diffusion of useful knowledge.

assured during the preceding seven years, and the original deposits paid by the shareholders being the component parts of such calculation, the result of which, on one or two occasions, has yielded a *liberal return* of the surplus income, which is either added to the policy or applied in reduction of premiums.

HOPE.

The assured in this office are entitled to *two-thirds* of the profits by septennial divisions, with the like option as to the application thereof as in the preceding office, which must, however, be formally notified to the office by six months' notice in writing.

EAGLE.

In this office *three-fourths* of the profits are allotted to the assured septennially, with the usual option of having the same added to the policy, or applied in reduction of premiums.

This office has also, for many years, adopted the plan of taking female lives at a reduced rate of premiums, under the prevailing opinion that their lives are of superior value to those of the opposite sex.

WEST OF ENGLAND.

The assured in this office are made participators in the disposable surplus; premiums
to be periodically ascertained, and *in such
proportions* as in the discretion of the directors
may be determined, with the like option as to
the application thereof, as given by the preceding office, to be formally notified by writing,
after such division shall have been announced.

NORWICH UNION.

The Norwich Union Society was the fourth
office established on the principle of mutual
assurance, and for a long season maintained
a distinguished reputation for permanently
yielding the most important advantages of
life assurance to its members, in comparison to
several of its proprietary contemporaries ; but,
when almost surfeited with success, individual
authority interposed its arbitrary sway, and, as
a natural consequence, aroused hostile feel-
ings, which put in motion a torrent of malig-
nity against the institution, and forced upon it
an investigation into its previous management,
the result of which disclosed circumstances
which led alike to the antidote and prospect

of resuscitation of its former high character. In this society, the *surplus funds* are shared among its members by periodical divisions, in proportion to the amount of premiums contributed by additions to their policies.

ATLAS.

This office, without binding itself to any specific apportionment of profits, professes to yield to the assured *a liberal* share thereof, but which is understood to be such a portion as shall remain, after a deduction for expenses of management and compensation for the guaranteed capital (*p*), to be determined by the directors, and to be ascertained every seven years, with the option of having the same added to the policies, or applied in reduction of future annual premiums.

NORTH BRITISH.
CALEDONIAN.

Both these offices were established at nearly the same period, and yield to the assured a

(*p*) According to the market table of shares, as regards the Atlas, the compensation here referred to is of no ordinary nature ; £5 per share originally paid, now yielding an annual income of nearly three times the amount subscribed.

share of profits, *four-fifths* of which are periodically set apart for the assured by the North British, and *four-sixths* by the Caledonian, with the usual option as to appropriation. Persons may also assure in these offices at a reduced rate of premium, without profits.

SUN.

Upwards of thirty years ago, the Sun commenced business as a proprietary establishment. In the life department, the assured were excluded from any share of the profits, the whole of which were allotted to the shareholder as a suitable return (to use their own words) for their capital employed in the formation of the society. Within a very few years, however, the Sun, like most other proprietary offices, determined on the expediency of holding out some more tempting inducement, as a means of competing with rival offices, and accordingly submitted to give up a moiety of the profits of the concern to persons who might thereafter assure with them; but, as if mindful of the olden adage, "to retain the spoon with the longest handle," the boon thus conferred was not without its precautionary reservation; thus, in case of necessity (quære, what necessity?), the society declares that a portion of the profits so proposed to be yielded, should be retained by them as a reserve fund; and by a recently published prospectus, this society now proposes to make a division of *such portion* of the profits only as in the discretion of the managers may seem most to the advantage of all parties interested (*q.*)

(*q*) The term "all parties interested" must be regarded as somewhat hypothetical, or a reservation pointing to the shareholders as the recipients of a large share of the proffered bounty, the natural inference being, that where their interests are so directly opposed to those of the assured, the discretion of the managers will lead to a preponderating bias in favour of the former; the loss to the one being a gain by the other in a corresponding ratio (vide Share List, p. 15, as it applies to this particular office); thus, where £10 per share was originally paid, it has been augmented by the periodical gatherings of dividends and profits to £47 capital, thereby yielding to the shareholder a per centage of £370 for the deposit so paid; a suitable return truly for the capital employed in the formation of the society, and for the protection of the assured against a risk as imaginary as the insolvency of the establishment itself. In the Hand-in-Hand Society, (which took up the business of life assurance about the same time, the Sun determined to concede a share of their profits), the Mutual Assurance principle was adopted, fortified with an already subscribed capital; and if it be assumed, as it fairly may be, that each of these offices makes a division of profits, say

SCOTTISH WIDOWS' FUND.

The Scottish Widows' Fund (r) and Life Assurance Society was the next in order established after the Equitable Society on the principle of mutual assurance, and claims affinity to that august establishment, as to its intrinsic merits; nevertheless, eschewing the errors of the latter as to the periodical division of the surplus funds, which in this office is septennial, when the assured who have been members five years become participants of *two-thirds, and entitled in expectancy to the remaining one-third*, the same being made a reserve fund until the next division of profits, when it becomes available as a divisible fund, in like manner as on the preceding division, with the

£30,000, at any given period the whole of that sum would go into the pockets of the assured in the one, whilst in the other less than one-half might reach that destination; and where the entire surplus fund is thus left to accumulate for the benefit of the assured, and to improve at compound interest, the result will considerably more than double the advantage to be derived, where one-half of the fund will be exhausted by the shareholders.

(r) This name is somewhat anomalous and unbefitting; it must be understood, however, that the society was originally modelled under a scheme for limiting its business to the making provisions for the widows of subscribers only.

option of having such profits, when declared,
applied in reduction of the annual premiums,
or added to the sum assured.

EUROPEAN.

The assured are entitled to *two-thirds* of the
profits by septennial divisions, to be calculated
on the amount of premiums paid, which will
be added to the sums assured; and may pay
their premiums by half-yearly or quarterly
instalments, or for a limited number of years,
at a corresponding increase of premiums beyond the ordinary rate, as may be agreed
upon.

BRITISH COMMERCIAL (s).

The assured in this office are entitled to
three-fourths of the profits by septennial divi-

(s) In the year in which this company was formed,
two societies commenced business on the principle of
mutual assurance, coupled with benevolent objects, such
as annuities and allowances to members and the like,—
namely, the *General Benefit*, and *Mutual Assurance*, which
have since been added to by the *Friends' Provident*, *National Provident*, *Provident Clubs*, *Provident Clerks*,
Temperance Provident, *Wesleyan Provident*, and *Operative
Mutual;* and it cannot be doubted that societies so constituted as these are, will tend greatly to diminish the

sions, to be appropriated either in reduction of the annual premiums, or in augmentation of the sum assured.

IMPERIAL (*t*).

In this office a return of *four-fifths* of the profits is made to the assured quinquennially by either of the following modes; that is to say,—by a present cash payment, or in reduction of the future annual premiums.

ECONOMIC.

The Economic as originally constituted was proprietary, allowing the assured a participa-

business and numbers of benefit clubs, as embracing all the essential objects of the latter, judicious management and undoubted security being now imposed on them by legislative enactments.

(*t*) In a case recently tried at the Warwick assize against this company, the point at issue was "spitting of blood." That trial being the third which had taken place on the same issue, in all of which a verdict was returned against the company, who sought to resist a claim upon a policy of £2000, the expenses of which trials most probably exceeded the amount of the claim. So determined a resistance, where the evidence was obviously equivocal, must not only tend to negative the belief that the directors acted with proper discretion, but also to show the importance of resorting to arbitration in such cases where practicable.

tion in the profits, to the extent of three-fourths, the remaining one-fourth being made a reserve fund for the final extinguishment of the originally subscribed capital. That object having been recently effected, the Economic now ranks as a mutual assurance society, by yielding to its members the full benefit of *all the surplus capital*, to be apportioned among them every five years, with the option of having the same applied in reduction of premiums or augmentation of the policy.

The year (1823) in which the Economic started, and following year, were fertile in the growth of assurance companies, namely, Law Life, Edinburgh Alliance, Asylum, Clerical, Medical, and Palladium, besides other societies of local interest (*u*), and it may not

(*u*) The *Leeds* and *Yorkshire*, *Manchester*, and *Kent*, are of the number established at this time; since which the *Yorkshire, Halifax and Bradford, Halifax, Bradford and Keighley, Preston and North Lancaster, Nottingham and Derby, Sheffield and Rotheram*, have been added to the list, and are chiefly of local interest and importance,—the three first and last of which promise to the assured a share of profits; the others are solely proprietary, and make no such promise or return. The Manchester has lately resolved on a dissolution, and to transfer the life department to the Pelican office, under the novel circumstance that their rules restrict them from taking a higher

be unfitting in this place to arrange under one general view the societies which have been formed under the immediate auspices of the legal profession ; that is to say,—

LAW LIFE,
LEGAL AND GENERAL,
EQUITY AND LAW,
SOLICITORS' AND GENERAL.

These rival institutions, each of which is supported by a large and influential body of the learned profession, (who, as shareholders, have necessarily an important stake in the success of the respective establishments to which they belong,) yield nearly the same benefits to the assured ; that is to say, *four-fifths* of the profits which are allotted every seven years, with the option of adding such profits to the policy, or in reduction of the future premiums to which the " Legal and General" adds the privilege of receiving the same in present money: its premiums are also a shade lower than the two first-named offices; female lives are also taken upon a lower scale. The " Solicitors and General "

dividend than £5 per cent. until a period which may be almost as remote as the union of the two poles.

add the option of insuring under the participation and non-participation scales of premium, and restricts the shareholders from taking any interest out of the profits fund beyond four per cent. for their guaranteed capital. The period of division of profits is also triennial after the first five years, and thus it approximates nearer to the principle of mutual assurance than the three other establishments; their premiums are also a shade lower than their contemporaries'. Another peculiar feature of this office, as it regards the shareholders' fifth of the profits, is, that a moiety of the same is made available to pay extra commission (x) to professional

(x) The practice adopted by proprietary offices, of allowing commission to solicitors and agents, has long been viewed with suspicion, as having a tendency to compromise professional integrity, or at least to influence their judgment; the bribe thus offered being intended as an inducement to recommend their friends and clients to select such offices as will allow the commission, in preference to those which not only refuse to pay commission, but regard such a practice as a misappropriation of funds properly belonging to more legitimate claimants; whilst, therefore, some offices have withheld the tempting bait, others have bestowed it with a liberal hand; hence it was not very marvellous that the professional community should have taken the business into their own hands, in order to secure as well the benefit of agency as that of shareholder; and although it is stated that many agents, as an inducement for them to bestow more than their ordinary zeal in promoting the interests of the society; and as the success of the office must essentially depend on the active and powerful aid and influence thus fostered, the boon so conferred being the voluntary gift of the shareholders themselves, it is reasonable to surmise that the assured will not be left without its beneficial influence.

EDINBURGH.

In this office the assured may either participate in the profits to the extent of *four-fifths*, or secure a precise sum at reduced rates without profits. The proprietors are also restricted from taking any part of the premium fund to meet the interest on their capital.

SCOTTISH UNION.

Two-thirds of the profits are periodically allotted to the assured in this society, with

thousands of pounds are yearly expended by the "Law Life Society" alone, in payment of commission, yet the success of that office shows, that whilst it trenches upon their funds on the one hand, it has at least yielded its beneficial results on the other by a vast extension of patronage, and proved beyond controversy that the business of life assurance is as successfully managed under a proprietary of solicitors as of mercantile men.

the option of adding the same to the sum assured, or applying it in reduction of the annual premiums, or persons may assure at a reduced scale of premiums without profits.

ALLIANCE.

After five annual payments of premiums the assured are entitled to a participation of profits, the quantum of which is in the discretion of the directors to determine, and not established by any fixed rule—with the usual option as to the application thereof. The proprietary of the Alliance, with a nominal capital of £5,000,000, except as to £50,000, which is paid up, rank as highly respectable.

ASYLUM.

The assured are not entitled to any share of the profits in this society. Persons of unsound health are insurable in this office, at premiums determined by the directors, according to the supposed risk; the assured have also the option of paying a portion only of the annual premium, for instance, one moiety, two-thirds, or the like, the unpaid portion being placed to his debit in the nature of a loan at interest, an inducement originated by this office and now adopted by several others, but which must not be regarded by the assured without danger, for when the time arrives for repayment of the loan, if he fails in so doing, he will most likely be driven to the necessity of selling his policy, and thereby defeated in the long-cherished hope of benefiting his family.

CLERICAL.

The Clerical, Medical, and General Society, in addition to the ordinary business of life assurance, also originated the plan for assuring the lives of persons of an unhealthy standard, in both of which departments the directors have very recently promulgated very flattering results, as an exemplification of the uniform progress and prosperity which have attended the society under their management, both as regards the selection of lives and prudent investment of their capital, coupled with sound data founded on twenty years of actual experience, by which the business as to the unhealthy lives can be safely and profitably conducted. The share of profits returned to the assured are estimated at *five-sixths* of the total, and are apportioned every five years. This office also affords the assured the almost exclusive advantage, by reference to their books, of satisfying their minds as to the genuineness of their periodical balance sheet.

PALLADIUM.

The assured in this office participate in *four-fifths* of the profits, which are added every seventh year to policies, or the same may be applied in reduction of the future annual premiums, at the option of the assured. In this society the paid-up capital being small in amount, the profits are not swallowed up to meet the interest and compensation for the same, as in many other offices. Policy-holders to the amount of £1000 may also attend and vote at the general meetings.

CROWN.

This company apportion among the assured, by septennial divisions, *two-thirds* of the profits, with the usual option as to the same being applied in augmentation of the sum assured, or in reduction of the annual premiums. The Crown also extends its business

to the assurance of the lives of persons de-
viating from the common standard of health,
and, unlike some proprietary offices, hold the
premium fund unfettered with taxation to
meet the compensation for the subscribed
capital, which is however small.

UNIVERSITY.

Persons assured in this office are entitled to
a periodical return of *nine-tenths* of the profits,
to be applied either in diminution of premiums or by an increase in the sum assured,
or, if preferred, by a present payment of the
value in money. This office also proposes to
advance loans at interest to the extent of nine-
tenths of the value of the policy, a practice
which, if generally adopted many years ago
by the older established offices, might have
avoided the forfeitures of thousands of policies
and the preservation of almost as many families from destitution, to which such forfeitures
too frequently lead (*y*).   The members of this

(*y*) The candid and open manner of giving publicity to
the internal management of the business of an assurance
office, as adopted by the University, Crown, Clerical,
and some other offices, cannot be too much appreciated,
as affording a test of their stability, and a due estimation
of public confidence.

society are almost exclusively confined to clergymen.

PROMOTER.

This office has yielded to the popular plan of giving up a share of the profits to the assured, *two-thirds* of which are apportioned to them quinquennially.

CLERGY.

This society appears to have been originated by clergymen, on the principle of *mutual assurance*, and under the patronage of some of the highest church dignitaries, having for its object the two-fold benefit of effecting assurance on the lives of clergymen, and raising a fund to secure provision for themselves, their wives, and children, either immediate, progressive, or deferred, and to meet almost every possible contingency, in cases of sickness, incapacity, old age, &c. &c., having also other benevolent objects in view, the ramifications of which are simplified by the prospectus of the society.

SCOTTISH AMICABLE.
LIFE ASSOCIATION OF SCOTLAND.
SCOTTISH EQUITABLE.

The parent establishments of these offices are on the other side of the Tweed, each of which, however, adopted the mutual assurance principle, by a periodical apportionment of *the profits* among the assured.

NATIONAL.

A policy of five years' standing in this society will entitle the holder to a share of the profits, *four-fifths* of which will in the sixth and every succeeding year be applied in reduction of the annual premiums (a plan of division to be preferred to many others at present in use), or persons may assure a given sum payable to themselves, should they attain a fixed or particular age, or at rates of premium to cease at a stipulated age; a feature somewhat new in the annals of life assurance.

ARGUS. (*z*)

This office holds out no inducement in the

(*z*) The Mentor, one of the defunct offices, some time since abandoned its great prototype by an alliance with this office, to which it transferred its business.

shape of profits; its rates of premium are however a shade lower than several other offices. (*a*)

MUTUAL.

The society which bears this name will not be misunderstood as to the principle on which it is based. Persons who are assured by this society for the whole term of life divide annually among themselves, in proportion to the number and amount of the premiums they have paid, *the whole of the profits or surplus funds;* and by a recently published statement of its operations for the past, the thriving condition of this society augurs fair prospects for the future, in which all its members have alike an equal interest and zeal in its maintenance.

(*a*) In reference to this office a case of a novel kind has lately occurred, in which the claim under the policy was resisted on the ground that the assured was affected with *hernia, rupture,* &c., and on the trial of the action the declaration was so adroitly framed as in legal etiquette to give the defendant's counsel the advantage of opening the case, and, as a consequence, the privilege of a reply, which had the effect desired on the minds of the jury, a verdict for the defendant being the result; but on a new trial that verdict was reversed. Such a course of proceeding surely needs no comment.

UNIVERSAL.
UNITED KINGDOM.

These offices, (*b*) although coetaneous with the Mutual, do not hold out corresponding inducements. The profits intended for the assured by the Universal being *two-thirds*, (*c*) and by the United Kingdom *three-fourths;* by the former, however, the profits become divisible annually after five yearly premiums shall have been paid, and in both offices the profits will either be added to the sum insured or applied in reduction of the future annual premiums. The United Kingdom also professes to have originated the plan of giving credit for half the premium, which has been since adopted by many other offices, and which has been found more especially convenient to persons who, although assured for the whole period of life, may yet contemplate the prospect of discontinuing the same when some particular object in connection therewith

(*b*) These offices are distinguishable for extending their business to India, in many parts of which an agency is regularly established.

(*c*) According to a published report of a meeting recently held by the directors of the Universal Company, £21,269 was stated to be the profits then divisible.

has been answered; for instance, a person may assure for £500, the annual premium for which may be £10, one half whereof only need be paid for five years, with interest for the other half, the assured being a debtor to the office for the unpaid half, and should the policy drop intermediately, the unpaid moiety becomes a loss to the office, which is still however a gainer of the other moiety.

LICENSED VICTUALLERS.

The Licensed Victuallers' Society was established by that particular class from whom it takes its name, and proffers the advantage of allowing the assured to participate in the surplus capital accruing in the fire as well as life department to the extent of *two-thirds;* but as the lives of that class of persons are admitted to be below the common standard of health, and are usually deemed exceptionable lives in other offices, and as such, subjected to rates considerably higher than the ordinary rates of premium, the Licensed Victuallers' Society does not hold out a sufficient inducement to that portion of the community who are more especially candidates for the blessing of longevity, the disproportion of doubtful lives in this society being too considerable.

METROPOLITAN.

This society was established upon the mutual principle, so far as that principle can be carried out as to profits, *the whole* of which are appropriated to the benefit of those members who shall have paid five annual premiums, and, as a pleasing adjunct, joins with the Scottish Widows' Fund Office in open disavowal of the practice adopted by many offices of exhausting its surplus income by commission to solicitors and others. (*d*) This society also adopts the now very general practice of having two classes of insurers, that is to say, members and non-members, the latter of whom being excluded from any share of profits, are chargeable with a lower rate of premium than the former. A distinguished feature of this office is to insure lives at a fixed per centage of premium, by which a corresponding increase is made to a sum assured, so as to make the same, perhaps, four-fold where the policy is of sufficiently long duration

(*d*) *Vide* note, page 438.

NATIONAL PROVIDENT.

The members of this society (e) constitute the assured, and as such are entitled to all the benefits of mutual assurance by the *entire surplus capital or profits* being divisible among them, with the choice of having the same applied either in reduction of the future annual premiums, or by additions to the sum assured, coupled with other wholesome privileges, which give to the society a high claim to public patronage.

PROTECTOR.

The Protector unreservedly retains out of the surplus fund *ten* per cent. for the subscribed capital before the assured can participate in the profits; the rights of the parties being however thus ascertained *in limine*, the policy holders are not absolutely left to the caprice of directors for the realization of the object desired.

(e) This society is almost exclusive in restricting the members from *selling* or *assigning* their interest therein by anticipation.

YORK AND NORTH OF ENGLAND.

This company does not profess to rank among those conferring a bonus on the assured; their tables of premiums are, however, somewhat lower than many other offices.

MINERVA. (*f*)

The Minerva makes a periodical return of *four-fifths* of the profits to the assured, which may be applied either by augmentation of the sum assured or in reduction of premiums. (*g*) This office also follows the plan of the National as to insuring sums payable to persons provided they attain a certain age, or to their representatives in the event of intermediate death.

(*f*) The importance of giving due notice to an office in cases of assignment or transfer of a policy has been recently made manifest in this office, the want of which having first led to a suit in equity, and next to that to an issue at law.

(*g*) In their last periodical apportionment of profits the Minerva afforded a notable illustration of the advantage of assuring at those offices which make a return of profits. Their next return, which takes place during the present year, will not, it is hoped, diminish their well-earned reputation.

HAND-IN-HAND. (*h*)

This old-established Society commenced the business of life assurance in 1836, fortified with their originally subscribed capital in the fire department, which is made subservient for the fulfilment of its engagements in the life department, wholly irrespective of compensation from the premium funds, so that the assured have the benefit of *the entire profits*, realized by their united contributions, and this not at distant periods, but yearly, where the policy is of five years' standing, besides the option of electing to have such profits applied in reduction of premiums, (*i*) or added to the amount of the policy.

NORTH OF SCOTLAND. (*k*)

The *entire profits* of this society are divided

(*h*) This office follows the practice of the Asylum, and one or two other offices, in taking up the business of assuring *anticipated bonuses* in the Equitable Society; thus, by payment of a small annual premium, the next bonus due in 1850 will be secured to the representative of the policy holder, in the event of his dying intermediately.

(*i*) The premiums on some of the older policies have been reduced nearly one-half.

(*k*) The Western of London has been amalgamated with this office.

among the policy holders of the participation class every three years.

BRITANNIA. (*l*)

This company commenced business in 1837, solely as a proprietary, and in its terms of assurance differed from the Argus in no material degree. The motive assigned by this office for adopting that system, is, however, singular, for whilst admitting that the principles on which life assurance companies are based are sound and unerring, it discarded the mutual assurance system only on account of the assumed liability of the assured to *calls* to satisfy deficiencies of funds, &c. This office has, however, in its zeal to do business, since yielded to the prejudice thus raised, and adopted a mutual assurance branch, by which the option is given of assuring, with or without

(*l*) The following notice has recently issued from this office:—"The transfer of the business of the *South of England* Life Assurance Society to this company having been now completed, the directors are enabled to make the same advantageous arrangements with the assured as were effected, to the satisfaction of the parties interested, on the two several occasions of the transfer of the business of the *Standard of England* Life Assurance Company, in 1841, and that of the *London and Westminster* Mutual Life Assurance Society in 1844."

profits, the latter being at a lower rate of premium.

FAMILY ENDOWMENT.

The legitimate object of this society is the business connected with family endowments, concurrently with which it undertakes the usual business of life assurance, in which department *a share* of the profits is periodically allotted to the assured by way of bonus. As to endowments, it may be observed, that since the rapid increase of investment, assurance, or deposit banks, the latter mode is calculated to diminish the practice of the former, as in the one case a total loss may arise which cannot happen in the other; for instance, payment of annual sums for a certain number of years, or a sum in gross under the head endowments, will entitle a child to a specific sum *on attaining a given age* only, but not otherwise, unless by convention of the parties, in which case the total loss may be guarded against by the office undertaking *to return* the premiums or sums actually paid, which is sometimes done. A peculiar risk is also provided against in this society, namely, the contingency of having future issue ; by

this new adaptation interests in property ex-
pectant upon the demise of persons without
issue may be made marketable.

NATIONAL ENDOWMENT.

This society embraces nearly the same objects as the preceding office (the Family En-
dowment).

LIVERPOOL.

This office has lately originated a plan by
which the assured will be entitled, after his
policy has been continued for ten years, to a
fixed annual bonus, and at the end of each
period of ten years, until its amount is doubled
it will be increased by the addition for every
year it has existed of a *stipulated bonus.*
A consummation devoutly to be wished.

ROYAL NAVAL AND MILITARY.

This Society, at the head of which are some
of the most honourable and distinguished men,
returns *four-fifths* of the profits to the assured,
and is eminently calculated to give the utmost

facilities to naval and military men going abroad, or residents in tropical climates, or British colonies (*m*).

THE GENERAL (*n*).

In making the periodical division of profits among the assured, this company appropriates, in the first instance, a tenth as a donation to Dissenting Ministers, who, as influential members, are likewise constituted agents, with the usual commission for recommending business to the office. These benevolent objects are, however, calculated to confine their operations to their own fraternity, although they openly invite persons of any other religious distinction to do business with them. The profits may be applied by additions to the policy, or in reduction of premiums, the choice of which must, however, be made when the policy is effected.

(*m*) Nearly all the offices declare policies void, if the parties whose lives are assured go beyond the limits of Europe, to obviate which additional premiums are charged, which in some offices considerably exceed those charged by this office.

(*n*) This office originally adopted the title of " Dissenters' and General," but have dropped the former term.

NATIONAL MERCANTILE.

This Society yields *two-thirds* of the profits to the policy-holders, either as a bonus, or to be applied in reduction of the premiums, the latter of whom have likewise the choice of paying half the premium only, for the first five years, upon the credit system. This office has also recently made its maiden division of profits, from which may be inferred its thriving condition, and ability to amplify the benefits of life assurance.

NATIONAL LOAN FUND.

In this society the assured are entitled to *two-thirds* of the profits by periodical divisions. The practice now very generally in use, of allowing the assured to borrow money on their policies, is adopted by this office to the extent of two-thirds of the amount of premiums paid, on his providing sufficient sureties.

SCOTTISH PROVIDENT.

This institution professes to be the only one which combines the advantage of mutual as-

surance and low premiums, and makes the
period of division of profits apply to the time
at which the premiums, with the accumulated
interest thereon, will equal the sum assured,
when the value of the policy is estimated, with
a view to the due distribution of the *surplus
capital* or *profits*, so that those of the policy-
holders who have contributed the largest
number of premiums, are entitled to the
greater share of profits; the effect of which
is to exclude therefrom those who die prematurely, or within the average duration of life;
and although the plan thus adopted is opposed
to the rule generally applied for distribution
of profits—namely, that of balancing the inequalities of life in such a manner that those
who do not live the average time shall be
participators in the good fortune of those who
do—yet it is an expedient well deserving of
imitation.

HAVING in the preceding pages travelled
through upwards of seventy offices, for the
assurance of lives, &c., we now come to the
year 1838 (the epoch of a new series of adventurers in that description of business), in
which the bubble mania, so prevalent among

railway projectors, had its kindred influence by giving increased facilities to the concoction of schemes which persons of a restless spirit of speculation or competition are ever ready to embark in, however supervened by danger, or doubtful in the result; thus, a person of such a cast, and having at the same time an eye to the enviable distinction of resident directorship, or even secretaryship, with his retinue of committee-men (o), solicitors, standing counsel, standing physician, &c. &c., may at once form the superstructure ; and whether he unfurls his banner under the proprietary or mutual guarantee system, no matter which, if he can add some new feature to make the project additionally attractive, it is more than probable that he will find proselytes. The most striking scheme, perhaps, among the new class of offices, is that of enabling a per-

(o) Few persons have perhaps forgotten the memorable Independent West Middlesex Life Assurance Company, who issued a prospectus with thirteen names as managers, all of whom with one exception passed under the title of esquires, but as to nine-tenths of that number, were in truth *non est inventus*. The public may thus take warning, not forgetting the fable of the Cat and Old Rat, the moral of which, it will be remembered, is this, " Be always on your guard ; Distrust is the mother of Safety."

son to make a provision, not for his surviving relatives, but for *himself*, by assuring a sum to be paid either at a given time in a certain year, or on his attaining a particular age, and as an adjunct after the similitude of savings banks, but under the more dignified title, *Deposit Bank*, or *Assurance Investment*, he may likewise make contributions to any amount, and as long as he pleases (*p*), and withdraw them when and how he pleases. The Scotch (*q*), who are ever alive to the turning their neighbours' money to good purposes, have the credit of originating these desiderata ; and however they may militate against the moral obligations of

(*p*) As the representative of an individual depositor in the savings' bank cannot, it seems, recover a larger sum than £150, the depositor must resort to a deposit office when his deposits exceed that sum.

(*q*) Our northern brethren (according to Peter Parley, a writer of no ordinary discrimination,) have ever been considered a money-getting race, and skilful in the management of that commodity. The Irish, with less apparent zeal for so important an acquirement, and with still less cravings for matters of life assurance beyond their native soil, are far behind the former in enterprizes of the kind; so that of the few assurance offices established in Ireland, some have existed for a brief period only, and of those now remaining, " *The National Assurance of Ireland*," " *Irish Commercial*," and " *Patriotic*" are the principal.

life assurance, yet when it is considered that policies are daily forfeited under the arbitrary rule, which limits the period for payment of the premiums as already stated (r), it cannot be doubted that the deposit system (s) might, in many instances, afford the best substitute for life assurances; but as the natural course of human events is ever and anon calculated to thwart mankind in their pursuits after wealth and independence, the having recourse to a withdrawal of such deposits as a present available fund, to meet any pressing emergency, being always a tempting allurement—the pecuniary object contemplated might thus, too often, be defeated. Were, however, life assurance offices (in the spirit of liberality towards the assured) more disposed

(r) Vide note, page 12.

(s) It is shown by a return recently issued, that in November last there were in number 1,062,930 depositors, and in amount nearly thirty-one millions of money in savings' banks; nearly tenfold the estimated number of policies of life assurance. In this branch of public polity, the French are not behind the English, although generally they repudiate all such traffic as speculations on human life for a mere pecuniary consideration, and at this time but few assurance offices exist in France. In Scotland, savings' banks are little known, owing to the facilities afforded by bankers in receiving deposits in small amounts, and allowing interest on them.

to meet the wants of the latter, either by a
loan on the policy, or purchase of the same (*t*)
on terms more nearly approaching the quantum
of premiums paid than they have hitherto done
(a benefit which the " City of London," and
one or two other offices propose to accord),
the latter mode of investment would generally
be preferred to the former, as few persons,
for reasons already adduced, would wish to
part with their policy, except in cases of ex-

(*t*) Assurance offices are always ready to purchase
their own policies, the advantage thereby being invariably
on their side, but which they justify taking, on the assumption that the risk they have already run, being
weighed against the risk they would have to run, based
upon the expectation that the life would attain the maturity they had calculated upon, must govern the price; it
usually happens, therefore, that a person who had paid a
premium for a number of years is surprised to find that
the utmost the office will give for his policy scarcely exceeds one third of the money he has actually paid (to say
nothing of the accumulations of interest); the difference
between that sum and the amount of premiums paid
being, *primâ facie*, clear gain to the office; nevertheless,
he will be told that he is one among a class of insurers
whose contributions at the outset were expected to continue permanently according to the supposed duration
of his life, and upon which the office relied for the fulfilment of its engagements to the assured generally, and if
by his own voluntary act he determines the original contract between them, he must submit to any price the office
may choose to offer.

treme pressure, or from inability to keep up
the due payment of the premiums.

It cannot be denied that the rapid increase
of assurance offices within the last seven years
has greatly outstepped a corresponding amount
of additional business, and this very naturally
leads us to surmise that with *some,* ultimate
success is more than doubtful ; and although
few cases have hitherto occurred in which
business of that description has come within
the immediate operation of the bankrupt laws ;
yet it is notorious, that whilst some have failed
in the fulfilment of their engagements, others,
under the apprehension of arriving at that
result, have either transferred their business
to neighbouring offices, or ceased to exist, by
their affairs being wound up, to the discom-
fiture of many.   It is indeed obvious, that the
low rates of premiums usually charged are so
near in affinity to the rate of interest which
the bulk of their capital can now realize in
the public market, that where the business of
an office is of inconsiderable magnitude, or
unaided by the most skilful and prudent
management, frequent insolvencies may be
expected, it being already shown that the
business of life assurance may be taken up on
purely speculative grounds, and almost with-

out capital (*w*) ; and where even a very limited amount of business is done, it might yield an ample fund to meet current expenses and ordinary and intermediate casualties, for a brief period, without seriously looking to the magnitude of their engagements, and assuming that none but good lives are assured, and that few of them would fall in within the first quarter of a century, the succession of premiums may accumulate to such an extent as not only to raise sanguine expectations of ultimate success, but a belief of their ability to yield a large per centage of profits at the very approach of a period when, should the lives fall in by quick succession, or the business of the office essentially diminish, or a season of unusual mortality happen, before an ample fund was accumulated to meet such unlooked-for events, insolvency would be the inevitable consequence (*x*); and should the expectations

(*w*) The English Widows' Fund proposes to issue £10,000 shares, of £20 each, on which a deposit of 2*s.* per share is first made, as limited by 7 & 8 Vic. c. 110, to be increased to £1 per share on complete registration, and which is nearly thirty times the amount required by the Scottish Widows' Fund.

(*x*) In the *Quarterly Review* (Oct., 1839), the writer has made a kind of arithmetical calculation, as a means for testing the stability of assurance offices, which he

of the policy holder be thus disappointed, he
must bear in mind that he may be told he
must submit to the will of the directors,
should they even resolve on breaking up the
concern ; because he is bound to be cognizant
of every clause in the deed of settlement under
which the company was carried on, one of
which might be their discretionary power to
dissolve the company, although he most probably never even heard of the existence of any
such a deed (*y*).

In conclusion, it will be only necessary to
observe, that nearly eighty offices for the
assurance of lives have entered the field as
candidates for public patronage since the year
1838, and most of them ulterior to 1840. Some
have survived a very brief period only, and

says may be classed under the following heads, viz. : of
*general stability—*a *salutary state—probationary—*and *ex-*
perimental. Under the first he includes all offices that
have existed twenty-one years and upwards; under the
second, those of fourteen to twenty-one years; under
the third, those of seven to fourteen ; and under the
fourth, those of an existence less than seven years.

(*y*) On the resolution being agreed to for the dissolution of the Manchester Company, it was stated that the
time had arrived when the mortality among the lives insured exceeded the business done in new policies, and
which would of itself lead to ultimate insolvency.

those which remain, with few exceptions, do
not possess any important feature calculated
to give them a very decided preference to
other similar establishments of longer standing (*z*), and must therefore, as to ultimate success, be left to time to develope (*a*), and which

(*z*) The enormous expense for advertising and allowance to agents, which attends every assurance office
during its infancy (and without which publicity it cannot hope to exist) must of necessity fall heavily upon a
growing fund, and, as a consequence, tend to lessen the
prospect of an early or material division of profits, and
although it may have the effect of augmenting the business, as is sometimes the case, by holding out attractive
and alluring terms (the Independent West Middlesex
Company, for instance, advertised their rates as thirty per
cent. lower than any other office, and as thereby conferring a boon to the public of £300,000 per annum); yet
as parent offices are not subjected to these preliminary
disbursements, the inference which follows is, that where
the office returns part of the profits to the assured, he
may be certain that, *cæteris paribus*, his share will be
greater in proportion as such expenditure is limited.

(*a*) The following advertisement, which has recently
appeared, is perhaps one of the most novel attempts at
procuring business for the office to which it refers:—
"The income of persons of respectability and influence
may be readily and greatly increased by promoting the
interests of a well established and highly successful
assurance office in London, the equitable and very advantageous terms of which offer great facility to persons of activity and intelligence for making a credit-
able increase to their present income."

will be arranged in the following manner (being the order in which they have been established in point of date), with a view to their respective merits being contrasted with those of their parent institution.

FREEMASONS.
CITY OF GLASGOW.

These societies may be said to be homogeneous, as holding out nearly the same inducements; and although proprietary, the shareholders of each are so avowedly philanthropic, as to do business on the system of mutual assurance, with the privilege of half credit as to the premiums payable, as likewise to assure sums to be paid at a period intermediate of death, or a particular age. The half-credit system, as already noticed, is, however, a dangerous expedient, except where the repayment of the loan is made to correspond with that of the claim under the policy.

VICTORIA.

The practice of extending the business of life assurance by the advance of small loans for a limited period on personal security is pursued by this office, whereby persons who require the advance must effect a policy for perhaps double the amount borrowed, and is thus made to pay interest varying from ten to twenty per cent., as the policy is usually discontinued on the return of the money borrowed: transactions of this kind, where the security is entirely personal, whilst improvident on the one hand, are not exempt from risk on the other, by the loss of both principal and interest. In this office, the assured are entitled to *a share* of the profits at stated periods, as may be determined by the directors.

STANDARD (*b*).

This office may be characterized as the Standard of Scotland, in contradistinction to the Standard of England, since the annexation of the latter to the Britannia office, as already noticed; and although existing in 1825, it has but recently established a branch office in the metropolis of London.

The profits being ascertained every five years, each policy holder has a claim upon the same, according to the number of annual

(*b*) The business of each of the two companies, the "Commercial Assurance of Scotland" and "York and London" has been transferred to this company.

premiums he has paid ; but what proportion it bears to the share conferred upon the proprietors may be best identified by the fact that policies of only five years' standing have had additions to the same somewhat exceeding eight per cent.

MARINERS.

The business of this office appears to refer chiefly to that description of persons whose pursuit in life is of a nautical character, and embraces philanthropic objects, highly deserving of consideration by that class, and in particular common seamen.

STAR.

This society is professedly formed by the Wesleyan Methodists' connection, and promises *nine-tenths* of the profits to its members, when a division thereof shall take place.

BRITISH MUTUAL.

In this institution, *the whole* of the profits belong to and are divisible among the assured, and the principle adopted in the distribution of the same is, perhaps, the most equitable of any at present in use, inasmuch as the members do not participate therein till the premiums they have paid, with the accumulation of interest, amount to the sum assured, when the share of profits is estimated according to the value of the policy; so that members who contribute the greater number of premiums will have the greatest portion of the profits, compared to those who die prematurely, and without having contributed premiums in an equal degree (c),—a plan somewhat analogous to a tontine.

(c) This mode of division will probably, ere long, become more generally in use. In the *Quarterly Review*, already referred to, the writer says, "The general use by insurance offices of the word 'profit,' is an abuse of the term, they being wholly contingent and remote. It cannot for a moment be questioned that instead of profit, the assurance office must sustain a loss by every insurer who dies before the amount paid by him in premiums, with the accumulated interest, shall be equivalent to the amount of his policy; yet in most of those offices the representatives share in the profits, should the insured die immediately after seven payments. The equitable rule would be to assign the bonus to such only as had survived the expectation of life, according to the generally received law of mortality, or who had paid in premiums with interest upon them a sum equal to that for which the life was insured."

GREAT BRITAIN, AND INDIA AND LONDON.

The Great Britain Life Assurance Society and India and London Assurance Company have been lately united, and now work together under one management, the former on the principle of mutual assurance, in which the members, after five annual payments or premiums, are entitled to share in the *entire profits;* and where their present means of paying the premium are inadequate, they may adopt the half-credit system, on approved security being given. The India and London is proprietary, and add to their ordinary business the assurance of invalid lives afflicted with mental or bodily infirmities, and persons resident in British colonies, India, and other distant parts of the world.

MERCHANTS AND TRADESMEN'S.

This office adopts the mutual assurance plan, as likewise the half-credit system for the first five years, for which period a portion of the premiums may remain unpaid. The *entire profits* are quinquennially divided among the assured.

CATHOLIC.

The Catholics, with the distinguished name of Earl Shrewsbury at their head, have followed the example of the Clergy and Dissenters by having an assurance office of their own creation; but, unlike the latter, as to any exclusive provision for their own clergy out of the surplus income; *three-fourths* of which this company apportion to the assured by septennial divisions and limits the interest on the paid-up capital to four per cent.

CITY OF LONDON.

As almost every new office possesses a distinctive feature indicative of something original, this office has adopted a system somewhat unique, under the title "Accumulative Assurance," which, in effect, partakes of the quality of a savings bank, in cases where the assured fails to pay up his premiums, by affording him the privilege of a withdrawal of the amount he has already contributed, but not with correspondent advantages; or the assured may continue his assurance under certain qualified terms, so as to avoid, in any case, a positive forfeiture of the policy. The division of profits is reserved *for future consideration;* but as nearly all the 5,000 shares were subscribed for almost *instanter*, the shareholders themselves are not, it is presumed, without a hope of being requited for the use of their capital. This kind of avidity for possessing shares is a striking illustration of the disadvantage persons labour under who assure with a proprietary company by involving in itself a sort of moral turpitude on the one hand, and more than ordinary credulity on the other.

GLASGOW.

The assured in this office are entitled to *four-fifths* of the profits.

LEGAL AND COMMERCIAL.

Allows the assured *four-fifths* of the estimated profits, which are to be ascertained and made divisible at the end of every five years, and applied either by additions to the sum assured, or in reduction of the premiums. Persons may also assure at a reduced rate of premium without profits.

LONDON AND PROVINCIAL LAW.

In this office *four-fifths* of the divisible profits will be allotted to the assured at the end of the first ten years, and at the end of every seven years following that period, on policies of not less than two years' standing. Residents at a distance from London may also effect assurance through any respectable solicitor. What need, then, is there for a board of thirty-six directors, twelve of whom only are to be excluded from remuneration at the forthcoming general meeting?

SOVEREIGN.

In addition to the usual business of life assurance, this office undertakes to receive deposits to improve at interest for the benefit of the depositor, as also to grant loans on its own policies for a limited period, on the borrower providing approved collateral security, and promises to the assured *three-fourths* of the profits, to be periodically divided and applied, either by addition to the policy, reduction of premium, or an immediate cash payment.

ALFRED.

Four-fifths of the profits are periodically awarded to the assured by this office, and applied either in reduction of premium, or augmentation of the sum assured. Persons may also assure a sum payable to themselves at a particular age (a practice now adopted by several other offices), and are exempted from extra premiums when resident in British colonies.

AUSTRALASIAN.

This office, like the preceding one, is essentially adapted for emigrants and colonial residents, and whilst embracing most of the useful objects of life assurance yields to the assured *one-half* of the profits periodically, with the privilege of leaving unpaid one-third of the first five years' premiums as a permanent debt against the policy at interest, and makes no charge for extra premiums as to residents in British colonies.

ENGLISH AND SCOTTISH LAW.

Two-thirds of the profits are apportioned to the assured periodically, with the privilege of half credit for the premiums. In this office a distinction is made as to Scottish and English residents as policy holders, the former of whom, besides participating in the profits of the Scotch business, share also with those of the English policy holders.

LONDON, EDINBURGH, AND DUBLIN.

The twofold system of proprietary and mutual assurance, as adopted by the Britannia, is also pursued by this company, in which the remuneration to the shareholder is limited to the surplus fund created by the nonparticipating class; the expenses of management being, however, thrown upon the mutual assurance class. A peculiar feature of this office is, that claims on policies on the lives of debtors held by creditors will be paid at the death of the debtor, although the creditor had been previously and irrespectively satisfied his debt, which, although in positive contravention of the law, savors much of justice.

ROYAL FARMERS.

As a strictly proprietary establishment this office makes *no* return of profits to the assured.

CHURCH OF ENGLAND.

In following the precedent of one or two other establishments of the kind as regard benevolent objects, this society sets apart one-tenth of the profits under the head "clergy fund," for the benefit of the less fortunate of their clerical members, and allows to the assured generally *four-fifths* of the remaining portion.

RELIANCE.

The *whole* of the profits are promised to the assured by this proprietary, but in what way the shareholders are to be requited for the use of their subscribed capital is not distinctly made to appear by their published prospectus.

MEDICAL INVALID.

This society is added to the number of those whose legitimate object is to assure unsound lives, and stipulates that after two yearly premiums shall have been made, policies shall not be subjected to a forfeiture by suicide, &c., but makes *no* return of profits to the assured.

MEDICAL LEGAL.

Whilst adopting the mutual principle guaranteed by a temporarily subscribed capital,
to be ultimately repaid with a bonus as a
compensation to the subscribers, the board
of directors of this office being composed
partly of medical men, assure unhealthy as
well as healthy lives, with, perhaps, more
than ordinary exactitude as to the rates of
premiums strictly applicable to each individual case.   The half-credit system is also
allowed to the extent of seven years, and,
when five annual payments have been made,
the *surplus income*, after setting apart £5 per
cent. for the subscribed capital, and a further
sum towards the liquidation of the latter, becomes divisible among the assured by addition to the policy or in reduction of annual
premiums.

COMMERCIAL.

The assured are entitled to a participation
of the profits realized by this association, to
the extent of *two-thirds*, by septennial divi-

sions (*d*), and have the privilege of credit for half of the premiums for the whole period of life, which is a less objectionable mode than the one in which a return of the money is stipulated to be made within a limited period.

ANCHOR.

The Anchor makes *no* return of profits, but grants loans on personal security, if accompanied with a life policy.

EXPERIENCE.

Proposes to divide among the assured *five-sixths* of the profits quinquennially.

WESTERN.

The assured in this office have the advantage of becoming entitled to *three-fourths* of the profits periodically, with credit for half the premiums during the first seven years.

(*d*) A septennial division of profits is perhaps the earliest which ought to be made by an office in its early growth. Earlier or large divisions of profits in the infant state of an office are not usually true indices of its prosperity or ultimate success.

MITRE.

This office makes *no* return of profits to the assured, who may nevertheless possess the privilege of leaving half the premiums unpaid at any time, and for an indefinite period, by payment of interest for the unpaid portion ; and where it becomes a permanent debt against the policy, it is, as already stated, a less objectionable plan than the one in which a return of the money is stipulated to be made within a short or fixed period.

TONTINE.

The business of this office is divided into two parts—Life assurance, and Tontine annuities. In the former, *four-fifths* of the profits will be allowed to the assured periodically. As to Tontine annuities, although hitherto very little encouraged in this country, yet, if placed under prudent and skilful management, they might be of singular utility to a certain class of persons whose chief object is to secure to themselves additional ease and comfort in old age. For instance, 500 persons forming a particular class, whose ages varied from twenty-five to thirty-five (or other given ages), and each paying £100, would, in the first year, receive an annuity according to their respective ages (say £4), but as some of the above number of persons (e) are expected to die every year, the annuities to the survivors would be successively increased by the persons so dying. So that those who might be favoured with longevity would have the benefit of their survivorship, by their annuities progressively increasing to ten, fifty, or, perhaps, one hundred fold (ƒ).

PROFESSIONAL.

This very recently formed company professes to identify itself more intimately than others with the professions, both clerical, legal, military, naval, and medical, and to hold out inducements not hitherto offered to the public; one of which is adapting its operations to the

(e) Out of 1000 persons of the age of thirty-five it is calculated that ten will die within the year.

(ƒ) A notable instance of this kind occurred in the Government Tontine, in which an individual, who had made no greater contribution than £100, was in the receipt of £600 for several years preceding her death; a similar instance to which occurred in the French Tontine, in which, for the original subscription of 300 livres, the last survivor, who died at the age of ninety-six, enjoyed an income of 73,500 livres.

formation of a fund equal to one-tenth of the profits, for the benefit of both proprietor and assured should indigence befall them. Persons may also assure against such bodily and mental visitations as may incapacitate them for business, such as blindness, or the like, by providing annuities; and, at the end of seven years, a division of the profits is to be declared, and *three-fourths* applied for the benefit of the assured.

THE ENGLISH WIDOWS' FUND (*g*).

It is stated that the object of this newly-formed association is to extend life assurance business to persons who constitute the *industrial class*, and to sums as low as £20, under the assumption that the pre-existing offices do not afford the like opportunities. In this office the assured will be entitled, after provision being made for a reserve fund, to *four-fifths* of the profits, after paying three annual premiums, to be divided among them periodically by the two usual modes of additions to the policy or diminution of the premiums.

(*g*) The advantages of the system of mutual assurance and the security of an adequate subscribed capital are promised by this association, the latter to be raised by 10,000 shares of £20 each.

BRITISH EMPIRE.

This is a non-proprietary company (if it may be so called), the interests of all parties being *mutual* and unfettered with the claims of shareholders for a subscribed capital, and the inducements are only lessened by the disadvantages which accompany a young office at the outset. At the end of the first five years a division of the profits will take place, after which they will be made triennially.

CONSOLIDATED INVESTMENT AND ASSURANCE.

In uniting the objects of a building society with that of life assurance, this office professes to enable mortgagors to extinguish their debts, and tenants to become landlords by the grant of loans; and the money so advanced to be repaid by equivalent annuities or yearly instalments; but as the ability of persons to fulfil such like engagements may be too often interrupted by events which they cannot either control or foresee, such transactions must necessarily be entered into with due caution.

The life department is of the ordinary nature, and *three-fourths* of the profits promised to the assured on policies of five years' standing, with the privilege of one-third of the premium being allowed to remain unpaid and accumulate, with interest, as a permanent debt against the policy.

DEFENDER.

This company was originated by pawnbrokers, and promises the assured *two-thirds* of the profits, and to allow the latter to pay their premiums in part only for the first five years, the unpaid portion remaining as a charge upon the policy, on interest, in the event of their dying within that time.

LONDON AND PROVINCIAL JOINT STOCK (*h*).

This company has recently commenced business in the twofold character of an invest-

(*h*) The similitude between this title and the "London and Provincial *Law* Society," has lately led to a suit in the Court of Chancery, in which the latter, as plaintiffs, unsuccessfully sought to restrain (by an injunction of the Court) this company from using the plaintiff's title,

ment bank and life-assurance office, but has
not at present developed its scheme of operations by a published prospectus.

on the ground that by so doing it might induce people
to mistake the one for the other.   It appeared the plaintiff's company was provisionally registered anterior to
the defendant's company; but the former did not discover the existence of the latter till August last, who it
appeared adopted the plaintiff's title in ignorance of the
existence of such a company.   His Honour the Vice-
Chancellor of England, before whom the application was
made, thought that when people went to insure, the first
thing would be to make an inquiry into the nature and
character of the company in which they intended to
insure.   In the plaintiff's title, lawyers were made the
prominent parties addressed; in the defendant's title,
the company had nothing especially to do with law, but
was merely a combination of persons purporting to be a
joint-stock society.

HINTS TO PERSONS ASSURING,

WITH

TABULAR ILLUSTRATIONS.

———◆———

AS it cannot be doubted that many persons who effect assurance on their lives or even on the lives of others, either through ignorance or inadvertence, do not bestow sufficient attention to the real essence of the contract which they are bound to perform, and on the due observance of which the validity of the policy depends, the following remarks may not be undeserving of attentive perusal. It is of paramount importance, that every person who may be about to effect an assurance should distinctly understand the nature of the terms he undertakes to perform on his part, which, however stringent and multitudinous, any the slightest departure therefrom, whether accidental or unintentional, if it essentially alters the nature or character of the risk, as it was originally understood by the office, may have the effect of vitiating his policy, and subjecting him to the loss of all the premiums he may have contributed ; and when it is understood that the strictest observance of candour and integrity is required of him by the office, and such fearful odds are against him, as that truth and falsehood will most likely at some time be weighed against him with scrupulous(i) exactness, he must in every respect abstain from making any *wilful* statement or *concealing* any fact or circumstance which may come within the category of the office, to avoid detection.

The preliminary information usually required by the office, and which the party is obligated to furnish with the utmost correctness, it being taken as the very basis of the contract between him and the office, is, a true statement of his *name, residence, profession or business, age,* whether *married* or *single,* in the *naval* or *military* service—whether the party has had the *smallpox,* or *cowpox, gout, fits, asthma, insanity, habitual cough,* or subject to *disease of the lungs, spitting of blood, rupture, hernia,* or any other *disorder tending to shorten life ;* to which he must likewise furnish the name of his usual medical attend-

(i) *Vide* note, page 51.

ant (*k*), if he has ever been attended by one in illness, which is not of the least importance, as the *substitution* of a medical man, who had not the like means of knowing his constitution might vitiate the policy. He must also show that his habits of life are *regular*, and *disclose* any circumstances touching his past or present state of health, which the office ought to be made acquainted with as tending to bias their judgment, in either accepting or refusing the proposal for the assurance. And in addition to his own statement, a corresponding one must be certified by one or two friends also, who must give reasons for their competency to make such statement; he must also procure a medical certificate of the soundness of his health, bearing in mind that it

(*k*) The medical certificate usually required by an assurance office has long engaged the attention of medical men as entitling them to their fees from the office, as in every case it is useful to the latter in determining either to accept or reject the proposal to insure; the professional reputation of the medical man, and the knowledge he is supposed to have of the health and constitution of the party being at all times the very basis of the assurance, irrespective of the judgment of their own medical officer, which is looked to as of secondary importance. Some offices have conceded this point to the medical profession by paying their fee.

will be preserved and found among the archives of the office, whenever his representatives shall make a claim under the policy.

Besides the above requisitions, the party is required to *sign a declaration*, to the effect that he is in a good state of health, and is *not afflicted with any disease tending to shorten life;* that the statement he has given of his health, age, and other particulars, is true, and that he has not *withheld or concealed any circumstance tending to render an assurance on his life* more than usually hazardous ; and that he agrees that the declaration shall be the basis of the contract between him and the office ; and that if any untrue averment is contained in the declaration or in the answers given, all sums which shall have been paid to the company shall be forfeited, and the assurance null and void.

From the preceding remarks, it may be naturally inferred, that a person can only venture to assure his life when under the full conviction, in his mind, that he is in a perfect state of health ; not so, however, as it must be understood that the door of an assurance office is still open to the *unhealthy* as well as healthy part of the community, and that *invalids* of almost every grade may alike avail themselves of the benefit, with this difference, that instead of the ordinary rates of premium, *extra* premiums are charged, according to the risk attendant on each individual case; hitherto business of this nature has been transacted in the Asylum, Clerical, Medical Invalid, Medical Legal, and one or two other offices.

If the proposal to the office, founded upon the above requirements, is accepted, the office becomes bound, by a policy in the nature of a deed poll, to fulfil the engagement on its part, as to the payment of the sum assured; nevertheless, *upon certain conditions* imposed upon the party assured, which are usually to the following purport, viz.

A policy becomes void if the premium for its renewal remains unpaid more than 30 *days* after it becomes due; but should proof be given, to the satisfaction of the directors, that the party whose life has been assured continues in good health, the policy may be renewed at any period within three calendar months, on the payment of a *fine*, to be fixed by the board of directors (*l*).

The policy of a person assuring his own

(*l*) In some offices the fine is fixed by their printed conditions and the period of grace extended beyond three months.

life, will become void if *he dies by his own hand, or by the hand of justice, or in consequence of a duel;* but in case of death, not *felo de se,* the board of directors may pay to the personal representative of the assured a sum *not exceeding* the value of the policy. But should such policy be assigned to other parties for valuable consideration, three calendar months (in some offices six calendar months) previously to the death of the assured, it remains in force to the *extent* of the beneficial interest therein of the party entitled to the same, when satisfactorily made out.

A policy likewise becomes void, if the person whose life is assured should die upon the seas (except in passing in time of peace from any part of Europe to any other part of Europe), or should go beyond the prescribed limits (which are usually between the Elbe and Brest), or should be employed in any naval or military services whatever, *without first obtaining a license in writing* from the board of directors, and *paying such additional premium* as shall be required by them.

When a policy shall become a claim, such proofs, evidence, and information shall be furnished to the board of directors as they may consider necessary to substantiate such claim, such as a certificate from the medical gentleman who attended the assured in his last illness, and the nature of the disorder with which he was afflicted, in addition to which many offices require due proof of his age, to obtain which is sometimes attended with difficulty; and as many assurance offices will waive the production of the proper certificate of register at the time of the policy being effected, the most prudent course to be adopted is either to produce the usual certificate in the first instance, or where that cannot be done, require the office to admit the age as stated, and indorse such admission on the policy.

The time required by most offices, for payment of the claims after due proof of the death of the party assured, is three months. The Equitable, Asylum, and Promoter extend the period to six months, and the Rock to eight months.

The following illustrations refer to the different modes of assurance now generally offered to the public, the calculations being made upon the participating scale of premiums (*m*) thus:—

(*m*) In almost every assurance office the option is given to assure *with* profits or *without* profits, a lower rate of premium being charged in the latter than the former.

A person whose age is 30 next birth day, may assure the sum of 100*l.*, to be paid at his death by a *single* payment of 45*l.* 9*s.*, or an *annual payment* during his life of 2*l.* 10*s.* 7*d.* If *without* profits, the premium will be 2*l.* 6*s.* 5*d.* only.

Or, a person of the like age may assure the same sum for one year only, by the payment of 1*l.* 3*s.* 8*d.*, or for five or seven years, by annual payments of 1*l.* 4*s.* 6*d.*, and 1*l.* 4*s.* 9*d.* respectively.

Or, by a limited number of annual payments (*n*), he can assure 100*l.*, payable at his death, as follows, viz.

		£	s.	d.
5 Annual payments of .	. .	9	19	0
7 ,,	. . .	7	8	10
10 ,,	. . .	5	11	4
15 ,,	. . .	4	3	1

Or, by the payment of an annual premium, *increasing* in amount, in periods of five years, and after a limited number of payments, then at a fixed rate for the remainder of life (*o*). Thus—

(*n*) This mode of assurance is intended to apply to persons having an income which, after a certain period, may terminate or become uncertain.

(*o*) Persons whose incomes are small in the early period of life, but who expect a gradual increase of the same, may find this mode of assurance useful.

	£	s.	d.
Annual premiums for the first 5 years	1	10	8
Ditto, second 5 years	1	17	3
Ditto, third 5 years	2	3	9
Ditto, fourth 5 years	2	10	4
Ditto, remainder of life	2	17	10

Or, by the payment of an annual premium, *decreasing* at the expiration of each period of five years, and terminating with a fixed payment for the remainder of life (*p*).   Thus—

	£	s.	d.
Annual payment for the first 5 years	2	17	0
Ditto, second 5 years	2	10	4
Ditto, third 5 years	2	3	8
Ditto, fourth 5 years	1	17	0
Ditto, remainder	1	10	4

Or, by the annual payment of a certain sum, until he attains a particular age—for instance, 4*l.* 14*s.* to the age of 50, or 3*l.* 2*s.* to the age of 60, with the option of receiving 100*l.*, or an equivalent annuity for the remainder of his life, which would be about 12*l.*

Or, under the head *Investment Assurance*, a person, by the monthly payment of 10*s.* for 12½ years, will be entitled to receive 100*l.* at

---

(*p*) This plan is adapted to individuals who, in early life, are in the possession of good incomes, but who, at a much later period, may expect a diminution of the same.

the end of that time; or in the event of his intermediate death, the amount of his payments, with interest, will be paid to his representatives.

Or, under the head *Joint Lives*, by the annual payment of 4*l.* 8*s.*, during the continuance of the lives of two persons, aged 30 and 40, 100*l.* would be secured at the *death of either*, whichever should first happen.

Or, by the annual payment of 1*l.* 15*s.* 7*d.*, during the continuance of the longest life, 100*l.* would be secured at the death of two persons of the like ages of 30 and 40.

Or, under the head *Survivorships*, by the annual payment of 2*l.* 11*s.* 4*d.*, a person aged 40 can secure 100*l.*, to be paid on his death, provided another person of the age of 30 shall survive him.

In most offices, assurances may also be effected for any sum from 20*l.* to 5000*l.*

The premiums may likewise be paid by half-yearly or quarterly payments, if desired.

The following stamp duty is charged on life policies, the inequality of which impost is glaringly absurd, and must afford a strong inducement to evade the same; for instance, a policy for 100*l.* pays *five shillings*, but for any trifling sum exceeding that amount, it pays a duty of 1*l.*, but if it be extended to 499*l.*, no more is paid. And if the policy is increased to 2999*l.*, an additional duty of 2*l.* only is charged, which must likewise be paid, if the policy is limited to 1001*l.*

STAMP DUTY.

	£		£	£	s.	d.
Not exceeding	50			0	2	6
Exceeding	50 and not exceeding	100	0	5	0
,,	100 and not amounting to	500	1	0	0
Amounting to 600	,,	1000	2	0	0
,, 1000	,,	3000	3	0	0
,, 3000	,,	5000	4	0	0
,, 6000 and upwards	.		5	0	0

For Product Safety Concerns and Information please contact our EU
representative GPSR@taylorandfrancis.com
Taylor & Francis Verlag GmbH, Kaufingerstraße 24, 80331 München, Germany

www.ingramcontent.com/pod-product-compliance
Ingram Content Group UK Ltd.
Pitfield, Milton Keynes, MK11 3LW, UK
UKHW021116180425
457613UK00005B/116